THE MAKING OF
THE PRIME MINISTER 1970

THE MAKING OF THE PRIME MINISTER 1970

ANDREW ALEXANDER &
ALAN WATKINS

MACDONALD UNIT 75 · LONDON

First published in Great Britain in 1970 by
Macdonald Unit 75, St. Giles House,
49-50 Poland Street, London, W.1

SBN 356 03495 X

Made and printed in Great Britain by
Waterlow & Sons Limited, London and Dunstable
Set in Monotype Times New Roman

TO R.
&
R.B.

CONTENTS

PART ONE – BACKGROUND

PART TWO – THE CAMPAIGNS

ACKNOWLEDGMENTS

I must express my gratitude to those friends who helped in various ways to make this book possible. Miss Julie Gooding, a researcher of awe-inspiring resourcefulness, deserves especial thanks.

As to the division of labour in this book, Alan Watkins and I would like to allot the blame and credit where they belong. He is the author of the two chapters on the Labour Party and its Campaign. I must take the blame for the chapters on the last four years in Government and on the Tory Party and its Campaign. My final thanks are due to the Tory Party for winning the Election and saving me from losing several hefty wagers.

ANDREW ALEXANDER

PART ONE
BACKGROUND

CHAPTER ONE

THE TORY VICTORY

'What all the wise men promised has not happened and what all the d . . . . d fools said would happen has come to pass'—LORD MELBOURNE.

The British public who sat down before its TV sets on the night of June 18 1970 had been inundated with assurances that the result of the general election was not in doubt. The only question to be settled was the size of Labour's majority. Virtually all opinion polls had agreed that there was a Labour lead, with some even predicting that Wilson would sharply increase his majority.

One notable exception to these predictions of a Labour victory was, significantly, the very last poll taken by Opinion Research Centre. The final sampling was carried out on the last two-and-a-half days before polling day itself. The prediction was a Tory lead of a fractional one per cent. But this was so far out of line with the general picture built up from the other polls that the political editor of *The Evening Standard*, which commissioned and published the sample, was disinclined to attach much significance to it.

Near incredulity therefore greeted the results as they started to flow in. By midnight it was clear that the Tories would win.

The final results were:		Old House (including two seats vacant)
Conservatives	330	262
Labour	287	346
Liberal	6	13
Speaker	1	1
Others	6	6

Explanations of what had gone wrong poured out from the press, TV and radio in rapid succession. Not all were convincing and not all paid attention to the obvious. As to the opinion polls, it was a plain fact that ORC had sampled voters' intentions after the publication of the bad trade figures published on June 15, which suggested that Tory warnings about the economy had to be heeded. That poll had, too, made emphatic allowance for the different enthusiasm for actual voting which was evident among Labour and Tory supporters.

In any case, some of the explanations of the result were missing the real point, namely, that the astonishing feature of the 1970 General Election result was not that the Tories won but that they had come so near to losing. It is a fact that the British electorate, probably because of an estimable desire for stability, almost invariably gives a political party two favourable votes in succession. This reluctance to turn a party out after only one period of office has been evident throughout the century. But at the same time the electorate has never given a party three victories in a row except after some remarkable successes. And by 1970 it was hard to find even any Labour politicians who believed that the period of the Wilson Administration could qualify for such a compliment.

The burst of wage inflation which had started in the Autumn of 1970 had induced a momentary feeling of prosperity because of the lag between rises in earnings and subsequent rises in prices. But it was hardly enough to compensate for the trials and tribulations endured since 1966.

CHAPTER TWO

GOVERNMENT; FOUR YEARS HARD SLOG

'His actions speak much stronger than my pen'—CHURCHILL, THE CANDIDATE.

As the results of the 1966 general election flowed in during the early hours of April 1, a mood of euphoria swept the Labour camp. Increasing its overall majority from three to ninety-seven, Labour had, for the first time ever, improved its strength after a period of office. Harold Wilson too had established himself as the dominant personality on the British political scene. Now it was the Tories for a change, uneasy under Edward Heath, who seemed to face chronic leadership problems. As for the economic outlook, had not Jim Callaghan, Chancellor of the Exchequer, already declared with the full authority of the Treasury behind him, that the balance of payments deficit would disappear in 1966? Above all, the nagging uncertainty was over. Here many Tories privately expressed their own relief. The country had seemed to be in a permanent state of electioneering ever since the Tory leadership crisis of 1963. At least politics would be less frantic from now on. Or so it was thought.

In the event, the calm lasted only a matter of weeks. By mid-summer, Labour found itself launched into a series of apparently endless crises which strained party loyalties to their limits, and soon had Labour M.P.s muttering their familiar complaint in times of constant trouble: 'Even God must be a Tory.'

But, for the moment, all this was unimaginable to the Government. As the news of the victory became final, Wilson, cultivating his image as the down-to-earth man-of-business, quietly smiled into the television cameras, declared the result to be precisely what he had expected, and set about forming his Administration. It was substantially the mixture as before, though one significant move was the introduction into the Cabinet of the ex-Minister of Aviation, Roy Jenkins. He became Home Secretary and was tipped by some as a possible eventual Prime Minister.

The Queen's Speech which opened the new Parliament did not suggest a particularly eventful session. There were several items left over from the previous Parliament like the Land Commission Bill and the Steel Nationalisation Bill. On the Foreign Side, it was reiterated that Britain would seek to join the Common Market, which depressed some Labour back-benchers. And the Government would ask the United Nations to impose mandatory sanctions on Rhodesia, which was still showing no signs of coming to heel.

The first major domestic event was the Budget. Callaghan began by explaining to M.P.s that it was necessary to take some further steps to safeguard the balance of payments—he seemed less optimistic now than just before the polls. Consumption at home needed to be curbed by some £300 million a year in fact. M.P.s became anxious. Income tax up? No, Callaghan had an entirely new impost: the Selective Employment Tax. All employers would pay a tax on every man and women employed. In the case of 'service' industries the Government would keep the lot. In the case of 'manufacturing' industries, the Government would return the tax in each case plus a premium. This ingenious (and, as the Opposition maintained, idiotic) new tax would produce £315 million in 1967. It would also steer workers away from service industries and into manufacturing. And of course, said Callaghan sternly, using a familiar if fundamentally dishonest formula, industry was not to pass the extra cost onto the consumer but to absorb it in greater efficiency. (This injunction turned his speech into an economic non-sequitur since, if a tax is not passed onto the consumer, it will not cut consumption. But it was not the first time—or the last—that this pious formula was to be used by a Chancellor.) The immediate effect on most Labour M.P.s was one of delight. But it was only a matter of about 24 hours before many Labour M.P.s had second thoughts. Those Socialist Members who were backed by the Co-op were swiftest to react. But while the Tories complained that this ogre of a tax was completely novel, one new Labour M.P., Mr. Christopher Rowland (Labour, Cardiff North) turned up a precedent: Lord North's Manservants Tax of 1777. This was applied, he said, along the lines of SET, differentiating between productive and service industries. At any rate by the last day of the budget debate in the Commons, it was clear that many M.P.s were not so happy with SET. The 18-strong group of Co-op M.P.s in the Labour Party held a heated meeting privately but ended up deciding to support the Government in the Lobbies.

A rather more serious problem for the Government was looming up on the industrial front. Wage talks between the shipowners and the National Union of Seamen had broken down and there was the possibility that a strike might follow. The pay rise demanded by the seamen was, in effect, 17%. The shipowners made an offer in early April to implement the 40-hour week in three stages.

Wilson called the Union leaders to Downing Street, but there was no progress. Ministers were worried but not alarmed. Under Merchant Shipping Law, the only way sailors could strike was by refusing to sign on again when reaching home port. So the effect of the strike on British trade would only be cumulative.

The Government had reached the decision that this was

the issue on which it would stand and fight—or at any rate get someone else to fight—for its incomes policy. The norm for rises was 3% and the NUS claim, if met, would make nonsense of that. Many Labour back-benchers however did not like the incomes policy at all and there were rumblings of discontent.

The strike, which was to last 47 days in all, began at midnight on May 16. That night Wilson made a television broadcast and pleaded for a settlement. The Union could have an interim award, a review of the old Merchant Shipping Act and a court of enquiry into conditions of work straightaway. But it was to no avail. Mr. Hogarth, General Secretary of the NUS, declared that it would be 'a fight to the finish'. The Government itself set up a committee under Lord Pearson to study the strike, the seamen's working conditions and the Merchant Shipping Act. The Committee was asked to make an interim proposal on pay as quickly as possible.

On June 8 the Committee produced its proposal: a 40-hour week within two years, with the first stage a reduction in working hours from 56 to 48. The cost of the interim plan, 9½% over two years according to the Committee, was certainly above the norm.

(Sir Keith Joseph, Shadow Minister of Labour, argued in the Commons that in fact the cost of the Pearson award was not 4½% in the first year and 5% in the second. Everyone knew that overtime would not in fact be cut as the Union pretended. The cost of the rise in the first year would therefore be 7% in fact, taking account of extra overtime rates.)

But any dilemma the Government might have had about its compatibility with its incomes policy was resolved almost at once: the Unions threw the proposal out. It was all or nothing, the executive council declared.

There was by now little sympathy in the country for the

strikers. Even Labour M.P.s who had been concerned in the beginning to collect 10/- a head for the seamen strike fund were beginning to get sour. And worried too. The trade figures for May came shortly after the strikers rejected the Pearson proposal. The deficit was £81 million. A month before, the deficit had been £70 million. And it was still too early to start putting the blame for this on the strike. Clearly, Callaghan had been optimistic in declaring that he had already taken enough steps to get the balance of payments into the black by the end of the year.

Wilson's tone with the NUS changed from one of pleas to one of fierce irritation. On June 20 he rose in the Commons and launched into a carefully prepared, though oddly oblique, statement about Communist influences at work in the NUS:

'A few', according to Wilson, were bringing undue influence on 'a select few' of the NUS Executive who in turn had been able 'to dominate that otherwise sturdy Union'. He went on to attack 'the tightly knit group of politically motivated men'. But many Labour left-wingers ridiculed the statement. Michael Foot (Labour, Ebbw Vale) acidly pointed out that 'tightly knit group of politically motivated men' was just as applicable to the Cabinet as to the NUS militants. (In fact, as events shortly afterwards were to show, Foot had overestimated the cohesive qualities of the Cabinet.)

With no sign of the strike lifting, Wilson named eight individuals to the House on June 28, including some Communist Party officials who were active in the strike. But by this time the Union was beginning to weaken anyway. The next day, the NUS Executive seized on a small concession proposed by the shipowners, an increase in the number of leave days, to vote to end the strike on July 1.

The Government heaved a sigh of relief and sat back waiting hopefully for the recovery of sterling, which had already slumped in the international money market to an alarmingly low figure. But scarcely was the NUS strike over than Wilson found himself faced with a Cabinet resignation. The Government had introduced a Prices and Incomes Bill in the Commons two weeks earlier which required advance notification of wage claims and price rises. It established the Prices and Incomes Board as a statutory body and gave it powers to defer increases but only for a short time while investigations of their merits were made. There was no thought, the Government insisted, of controlling such rises, only of keeping track of them so that the Government could try to use informal powers of persuasion. Frank Cousins, Minister of Technology, rather abruptly decided that this was too much for a man of his Union background. In a curt note to the Prime Minister on July 3, he declared that he could have nothing to do with the policy.

It was an early jolt for Wilson. But more worrying still for him as he reshuffled his Cabinet to fill the vacancy was the fact that the recovery of sterling had not materialised since the end of the strike. Nor did it look like materialising. International holders of sterling were unconvinced that the poor trade returns were due to the shipping strike, as the Government maintained. After all, even by the end of the dispute, little more than one third of the British Merchant Marine was actually tied up in port.

Help was soon at hand from the Central Bankers who made available a further $1,000 million of credit to protect sterling. But the run on the pound only faltered, it did not stop. By the middle of July it was clear that something drastic would have to be done. Bank Rate was hoisted from 6% to 7% on the 14th. But sterling continued to be sold heavily and the Government now let it be known that there would be an emergency budget in a week or so. Wilson himself had to leave almost immediately for Moscow on a trip he had arranged a week before following severe back-bench criticism of the Government for failing to condemn American bombing in North Vietnam. He was to have talks with Kosygin, the Soviet Premier. They were to yield nothing at all, but at least Wilson was spared some of the inter-departmental battle over the cuts. A striking indication of the decline of the Government's popularity came on the 14th, in the Carmarthen by-election. It fell to the Welsh Nationalists. It was an astonishing swing which shook the Welsh Labour M.P.s, who had hitherto regarded their seats as safe for life. But their alarm was ill-founded. Gwynfor Evans proved the first and last Nationalist Welsh M.P. in the current Parliament and made no great impact.

Wilson returned on the 19th to find the Cabinet sharply divided. He held a meeting that day and the following day. Discussion was prolonged and at times bitter, with George Brown proving particularly difficult. Finally, on July 20, Wilson rose in the Commons to unfold the new emergency measures. 'Where's George?' cried a Tory M.P. jovially at the outset, noticing the First Secretary's surprising absence from the Treasury bench. The laughter at this sally was soon replaced however with gasps of disbelief and dismay as the Prime Minister, his head firmly in his notes and refusing to be deflected, listed the measures to be taken one by one. There was to be:

a six months' wage and prices freeze.
statutory prices and incomes controls.
a £50 foreign travel limit.*
a 10% surcharge on surtax for the year.
duty on tobacco, wines and spirits to rise by 10%.
higher postage rates.
building controls extended.
nationalised industries' programme cut.
local government expenditure programme cut.
overseas spending on aid, defence and embassies to be cut by £100m.

cuts in BAOR, unless the German Government would increase its share of the foreign exchange cost.

The way in which the Ministers reached agreement on the travel limit provides an interesting insight into Cabinet Government. As the plans were being finalised in Cabinet, Wilson turned to the travel limit. £50, he said turning to his colleagues for comments, had been suggested as the figure. One of the less well-heeled ministers promptly commented, 'Well, no one could possibly need more than that.' Several of his more affluent colleagues stared at each other in awkward surprise—and silence. 'Right, then, £50,' said the Prime Minister, moving on to the next item.

Howls of 'resign' from the Tories and a sullen hostility from Labour benches greeted the programme. Pressed to explain the probable effect of these deflationary measures, Wilson said that of course they would mean higher unemployment. $1\frac{1}{2}$ to 2% ought in fact to be acceptable, he thought. British industry needed what he called a 'shake-out which will release the nation's manpower, skilled and unskilled, and lead to a more purposive use of labour'. The reaction was not only astonishment at the measures but also at the way in which Wilson had broken his undertaking to the electorate three months previously. Wilson had said in a television interview just before the Election: 'As to the idea of freezing all wage claims, salary claims . . . I think this would be monstrously unfair . . . I do not think you can ever legislate for wage increases and no party is setting out to do that.'

There were internal troubles too in the Cabinet. Once Wilson had finished his statement in the Commons, the cry of 'Where's George?' was found to be more significant than had been thought. Brown was in fact considering his resignation—or rather re-reconsidering it. He had, it transpired, declared on Tuesday that he would resign. But on Wednesday he had turned up at the four-hour Cabinet meeting and taken part in the proceedings as if he had intended to stay on. On Thursday however he returned to his original decision and appeared at 10 Downing Street at 6 pm with a letter 'offering' his resignation. Wilson would not accept it and asked him to think again. At 10.30 pm Brown returned to No. 10 and after a long talk with the Prime Minister, the Leader of the House, Herbert Bowden, and the Chief Whip, John Silkin, he emerged to tell the waiting press that he was not resigning after all. It was, he said, his duty to stay.

The reaction in the country generally was extremely bitter. Labour's lead in the Gallup Poll in May had been a striking 18%. After the emergency budget, a massive swing took place putting the Tories just ahead by 1.5%. In Parliament, Labour back-bench hostility was soon translated into votes. The nominal majority of the Government dropped from 95 to 52 when the Opposition tried to stop the new freeze proposals being added to the Government's existing Prices and Incomes Bill, then proceeding through the House. There is little doubt moreover that the vote would have been substantially worse for the Government had the real future of the legislation been understood at the time. As the Government presented it, the powers to impose a freeze were essentially reserve powers, just in case Unions and firms did not co-operate. The Government did not anticipate, said Brown in later debates, that it would have to *activate* these powers. Activation would involve an Order in Council and consequently a confirmatory vote in the Commons. Nor would the powers last more than a year, he insisted.

Brown's sincerity was certainly not to be doubted. He clearly meant all he said. However by the time the Prices and Incomes Bill passed its third reading on August 10, these personal assurances were somewhat devalued by a Cabinet reshuffle in which Brown was moved away from the Department of Economic Affairs. His new post was that of Foreign Secretary. It was a post he had always coveted. (In 1962, when Wilson won the vote for the leadership of the Labour Party after the death of Hugh Gaitskell, Brown had asked that he should be made Shadow Foreign Secretary as a consolation prize. Wilson, however, had thought him too excitable for the job.)

Crossman became Leader of the House and Bowden took over the Commonwealth Office from Arthur Bottomley. Bottomley's excursions overseas had proved something of a hazard. In December 1965, he had visited Zambia. He kept referring to the country as Gambia in his public comments and informed one audience there that Zambians were 'noble creatures'. Earlier that year, on a visit to address some chiefs in Rhodesia, he had produced to a bewildered audience what he thought were local proverbs, including obscurely, 'the breast of man is a granary'. The caustic comment of one chief was that Bottomley might remember that a little learning is a dangerous thing.

The final stages of the Prices and Incomes Bill in which abstentions repeatedly halved the normal Government majority were marked by hot debate and many back-bench warnings. There was, however, a diverting interlude. In one debate Brown had the task of winding up for the Government. It was a disaster; 'For almost two years now', he declared earnestly, 'we have tried to manage the economy in a way that no economy has ever been managed before.' The evening ended, needless to say, with the Opposition almost helpless from laughter. It was in this debate that the first, if oblique, reference was made that the National Plan of 1965 was dead. 'The rate of growth (in the Plan)', admitted Brown when goaded, 'is no longer available to us.'

It was with considerable relief that the Government was able to end the Parliamentary session on August 12. It was almost immediately obvious that, sooner or later, the Government would have to implement Part Four of the now enacted Prices and Incomes Act with its penal clauses, whatever Brown may have assured the Commons. Predictably, several groups of employees were not prepared to forego wage increases promised before July 20 to take effect after that date, and the courts agreed that these increases had to be paid.

On October 5 a Cabinet meeting was convened in the unlikely surroundings of the Grand Hotel, Brighton, during the Labour Party Conference. Crossman, Lord President of the Council, and Sir Elwyn Jones, Attorney General, were despatched to the Queen at Balmoral next day for the ritual of an Order in Council making Part Four operative. The simultaneous Conference debate on the Prices and Incomes Policy passed off surprisingly smoothly. The Government won the vote after an assurance that the measure was only temporary. The rest of the proceedings during the Conference passed off relatively easily, though the Government was defeated, as expected, on a Vietnam motion.

It was the turn of the Tories at Brighton the next week with Heath himself under some fire for unenterprising leadership. It was, some of his closest colleagues felt, a dangerous period for him personally. But although there were critical motions down, the Conference followed usual form and accorded the leader a long ovation at the end of the proceedings. It was noticeable of course that Powell, the maverick Shadow Defence Minister, got a particularly warm ovation. He was then, as he had been for years, one of the favourites of the rank and file.

Parliament returned in a critical mood in October, with the motion to approve the Part Four order provoking an angry debate. Only one Government back-bencher, Gordon Walker, the ex-Foreign Secretary, gave the Government his full support. Otherwise the reaction varied from bitterly hostile in the case of Cousins to cautious disapproval in the case of the right wing Socialists. The Government's majority approving the Order dropped sharply, the by now familiar thirty members of the Tribune Group abstaining.

At the same time, restlessness was beginning to appear about unemployment. Wilson's statement about the need for a 'shake-out' had been badly received anyway and the Unions were getting worried at the growth of unemployment. The beginnings of what looked to some Trade Unionists as a steady rise in the number of jobless was apparent.

Nor did Wilson's European initiatives do anything to unite his Party. At the Lord Mayor's Banquet on November 11, he announced that Britain was formally applying for membership of the Common Market. In the Cabinet itself, Douglas Jay, President of the Board of Trade, and Fred Peart, the Minister of Agriculture, were hostile. There was doubt too about Wilson's own real position. Ambivalent—or shifty, according to the Tories—on his attitude towards Europe in the past, he appeared to be now committed to the ideal of the European Economic Community. But Europe, as his followers recalled—with satisfaction or concern, according to their own position— was not the only issue on which he had shifted his view.

The Road to HMS Tiger

The Rhodesian issue on the other hand was to provide the Party eventually with some much needed cohesion in the Commons itself. The predictable and predicted Unilateral Declaration of Independence by the Rhodesian Government in November 1964 had been roundly condemned by all the political parties in Britain. Among the Labour left wingers there was even a demand for the use of force. The Government rejected that firmly and resorted to economic sanctions instead. The Opposition was prepared to support this action up to a point, though there were some very sharp differences inside the Tory party.

Wilson, carried away as usual by his own optimism, was unnecessarily enthusiastic about the prospect of ending UDI by the imposition of oil sanctions. He told the Commonwealth Prime Ministers at a meeting in January 1966 that the rebellion would be 'over in weeks rather than months'. A Commonwealth Office official concerned with advising the Prime Minister on this matter was heard to put the prospect even more plainly: 'They [the Rhodesians] will crumble like a piece of old wallpaper', he said. The official has since been promoted.

The weeks and months went past with little sign of the rebellion ending, rather the Rhodesians seemed to be in a more determined mood than ever. The British Government, which had been in intermittent contact with Smith and his regime throughout, decided in June that another attempt at a settlement should be made. Talks however proved abortive.

Wilson was now left to face the Commonwealth Prime Ministers' Conference in September 1966 with nothing to show for his promises or efforts. The Conference was extremely hostile. In effect it dictated orders to him. He was given three months to settle the crisis, otherwise the United Nations would be requested to impose mandatory sanctions and to require Britain to refuse Rhodesia legal independence until there was majority rule—the previous British negotiating position had been that independence would be granted in the light of guarantees of *unimpeded progress* to majority rule.

Towards the end of November Salisbury was visited, first by a senior Commonwealth official and then by Bowden himself. There was nothing in Bowden's report, when he returned on November 28, to justify optimism. The Rhodesian economy seemed firm, morale there was high and the Smith regime certainly did not appear to be in the mood for making the sort of concessions which Wilson required in order to 'sell' a settlement to his own Party or to the Commonwealth Prime Ministers. But with time running out, Wilson decided on a typically dramatic gesture.

On December 1 he announced to the Commons that he was flying to meet Smith at an undisclosed destination.

Instant suspicion was the reaction from many Labour back-benchers. Was the Prime Minister going to abandon the six principles? (These principles were: unimpeded progress to majority rule, guarantees against retrogressive legislation, immediate improvement in black Rhodesians' political status, progress toward ending racial discrimination, acceptability to the Rhodesians as a whole of any solution, and no oppression of one race by another.) Wilson was adamant: there was no danger of any abandonment, he insisted. The negotiations themselves took place on board the cruiser *HMS Tiger*. At first it looked as though settlement was possible. Smith and Wilson worked out a basis for an agreement and for a return to constitutional rule. But then Smith announced, after exchanges with Salisbury, that he would have to refer the final decision to his own Cabinet. It had been thought that Smith had his colleagues' full authority to reach a settlement, so there was some irritation at this. But there was no alternative to ending the meeting and hoping for approval of the provisional agreement from Salisbury itself. The two sides returned home. Salisbury's final message came: the *Tiger* terms were not acceptable.

This left Wilson in the most exposed of all possible positions since, with the inevitable publication of documents, it immediately became clear that he had in fact abandoned the six principles without even the consolation of reaching a settlement. It became quite clear that the provisional settlement would not have 'guaranteed' unimpeded progress towards majority rule. All that would have been necessary for a white-dominated government to do, as the number of qualified black voters threatened to become a majority (in about ten to fifteen years' time), was to ditch the Constitution. Nothing in the provisional agreement between Smith and Wilson could have prevented that, since Rhodesia would, by the agreement, then be an independent nation outside any real or even nominal United Kingdom sovereignty. As for deciding whether the settlement was acceptable to the majority of Rhodesians, that was to be decided by a Royal Commission appointed by a joint decision of the British and Rhodesian Governments.

Ironically, it seemed to be a set attitude to legal niceties, a determination *not* to 'settle now and scrap it all later' which led Smith and his colleagues to refuse the proposals. As Michael Foot put it in the Commons later, the whole plan would have involved placing trust in Smith's word. The issue which the Rhodesian government chose to base its rejection of the package on was, ostensibly, that of the conditions governing the return to legality.

In the subsequent two-day debate in the Commons it emerged, as one Labour back-bencher put it, that many of his fellow Socialists were 'delighted' that the talks had broken down. They thought that the Prime Minister had gone already far too far in his proposed concessions to the Smith Government.

The Commons debate released feelings which had been pent up during the many months of negotiations when not rocking the boat was the cardinal rule. Wilson chose to turn the occasion into a purely Party battle, successfully finding the issue on which his own side was united in the fiercest distrust of the Tories. Wilson's attack on the Opposition as 'supporters' of the Smith regime was a masterly piece of political tactics which brought his own side to its feet in a standing ovation. Fortunately for the Tories, Heath hit back just as hard. He scoffed at Wilson's high moral principles. They were so high, Heath said, that he was in favour of sanctions against Rhodesia though not against South Africa which was important to the British economy. The debate resounded to sharp shouts of 'traitor' at Heath and 'hypocrite' at Wilson. There was near pandemonium at the end. But for Wilson it was an undoubted success. He had found the one issue which united his own side and ruthlessly exploited it.

The most contentious Parliamentary measure at the time, however, was a private member's Bill which exempted from the criminal law homosexual acts between consenting adults. A small band of back-benchers, mainly but not wholly Tory, fought it fiercely, solemnly predicting all sorts of dour consequences. But the Government, at the instigation of Jenkins, decided to give the Bill the required Parliamentary time and its safe passage was thus assured. Reforms on abortion and divorce were also to be carried through later by private bills given special Government time.

December also marked the end of the import surcharge scheme first introduced by Callaghan in November 1964. The measure had been fiercely attacked by overseas governments as a violation of trading agreements. Callaghan, under strong international pressure, had announced the impending abandonment of the scheme in May. But, in any case, the Government was beginning to feel reassured about the economic situation. The Chancellor was talking of 'not just a bare balance in 1967, but a surplus'. At the same time the Government announced small increases in capital investment grants for industry.

But these were very minor changes. The year went out on an uneasy note. Wilson himself was now widely distrusted within his own party. The minister who had perhaps made the most impression was Jenkins. The epithet 'smooth' was much applied to him in the press. It was appropriate in some ways. He had a certain elegance of manner and was popularly (and correctly) credited with being unusually at home in ducal drawing-rooms for a Socialist. But at the same time, his acute intelligence and debating skill were widely recognised in politics.

Brown on the other hand was arousing a certain amount of

anxiety. A combination of boisterousness and unpredictability was all very well in the Minister for Economic Affairs. But in a Foreign Minister it was rather different. Stories of 'outbursts' at ambassadorial dinners where Brown was 'overwrought' were rife. There were also stories of jovial advances made by him to diplomats' wives.

1967: The Road to Devaluation

Officially 1967 marked the end of the 'freeze' and the beginning of the period of 'severe restraint'. This was supposed to mean that though all prices and incomes were no longer frozen, actual increases were to be approved only in very special cases. But there was very little 'severe restraint' in Government management of the economy, whatever discipline may have been demanded from the private sector. Bank Rate was cut three times between January and May, bringing it down from 7 to 5½%. Government spending for the forthcoming financial year was raised by £600 million and there was some easing of the supply on house purchase funds from the central Government as well as a sharp acceleration of the speed with which investment grants were paid out to industry. At the same time funds for general local authority borrowing were made more readily available. In short, as it was to be emphasised later, the Government was making very little effort to control the general money supply.

These relaxations did something to help the Government's popularity at first. Indeed, in February, a Gallup Poll showed Labour back in the lead by 11½ points. Heath's personal standing was particularly low. In the Parliamentary Labour Party, however, Wilson was still having some trouble with vociferous rebels who were particularly irritated by the Prices and Incomes Board's activities. In March, the Prime Minister even went so far as to deliver what sounded like an ultimatum on discipline. He told a Parliamentary Labour Party meeting: 'All I can say is, watch it. Every dog is allowed one bite but a different view is taken of a dog that goes on biting all the time. If there are doubts that the dog is biting not because of dictates of conscience but because he is considered vicious, then things happen to that dog. He may not get his licence renewed'.

It sounded ferocious. But it turned out to be reminiscent of Ambrose Bierce's definition of an ultimatum: 'The last warning before resorting to concessions.' Far from the Government whip, Silkin, disciplining back-benchers more fiercely, he seemed to be anxious to devise excuses for avoiding confrontations. Any conviction on the part of Wilson that his position in the country was now becoming more secure was also dashed shortly after his 'dog-licence' speech by the Greater London Council elections. The Tories were swept to power in the April elections, gaining 82 of the 100 seats. Even the most optimistic Tories were taken aback.

It was clear that Spring that the Government was slipping back into its habitual condition of wild optimism about the economy. Having already embarked on these substantially reflationary measures, it was not surprising that the actual budget itself had little to add. Bank borrowing was made marginally easier and hire-purchase restrictions on motor bikes and three-wheelers were eased.

There were so few changes in fact that the Commons was stunned; and the well-known capacity of M.P.s for saying a lot about a little was strained to the utmost in the subsequent ritual of a three-day debate on the budget proposals. Callaghan's own view was that 'we are emerging from the valley of gloom'. The nation was 'back on course' and the motto for the future was 'steady as she goes'. Only a few days later he was maintaining that 'there will be a surplus this year and a bigger surplus next year'.

Nor was he alone in his optimism. In February, Wilson,

whose optimism could be called impressive or alarming, according to one's political and economic views, spoke in February of Britain's growing economic achievements. In March, he added, in a television interview, 'the whole world knows that we are in a balance of payments surplus this year'. Many back-bench Labour M.P.s on the other hand, were not so sure. Even if there was going to be a surplus—and several still had their doubts—it was being achieved as they saw it at the cost of too high a rate of unemployment and too slow a rate of economic growth. Substantial swings against Labour in the Glasgow, Pollack, and Rhondda by-elections suggested that a lot of electors took the same views. A number of Labour M.P.s hinted strongly at the need for devaluation at the end of July. But they were sternly refuted by Callaghan, who insisted that such a step was inconceivable and would be self-defeating.

On the foreign side, Wilson faced substantial divisions within his own party on two issues: Vietnam and the Common Market. There was mounting hostility among Labour back-benchers at the Government's refusal to dissociate itself firmly from American action in Vietnam. An opportunity for one of those many British 'initiatives'—almost invariably unsuccessful but useful for domestic consumption—arose when Kosygin paid an official visit to Britain in February. The Guild Hall witnessed the rather unedifying spectacle of a Russian Premier using it as a platform for an attack on 'American aggression'. But Wilson, to the alarm of some Foreign Office officials, seemed to be forming a positive fondness for Kosygin. In public the Prime Minister said that Kosygin 'had almost become a part of our way of life'. Certainly the Prime Minister seemed convinced that the Soviet leader wanted peace in Vietnam. But the only positive achievement of Wilson, and that was largely prestigious, was an obliging acquiescence from Kosygin for a hot-line to be installed between Downing Street and the Kremlin.

The Common Market negotiations involved Wilson and Brown in a further series of 'initiatives' as they made a rapid tour of the capitals of the Six. Except in Paris, where the atmosphere was cordial but non-committal (as might be expected), the two men found enthusiasm for the British application (as was again to be expected). The only jarring moment for the Government came when, taking advantage of their absence, Douglas Jay chose to inform a meeting of the Parliamentary Labour Party that membership of the EEC would involve immense balance of payments costs and no advantages to speak of.

However, on May 2 the Prime Minister announced to the House after a Cabinet Meeting that Britain was now sending in the formal documents to Brussels with Britain's application. This seemed to be about the third time the Government had announced that it was actually applying for membership (previous occasions had been the Queen's Speech in April 1966, and in November's speech at the Lord Mayor's Banquet); the statement provoked no particular reaction in itself. But at least it provided the Commons with a chance for a two-day debate. In this both Tory and Labour opponents of the Common Market united; with some M.P.s threatening undying opposition to the application. And though the vote in favour was 488 to 62, the Government noted with some anxiety that there were 51 Labour M.P.s who abstained as well as the 34 who voted against; and this was despite a three-line whip. Seven Parliamentary Private Secretaries who joined the rebels were forced to resign on the Prime Minister's instructions.

The sudden eruption of Israel-Arab hostilities in June had found very little division in Parliament. The ordering out of the United Nations peace-keeping force by President Nasser, the closing of the Straits of Tiran to Israeli shipping, and the build-up of Egyptian forces provoked a ferocious pre-emptive strike by the Israelis which few felt inclined to call unjustified. The brilliantly conducted *blitzkrieg* by the Israelis lasted six days and brought her to the edge of the Suez Canal and to the bank of the Jordan. As one of the Four Powers which had given the original guarantee of Israeli integrity in 1948, Britain busied herself diplomatically, talking of arms embargoes and peace initiatives. But since the Arabs were in no mood to negotiate and the Israelis were prepared to consider only direct negotiations with the Arabs, these activities were fruitless.

There were two important economic aspects of the war for Britain. One was the closure of the Suez Canal. The other was the disruption as the oil-producing nations of the Middle East, in a display of Arab unity—and therefore temporarily—suspended oil supplies to the West because of its supposed pro-Israeli activities.

After severe restraint

The Middle East troubles did not, however, in the Government's view mean a serious blow for Britain. July 1 officially marked the end of the period of 'severe restraint' and ministers were convinced that the economy was on the mend. Caution on the Government's part was marked by only one major decision, to renew the Prices and Incomes Act and its powers. Both Tories and left-wingers were quick to point out that this constituted another broken pledge. Last year Brown had promised no further prices and incomes legislation. This year, though, it was Michael Stewart as Minister for Economic Affairs who brought forward the Bill. The order implementing these powers provoked a fierce debate. The most formidable threat to the widespread use of these powers came from Iain Macleod, Shadow Chancellor, who pointed out that under the Act the Commons was entitled to debate every individual price or incomes order that the Government chose to bring in. If, he said, meaningfully, the

Government chose to use these powers extensively, the Opposition would use these occasions to the full, with the result that very little other business would be transacted in Parliament. Stewart reacted to this by a promise that of course the Government did not intend to make many such orders. This, logically, seemed to the left-wingers to make the Act superfluous as well as obnoxious and in the subsequent division the Government majority fell to 56, with 22 Labour abstentions despite a three-line whip.

However, the Prime Minister was so convinced that matters were going well that, in a staggering masterpiece of mistiming, he announced on August 28 that he was to become the 'overlord' of the Department of Economic Affairs, appointing Peter Shore to run the Department on a day-to-day basis. The comparison he chose was the decision of Sir Winston Churchill, during the war, to be Minister of Defence as well as Prime Minister. Some Tory leaders also asked, rhetorically, if the Prime Minister was saying that he had not been in overall charge of the economic situation hitherto. There were derisive comments too when hire-purchase relaxations were relaxed three days later for cars, furniture, household goods, and so on. The Prime Minister, it was said, was trying to boost his own standing by taking over the management of the DEA just as reflationary measures were being planned in any case. A week later Wilson insisted that the balance of payments was 'in a position of basic balance and growing strength'. The hire-purchase moves and the Prime Minister's statement were followed however a week later by ominous figures which even the Prime Minister should have been able to read. The overall balance of payments accounts for the second quarter, which largely excluded the effect of the Suez Canal closure, were published. They showed a heavy deficit. Since the first quarter's surplus had been considerably due to fortuitous elements, as various economists and Heath too had warned at the time, this was not surprising. Industrial trouble came too with the beginning of an unofficial dock strike on September 18, though it was confined to Liverpool and only a part of London docks.

As a prelude to the Party Conference season, Wilson had the dismaying experience of seeing the Tories win the Cambridge and Walthamstow by-elections with huge swings. For Heath, on the other hand, who was still under fire from some of the Tory rank and file, this was a splendid windfall. There was no arguing with success, as one of his strongest supporters in the Party kept putting it.

The Tory expectations of a hard time for Wilson and his Party Conference at Scarborough were dashed. The Labour Party was glum, but it was not feeling particularly rebellious. Matters were certainly helped by Callaghan, who made a superb speech, bristling with apparent confidence and competence. The Prime Minister, too, was in excellent form. The net result was that the hostile votes against the Government were few, considering all the circumstances and considering the form of the Unions, who had been in a militant mood only a month before at the Trades Union Congress. There was, however, one unfortunate incident involving Brown. This time it was a public row with press photographers, first in the Scarborough Ballroom and later in his hotel. There, in a scene reminiscent of a French farce, he kept denouncing the assembled photographers to their faces and marching off up the hotel stairs, only to keep pausing and marching down to renew his denunciations.

How long could a Foreign Secretary like this survive, M.P.s kept asking? A rumour flew around that the Prime Minister had carpeted Brown. This was promptly denied with assurances that the Prime Minister and the Foreign Secretary were on more than usually friendly terms. Cynics declared that this was quite probably true. Each incident involving Brown meant that Wilson could the more safely ignore any challenge to his leadership from his one-time rival.

There was a further blow for Wilson's prestige on November 3 in three simultaneous by-elections. In one the Tories won a Labour seat, in another a very safe Labour seat was only just held; in the third, Hamilton, a substantial Labour majority was converted into a substantial Scottish Nationalist majority. It was to prove the only victory for the Scottish Nationalist Party but it was such an impressive result that Scottish Labour M.P.s became very nervous.

When the new Parliament reopened on October 31, Heath made warning noises to the Government about the prospective balance of payments deficit. Already the September trade figures had shown a deficit of £52 million, following a June deficit of £105 million. The total balance of payments deficit on current account for the year, he said, could be £200 million. Wilson was scornful about this and other warnings. There was widespread recognition that the economy was 'on the turn', he insisted. He thought the unemployment figures were not as discouraging as they seemed. Callaghan also tried to be reassuring. In the event of any sterling difficulties the funds available for Government borrowing and buttressing of the pound were more than ample.

But a few days later the trade figures for October were published. The deficit this time was £162 million. It was an all-time record; and though the dock strike was estimated to have been responsible for £100 million of the deficit, it still left a figure—following the result for September—which was thoroughly alarming. In anticipation of the deterioration, Bank Rate had been raised twice, to 6% in early October and to 6½% in early November. But neither this nor tangible evidence of support for sterling from overseas bankers could stem the run on the pound. Indeed, Callaghan and Wilson had already reached the decision that devaluation was inevitable. The most secret instructions for putting the process in train were issued on November 8 and the Treasury started to work by the 'War Book' which had been prepared for this contingency, turning over the page for each day in preparation for the final announcement. Nominally the decision was taken on the 15th at a Thursday meeting of the Cabinet, where the plan was unanimously approved. But international financial circles had already got the jitters and sterling was draining away. Worse, there was a last minute stampede on the Friday. This resulted from the most unfortunate exchange in the Commons involving the Chancellor. Mr. Robert Sheldon (Labour, Ashton-under-Lyne) had tabled a Private Notice Question asking whether it was true that the Government was negotiating another $1,000 million loan for buttressing the pound. As with all PNQs, it was up to the Speaker to decide whether the Minister should have to answer it. A message was sent into Callaghan during the Cabinet meeting. He glanced at the question but put it aside. By the time he emerged from the meeting over an hour later, the Speaker had decided to accept the question. It was to prove one of the most costly decisions ever taken by a Speaker of the House of Commons, though Callaghan too must share much of the blame. He made no attempt to get the question postponed.

Callaghan's answer in the House was that he could not say anything in the circumstances about the rumours in the press about a further loan. The supplementaries included these exchanges:

MR. DICKENS: Is the Chancellor aware that some of us at any rate are totally opposed to—[An Hon. Member: Everything.] this country having further money from foreign bankers.

MR. CALLAGHAN: Yes, I understand my Hon. Friend's point of view. I have no further comment to make.

MR. THORPE: Whether or not there are any negotiations under way could the Chancellor say how much longer the Government will rely upon borrowing to maintain confidence in the pound? Is he aware that there is a general feeling that to sacrifice full employment and economic expansion for the sacred cow of sterling is something to which many people are opposed.

MR. CALLAGHAN: That does not arise out of my original answer.

MR. ORME: Would my Right Hon. Friend agree that if the difference is between a reduction in public expenditure at home, a wage freeze and the introduction of a regulator and devaluation, devaluation is preferable to those three things.

MR. CALLAGHAN: I have nothing to add to or subtract from anything I have said on previous occasions on the subject of devaluation, and in any case it does not arise from my original answer.

MR. STRATTON MILLS: The Chancellor's original answer is quite incredible. Will he clear up whether negotiations are or are not progressing? When he makes his statement, will he give full details on all the outstanding short-term loans which this country has incurred and which have not been revealed to the public?

MR. CALLAGHAN: I have nothing to add to my original answer.

This was a very different Callaghan from the one who had previously dismissed the whole idea of devaluation with vehemence. What ensued in the City the next day was little short of panic. Selling of sterling reached a frantic rate. That day of speculation cost Britain over £300 million.

The actual announcement of devaluation came on the Saturday evening. The size of the devaluation was 14.3%. At the same time Bank Rate was raised to 8% and there were to be severe cuts in bank lending. The reaction in the Commons on the Monday was very mixed. The Tories howled for Callaghan's blood, but many M.P.s who had been devaluation enthusiasts for some time in the Labour Party cheered him loudly. Callaghan himself quickly acknowledged that he could not now remain Chancellor for long. (In fact, his letter of resignation had been handed in at 10, Downing Street the previous Saturday.) But at least he was going to defend devaluation for the few days left to him; and this he proceeded to do with considerable dignity in the face of a very genuine Tory fury at what they regarded as a betrayal of the nation's faith.

Wilson's own performance in the controversy was maladroit. In a television transmission he declared that devaluation 'does not mean, of course, that the pound here in Britain, in your pocket or purse, or in your bank has been devalued'.

Later in the House, he tried to portray devaluation as if it were some sort of brilliantly conceived panacea. He attacked Heath who had condemned devaluation in a bitter and effective television broadcast two days before. Heath would regret his views, said the Prime Minister. Why, in a year's time, the problem would be shortage of labour. This was Britain's chance for real and sustained economic recovery. He added: 'Since early Autumn, there was no doubt that the economy was moving upwards. As I told the House last Thursday, on the basis of existing policies—that is before devaluation—we could look forward to a substantial increase in production over the next year—well above the five per cent which we had envisaged earlier.

. . . Now of course with the opportunities of export-led expansion resulting from devaluation, it is right to tell the House that the problem which we shall be facing in a year's time is far more likely to be not deflation and unemployment but expansion to a scale which might lead to labour shortages in many areas.'

It was clear that some M.P.s believed Wilson. More important, perhaps, was that Wilson clearly believed Wilson.

Administratively, the immediate and pressing problem for the Prime Minister was to chose a new Chancellor. He had three candidates in mind, Denis Healey (Defence Secretary), Anthony Crosland (President of the Board of Trade) and Jenkins. Healey had the distinct disadvantage that he tended to bully the Prime Minister even in front of his colleagues. On the whole, the Prime Minister preferred Crosland to

Jenkins. But the latter had a considerable following on the back-benches which the Prime Minister thought it might be as well to appease. Certainly Jenkins's performance as Home Secretary had been consistently competent and the Opposition had rarely been able to get the better of him in the House. In any case Callaghan was showing some enthusiasm for the idea of swopping the Treasury with the Home Office. So Wilson decided on the straight swop between the two.

Jenkins's start was, however, vigorous rather than accomplished. The International Monetary Fund loan which had been negotiated to tide sterling over the post-devaluation phase was, of course, made available on the basis of a Letter of Intent written on behalf of the British Government by Callaghan just before resignation. The Letter of Intent was published by Jenkins in Hansard, but the day before he was rash enough to tell the House that 'despite misleading reports to the contrary, the Fund has not attached conditions to this credit'. Nor, he said, did the policy set out in the Letter of Intent involve any net deflationary policies. Both statements seemed palpably silly to M.P.s who could hardly see why the Fund would lend yet further sums to Britain without conditions. An emergency debate proved gruelling for Jenkins. The essential points in the Letter of Intent were that home consumption was to be cut by £750 million according to the Government's promise. There were, in effect, conditions attached to the loan and there was an undertaking by Britain to deflate. Nigel Birch (Conservative, West Flint), with his usual scorn, commented that 'to tell a fib when one is bound to be found out within ten minutes is pathetic, childish'. It proved an uncomfortable time for the Chancellor and at the end of the day eighteen Labour M.P.s actually voted against the Government's deflationary strategy and at least as many others abstained. During this period Wilson's leadership was inevitably under attack inside the Party. Unfavourable contrasts were drawn between Callaghan's dignified acknowledgment of a defeat and Wilson's own attempted presentation of the move almost as if it were a carefully planned manoeuvre. 'We have the chance now', Wilson had declared cheerfully on television, 'to break out of the straitjacket of these past years'. There was even some speculation by political correspondents that there would be an attempt to replace Wilson with Callaghan. It was an inherently improbable rumour to start with, but the fact that it gained currency at all showed the weakness of the Prime Minister's position.

To make matters worse, Wilson also faced a rebuff from President de Gaulle at about this time. In a speech in which many detected an unpleasant element of *schadenfreude*, the President said that Britain was not ready to join the EEC and the community could not take on the burden of British problems at the time.

The Tory lead in the Gallup poll, 7½% before devaluation, was now standing at 17½%. Nor was the Government position likely to be improved by the economies in public spending which now had to be arranged. The Chancellor fixed the target for cuts at £800 million over two years; and after a Cabinet meeting just before Parliament rose, Wilson announced that no area of expenditure could be regarded as sacrosanct. But at least one aspect of the situation had turned out very conveniently. The decision, though forced on the Government, not to sell arms to South Africa was treated by the Prime Minister as a sort of moral crusade. Stern, hard measures to deal with the economy might be required, he said in a subsequent Commons debate, but the Government, unlike the Tories, would not try to make money out of selling arms to South African racialists.

1968: The Two Years' Hard Slog

For Ministers it was a miserable Christmas and New Year. Finding economies at short notice was difficult without disrupting a whole series of departmental programmes.

Foremost were cuts planned in defence. Wilson who had once even talked about Britain's frontiers being on the Himalayas, and who had vigorously supported an East of Suez role as late as mid-1967, now made a complete about turn. Healey, who had said even *after* devaluation that Britain must keep faith with its eastern allies for at least a decade, was given the task of preparing for a total British withdrawal from the Far East (except Hong Kong) by the end of 1971. The Prime Minister of Singapore personally flew to London in early January in an unsuccessful attempt to change Wilson's mind. The Australian Prime Minister, John Gorton, protested publicly and President Johnson urged the Government to reconsider its decision. It was to no avail. Defence cuts topped the list of economies which Wilson announced in the Commons on January 15. Apart from the withdrawals from East of Suez—which Wilson was soon presenting as yet another well-planned manoeuvre and abandonment of Tory post-imperialist fantasies—there were to be large cuts in the armed forces, aircraft carriers were to be phased out, and the order for the F111 American aircraft was to be cancelled. Prescriptions charges were to be reintroduced at 2/6d. an item, subject to some exemptions, the national insurance stamp charge was to be raised by 1/6d. and free school milk ended. The raising of the school-leaving age was deferred until 1973. The housing programme was to be cut. The main section of the Territorial Army was to be disbanded and the Civil Defence put on a care and maintenance basis. Over twenty Labour M.P.s abstained from supporting the Government in the subsequent debate. There was only one Cabinet resignation, that of Lord Longford, Lord Privy Seal. For him the breaking point was the deferment of school leaving age. Miss Jenny Lee, Minister for the Arts, had broadly hinted at her resignation before the decision was finally made but in the event she found it her public duty to stay.

As if this was not bad enough, Mr. Jenkins warned the

nation that the budget would be a harsh one and would be brought in rather earlier than usual.

When the budget came in March, it turned out to involve the most swingeing increases in taxation the country had ever faced on one single occasion. The changes were:

Petrol up by 4d. a gallon.
Cigarettes up 2d. for 20.
Whiskey up 2/6d. a bottle.
Road Fund Licences up £7 10s.
Corporation Tax (as foreshadowed in November) up 2½%.
SET was increased by 50%.
Betting Tax was doubled to 5%.
Income Tax allowances were cut so as to neutralise the previous family allowances except for the poor.

There was to be no increase in Income Tax, however, to the relief of all. But there was to be a special surcharge on large investment incomes which amounted to a Capital Levy. This last item, skilfully kept until the end of the Budget statement, so delighted Labour left-wingers, who had longed for such a levy for years, that Jenkins was actually given a standing ovation by this section of the Party at the end of his speech. The satisfaction of course did not last long. Soon the Government was facing as fierce an attack as ever from back-benchers and the Unions for deflating the economy so fiercely. The realisation was at last dawning even on the most obtuse supporters of devaluation that Callaghan had spoken the truth when he said that devaluation could only be made to work by deflation. Nor, to complicate matters, did the measures seem even to get the balance of payments right as the months went by. As 1968 progressed, the trade figures got worse not better. The initial rise in the price of imported raw materials due to devaluation was inevitably to be expected. But as the months rolled by and the trade figures persisted in large deficit, the Government's anxiety increased. To add to the difficulties there was an international financial crisis in the air too. For some time the International Monetary System had been showing weakness. It was still based on the now somewhat obsolete structure drawn up at Bretton Woods in 1944; the gold price was artificially low; and the Americans' involvement in Vietnam was causing them to run a huge balance of payments deficit. This led to a steady diminution of the Washington gold reserves. The British devaluation had the effect of sparking off world-wide speculation about the future of other currencies, including even the dollar. The crisis came in March when the US Government decided that it could no longer redeem dollars in gold except for other governments. The decision of the main Western governments which followed this involved the closing of the gold and stock markets for twenty-four hours. This decision in the case of Britain, taken precipitately, supplied Wilson with at least one blessing. George Brown resigned. He had taken extreme umbrage at being left out of the Privy Council quorum that went to the Palace to arrange the closing of the markets.

In a curt note to the Prime Minister, he said he did not like 'the way this Government is run and the manner in which we reach our decisions'. In the subsequent reshuffle Wilson appointed Michael Stewart to the Foreign Office again and wound up the Department of Economic Affairs. He merged its earthly remains with the Ministry of Labour to create a new department, the Ministry of Employment and Productivity. Barbara Castle was raised from the Ministry of Transport to run this new department and Ray Gunter was moved to Transport. He did not stay long and handed in his resignation in June, because of his feelings about Wilson's leadership. Neither Gunter nor Brown, in fact, ever proved a threat to the Government. Brown was no longer a force to reckon with; and Gunter chose to remain very quiet.

The gold crisis itself had left considerable uneasiness in

financial circles everywhere. There was little or no signs of a British balance of trade recovery either. Sterling became increasingly vulnerable to pressure. The Government had been able to cut back Bank Rate by a ½% to 7½% in late March. But part of the motive had been to achieve a position from which Bank Rate could be once again raised without setting an even higher record and without provoking talk of yet another record high level of interest rates. In May, the Government felt obliged to put a further squeeze on bank lending. At the same time, to the disgust but not this time the surprise of its own side, it said that further Prices and Incomes powers would be necessary. The Act would now be extended another one year. It was exceptional, it was explained to the House, because this was the post-devaluation period. In such circumstances previous pledges must be treated in a special light. There always seemed to be special circumstances, either the express necessity of devaluation or of making devaluation work.

After a Commons debate in which charges of broken faith rained down on the Government as fiercely from its own back-benches as from the Tory side, the Government secured the second reading of the Bill but only by a majority of 35. The Amalgamated Union of Engineers and Foundry Workers even called a one day national strike in protest. The disillus-sionment of the electorate too seemed absolute. In the local Government elections in May, the Tories swept the board. After the polls, Labour was found to be in control of scarcely any of the large cities.

In April, however, the Tory Party was bitterly divided over a domestic issue. Race. Just before the passing of the Race Relations Bill, which made discrimination in employment and housing illegal, Enoch Powell launched into a ferocious attack on the whole immigration policy. Passing the Bill, he said, would be to risk throwing a match onto gunpowder. 'As I look ahead I am filled with foreboding. Like the Roman,

I seem to see the river Tiber foaming with so much blood.' There must not only be a complete stop to immigration, he insisted, but large sums must be diverted to encourage re-patriation. Many Tory M.P.s, some privately and some publicly, agreed with Powell's views, though many of those thought that bringing into his speech examples of British citizens having excrement thrust through their letter-boxes by hostile immigrants was sensation-mongering of the worst type.

Asked many months later if he did not regret this speech, Powell said that the only thing he would have changed in retrospect was the reference to the Tiber. He should, he said, have quoted the remark in Latin to emphasise that he was only recalling a classical prophesy of doom, not actually predicting a blood bath.

But the gunpowder which this incident ignited was not racial but political. Heath instantly dismissed him from the Shadow Cabinet and not without some relief to most of his colleagues. Powell had proved a difficult colleague, publicly attacking adherence to any sort of incomes policy as absurd, implying that an East of Suez role was folly and generally acting as a maverick of the most disturbing kind. Moreover, several of Powell's colleagues recalled that, as Minister of Health, he had cheerfully encouraged the immigration of coloured nurses and doctors to supply the needs of the Health Service. Some were inclined to mutter about hypocrisy. But they rather ignored a very striking trait in Powell's character. If he had concluded, after a rigorous analysis, that his own views had been wrong in the past, he put his new case with greater vigour than ever. Having been a minister in a government which followed all sorts of consensus policies he now considered wrong, he set out to attack them with unremitting ferocity. His intellectual integrity seemed to drive him to the point where he had to be able to say to himself on any and every issue: 'I have not trimmed today'. Indeed on many issues, this driving urge seemed to push him into overstating his case.

But in the country as a whole there was a reaction which shook the leaders of both parties. A march of several hundred dockers and Smithfield meat porters converged on the Commons shouting 'Good old Enoch' and demanding his reinstatement. Wilson after a savage attack on Powell urged that race should be 'taken out of politics'. (It was an unusual line for Wilson, indicating that he was on the defensive.) Many leading Tories publicly disowned Powell. Quintin Hogg, Shadow Home Secretary, was one of them. But whether Hogg and the Shadow Cabinet were maintaining their balance seemed open to doubt. In a burst of indiscriminate liberalism, Hogg officially moved in the committee stage of the Race Relations Bill that discrimination should not only be banned on grounds of race but also of age, sex and religion. This fatuous amendment, as *The Daily Telegraph* acidly pointed out, would have the effect of compelling the Young Women's Christian Associations to admit elderly male atheists.

The fierce row over race relations tended to obscure to some extent the abiding public concern about the economic situation. In the Commons, the Tories attacked the Government constantly over the way in which every undertaking given at the 1966 election had been or was being abandoned. The Tory Front Bench was particularly determined to brand Wilson as the man no one could trust. Terms like 'cheat', 'twister' and 'fraud' were systematically hurled at the Prime Minister in debate after debate. It was certainly the easiest thing possible to quote the Prime Minister against himself. But whether these were the right tactics was open to doubt.

The first of the conferences that autumn, the Trades Union Congress, gave the Government a rough ride on most issues. The fact that the Government had just negotiated a further central bank credit of £800 million worried the

Labour movement more than ever. The idea of being in pawn to 'bankers' was bad enough but being in pawn to 'foreign bankers' roused xenophobic as well as anti-capitalistic instincts. But though the votes of the TUC were fiercely critical, ministers were given a relatively easy time at the Labour Party Conference shortly afterwards. The Prime Minister, in his usual aggressive form, set the tone by announcing in his speech at the outset that this would be known as the year when Labour 'started to fight back'. The Conference seemed to take its cue from the Prime Minister's theme.

But the electorate did not. Crushing swings against the Government at by-elections continued. In the Bassetlaw contest in late November, Barbara Castle made a serious boob by telling electors that 'there was no economic freeze on the way'. In the literal sense this was perhaps true. But the Cabinet was in fact preparing plans for a still tighter squeeze at that moment and when it materialised a few days after the contest in the form of tighter hire-purchase controls, it provided the Tories with still further ammunition for their persistent campaign against Labour ministers as untrustworthy—not even trustworthy for 24 hours.

Worse was to come. On November 22, after an urgent meeting at Basle precipitated by further international unrest over currencies, particularly sterling, Jenkins rushed dramatically back to London on a Friday afternoon to announce further severe restraints. Again they were worse than anyone had anticipated. There was 5d. extra on petrol, 5d. on cigarettes, 6d. to 1/- on wine, 10% increases in purchase tax. In addition, there was to be a new 50% deposit-in-advance scheme for imports and yet another attempt to squeeze bank lending further. In the Tory camp the talk was mainly of the sort of majority that seemed inevitable at the next general election.

The Tory Conference that autumn had been largely

eclipsed by another of Wilson's dramatic attempts to settle the Rhodesian question. The general conclusion that Wilson had contrived this timing was rebutted by, characteristically, Sir Alex Douglas-Home. He would ascribe no such motives to the Prime Minister and wished his endeavours the best of luck.

Informal discussions between British semi-official envoys ranging from Sir Alec himself to Lord Goodman, Wilson's own solicitor, had been proceeding sporadically since shortly after the collapse of the *Tiger* talks. Fifty-nine Labour M.P.s had fired a warning shot across the Prime Minister's bows at the end of the summer session by signing a motion warning him not to settle the Rhodesian question during the recess. Emphasising that any settlement would be subject to Parliamentary approval, Wilson flew to Gibraltar again, this time to negotiate with Smith on board HMS Fearless. But the Rhodesian leader was in a tougher frame of mind than ever. Rhodesia seemed to be surviving sanctions remarkably well. In fact, when Britain devalued in November 1967, Rhodesia had not been among the other twenty-four countries which had followed suit. The two leaders made their offers to each other and returned to their respective capitals. Wilson was greeted in Parliament with compliments from the Opposition, first for trying to reach a settlement, and second for a more conciliatory bearing. Certainly it was becoming clear that the Government was now ready to give way to Smith on several points. It was prepared to drop its demand that there should be an interim period of return to constitutional rule before Rhodesia became independent. The point at which Smith jibbed was the insertion in the proposed constitution of a guarantee against amendment to the entrenched clauses guaranteeing African rights. The readiness of the British Government to have settled on these terms led, after the apparent collapse of the talks, to angry Labour attacks on Wilson and Thomson as the full details unfolded. If the Government persisted in offering such terms, there would clearly be several resignations. In the Commons fifty-one Labour M.P.s voted against the Government on a procedural motion to signify their disapproval of the terms offered. It was the biggest rebellion the Government had faced yet. Combined with continuing reverses at by-elections, it brought Wilson's leadership to another low ebb.

At least it was some consolation to Wilson during this period that Heath also was far from flourishing as Tory leader. Splendid as the by-election results were, the opinion polls continued to show Heath unable to gain a good personal rating. The Tory Conference had shown the great majority of delegates ready to give Powell a standing ovation at the slightest opportunity. Heath survived the Conference comparatively unscathed, making the usual last day speech. It was a good one and he deserved the customary ovation. Powell had to contend with boos as well as cheers. In the Commons, Heath was still not a consistently impressive performer. Sometimes he would produce a first-class speech, but he could never match the cool mastery of the House which Wilson displayed, often by cheap sneers perhaps, but effectively just the same.

On one foreign affairs issue a substantial group of back-benchers on both sides was prepared to battle with the combined force of both front-benches: Biafra. After the brutal overthrow of the original and democratic Nigerian Government in 1966 by a group of army officers, a majority of whom were Ibos, tribal tensions which were never far below the surface in the country grew rapidly. One further military coup and many months later, a savage massacre of Ibos took place in northern Nigeria conducted by Hausas. This horrific occurrence, involving the death of over 10,000 Ibos, led later to the breakaway of the Ibo-dominated eastern province. Under its leader, Colonel Ojukwu, 'Biafra' demanded independence and prepared to fight for it. In the subsequent bloody civil war, which only ended with the eventual triumph of the overwhelmingly stronger federal army in January 1970, some 2,000,000 are reckoned to have died, mainly from starvation. The British Government, generally but not in every way supported by the Tory front-bench, sided with the Federal Government to the extent of supplying it with arms in almost limitless quantities and on credit. From a Government which prated about the virtues of self-determination for all, this policy seemed objectionable and appalling; to say nothing of hypocritical. Periodic debates took place in the House in which groups of Tories, Socialists and Liberals continued to assail the Government. But the rebels never mustered more than 51 votes.

1969

In his 1969 New Year message, Wilson emphasised that for Britain this year, he was proud to say, the Government would introduce its new earnings-related pension scheme: 'the culmination of a generation of Socialist innovation in social provision'.

A more pressing problem of internal unity arose a week later when Mrs. Castle published her White Paper 'In Place of Strife.' For some time the rumours had been circulating that the Government was intending to follow up the autumn report of the Royal Commission on Trades Unions with legislation to curb wild-cat strikes. There was talk of Government powers to impose cooling off periods and compulsory ballots and to increase the liability to legal enforcement in union-management agreement. The rumours were however received with incredulity in the Party at first. 'Not with Barbara at the DEP' as one left-winger used to say confidently. But when the White Paper appeared, it turned out to contain precisely these 'penal proposals', as the Trades Union

M.P.s called them. There was an immediate outcry from the Unions and Labour back-benchers to say nothing of less public protests from several ministers. Six weeks later the Commons debated the proposals and gave the Government its roughest handling yet. The Tories, whose document 'fair deal at work' contained some similar but by no means identical plans for curbing union powers, abstained in the vote, but sixty-two Labour M.Ps braved a three-line whip and voted against the motion to approve the White Paper. More than thirty others abstained. Opposition in the Cabinet began to grow too. An extraordinary display of disunity came when the National Executive Committee of the Labour Party met a few weeks later. Callaghan voted with the majority at that Committee to say he could not support the proposals. It was an almost unprecedented flouting of the Prime Minister's authority. But with so tenuous a grip on the leadership the Prime Minister was in no position to dismiss Callaghan. The most he could do—and it took him some weeks to pluck up the courage for that—was to exclude him from the Inner Cabinet, the group of six senior ministers who met to discuss the most important topics. Otherwise the Government displayed a mood of stern determination. When Jenkins came to introduce his Budget on April 15, he devoted a special section to 'In Place of Strife'. The Prices and Incomes powers were being dropped at the end of the year. To take over from there, new curbs on the Union powers would be 'essential', he explained.

Mrs. Castle was no less dogmatic in her speech the next day, though she did make one concession: the Government would drop the power to order ballots. Wilson himself had rarely been in a more determined mood, it seemed. In the Commons, on television and on public platforms, he emphasised again and again that the measure was essential. It was essential to economic recovery, to the balance of payments, to full employment. It was a question of whether any Labour Government could survive without such legislation, he said. He told the Parliamentary Labour Party that the Government would treat the Bill, as 'a matter of confidence'. If he failed to get it, he would go to the country. It seemed inconceivable after this that Wilson would retreat, but the pressure on him to do so became intense. The one-hundred-and-thirty strong Trade Union group of M.P.s publicly urged him to drop the Bill. Douglas Houghton, Chairman of the Parliamentary Labour Party, warned him that the Party might disintegrate if he tried to put his measure through. Indeed, the party Liaison Committee warned him that it did not see how he could get his measure through at all, no matter how late into August the Commons was kept sitting. Wilson seemed now in an impossible position. His threat to go to the country even led his colleagues to the point of brushing up on constitutional practice. They found that the established precedent was not, as Wilson told them, that a Prime Minister going to the Sovereign could demand a dissolution at any time whatever the advice of the Cabinet. Matters reached the point where ministers were pointing out to each other that 'if Harold rushed off to the Palace' they would be within their rights to ring the Queen's Private Secretary and say that he did not ask for a dissolution with their approval. On the contrary, the Government could be carried on with the Party choosing another leader.

Of course, matters never reached quite that pitch. Following more attacks on the proposed Bill, Wilson held a series of meetings with Victor Feather, General Secretary of the TUC, and his colleagues. On the grounds that the TUC leaders had given 'a solemn and binding undertaking' to try and conciliate in strikes of all sorts and reduce their numbers, Wilson then announced that the measure would be abandoned. The reaction from the Opposition and from the Press was one of scorn and derision. In a phrase which he kept repeating in subsequent speeches, Heath scoffed at Wilson as 'a man of straw, a pushover'. In the Labour camp, on the other hand, the relief was almost universal.

During this row, which dominated most other events, Jenkins's Budget had also provoked a considerable revolt. It was yet another deflationary move. There was over 2d. a gallon on petrol, 1/- on wines, an extension of Purchase Tax, a 2½% rise in Corporation Tax and an increase of over 25% on SET. Announcing the last, he pointed out with some malicious satisfaction that this brought the revenue raising capacity of the Tax to over £600 million a year. So how would the Tories now keep to their promise to abolish SET? But Macleod reiterated firmly that the Tax *would* go if the Tories got back.

Forty-one Labour M.P.s more and more disenchanted with the working of SET with all its anomalies, abstained on the resolution raising the rate and the Government majority fell to 28. Letters of suspension were sent to some of the more persistent Labour M.P.s by Silkin. But singling out a few—and the selection seemed strangely arbitrary—angered some of the other Labour rebels who seemed irritated that they were not to figure in the proposed martyrdom. It was hardly egalitarian discipline. The difficulty was solved by Wilson sacking the Chief Whip instead, though the move was disguised as a promotion. Silkin moved to the better paid but less important post of Minister of Public Buildings and Works, while Robert Mellish went from the Ministry to the office of Chief Whip. He immediately withdrew the letters of suspension and declared that it was a chance to start with a clean slate.

In the foreign affairs field, the Biafran War was continuing to cause some agonies. In the Commons with a number of M.P.s from both sides savagely critical of the Government Wilson himself went to Nigeria in an attempt to mediate between the two sides and to improve the prospects of starvation relief getting through. He also offered to meet Colonel Ojukwu on a British warship. But the Biafran mistrust of the British was intense and nothing came of the move. That there should be any Biafran mistrust of the British, so often dismissed in the Commons as unreasonable, was hardly surprising. Indeed confirmation of some underhand dealing came a year later. One of the British Government's military observers in the civil war, sent in a supposedly impartial role to watch for any atrocities by the Federal forces, had complained to a Social Security tribunal in early 1970 of having been unjustly dismissed from that job by the Foreign Office. It stemmed, he said, from his refusal to act as a spy. The tribunal held that the Foreign Office had not acted improperly in dismissing him. But, pointedly, the chairman of the tribunal emphasised that this did not mean that the tribunal disbelieved Major Walsworth Bell's account of his having been asked by the Foreign Office to spy on the Biafrans.

It was not so much Wilson himself who came under fierce attack, but Stewart, whose pronouncement on the individual events of the Nigerian war nearly always showed the Biafrans in the worst possible light. His comments were widely mistrusted.

The Anguilla Affair

'Would the Foreign Secretary convey to the Prime Minister, the House's congratulations on at last taking on someone of his own size?'—Nigel Birch, M.P., on the announcement of the British invasion.

It was shortly after this that the nation's attention was diverted by a foreign affairs foray of Stewart's which was of almost sublime dottiness. The nation woke up one Monday morning to find that it had invaded, on the slenderest pretext, a minuscule island in the Caribbean which many had never even heard of and few could find with ease on the map.

The trouble began in 1968 when the Island of Anguilla declared itself independent of the newly formed Commonwealth nation: the Federation of St. Kitts, Nevis and Anguilla. Problems stemmed from a dislike of St. Kitts in general and of the Federation's Prime Minister, Mr. Bradshaw, in particular. The representatives of St. Kitts were sent packing from Anguilla and an attempt by twelve policemen from the capital to restore Federal sovereignty was repulsed. At this point, the British Government's sympathies were clearly with the Anguillans. But not for long. There was an almost paranoiac suspicion of Americans on the part of the Foreign Office. It was allied with an inability to distinguish between a Mafia suspect and a university lecturer of the same name visiting the island and led to acute suspicion in Whitehall that Anguilla was about to become a Mafia base. William Whitlock, Minister of State at the Foreign Office (known unkindly by the nickname of 'Bill Deadlock'), was despatched to the Caribbean to try and mediate between the island and the Government of St. Kitts. Flying in for his first visit to Mr. Bradshaw, Whitlock and his party were met by Mr. Webster, the Anguillan leader who had, in honour of this occasion, donned full evening dress. This well-meant, if uncomfortable gesture (it was mid-day at the time) led to further difficulties since a rather hysterical Foreign Office source subsequently inferred that this extravagant sartorial touch indicated that Mr. Webster was a Black Power enthusiast. The breezy cheerfulness of the airstrip meeting was married by an official in Whitlock's party who had insisted on immediately distributing around pamphlets. Mr. Webster interpreted this as an attempt to undermine his authority. There were recriminations, the negotiations seemed unproductive, and that evening someone fired a shot at Whitlock's bungalow. This resulted in a premature and undignified withdrawal by the British party at dawn. The British public, regaled two days later with pictures of Whitlock at home, collecting the early-morning milk in dressing-gown, slippers (and socks), seemed only amused. But in Michael Stewart, the incident provoked an almost Palmerstonian reaction.

A hastily summoned Inner Cabinet was confronted by Stewart. The Mafia, he declared, was taking over Anguilla. Moreover, he said, Britain had been urged at the last Commonwealth Prime Ministers Conference to discourage islands from seeking independence: the Premiers in question not surprisingly feared the contagion might spread to their own insecure federations. Stewart's colleagues were incredulous. The Mafia? Yes, insisted Stewart, the Mafia. But what right had Britain to invade, they asked, when he suggested this drastic step. The Federation's constitution, he pointed out, allowed the Federal Government to call on British assistance in the event of outside interference. The handful of American Mafia-ites, it could be argued, were the outside threat. Mr. Bradshaw himself—despite Britain's consistent declaration that the Anguillans should not suffer a government they did not want—would agree to make the necessary demand for aid. Uneasily, Stewart's colleagues agreed. So on Monday the nation learnt on its morning news bulletin that British paratroopers had been despatched to the area.

That afternoon Stewart confronted the Commons, made a formal statement and was cross-questioned (Commons rules forbid speeches on a Ministerial statement). The House was bewildered and uneasy. Stewart tried to reassure M.P.s. Law and order, he said, had broken down in Anguilla. Undesirable elements had come to the island, including 'Mafia-types'. This phrase alarmed his Cabinet colleagues who recalled that only a few days before he had talked to them of 'The Mafia', without qualification. But M.P.s. were not to know that. There were, continued Stewart, unsolved crimes including murders on the island. And there were caches of firearms there too. The reaction of M.P.s. ranged from wary support to scorn and ridicule.

In the world at large the general reaction was a mixture of satire and contempt. The American press dubbed the expedition the British 'Bay of Piglets'. The Caribbean Prime Ministers, predictably, dissociated themselves hastily from the British invasion once it had taken place. On the island itself, the British paratroopers were soon replaced with City of London policemen, complete with blue serge uniforms and a moustachioed Commandant. Some Royal Engineers were also flown in to replace the more formidable looking invasion force. At first the British forces encountered a mixture of personal geniality and mob hostility. The British High Commissioner, Tony Lee, went down so badly with the population that he had to be replaced shortly afterwards. The expulsion of several Americans from Anguilla, including a Baptist Missionary 'Mafia-suspect', was also resented. After a time, however, the island more or less settled down, with the Royal Engineers building some much-needed roads. No significant arms haul was ever found, in fact, despite careful searches. And the murders which Stewart referred to turned out to be one *crime passionel.*

By mid-year, Britain's financial position was still causing alarm. Jenkins maintained his confidence that the balance of payments would soon come right, though by that time he had twice had to downgrade his forecasts. But the vulnerability of sterling to external pressure was still painfully apparent on the foreign exchange market. Yet a further IMF standby would be required. This time, however, there were rumours that the IMF's patience was exhausted. It would insist on conditions for the loan, involving the sort of close supervision and 'trigger clause' which were normally only applied to chronic debtor countries such as Ghana. Harold Lever, the urbane Financial Secretary to the Treasury, flew to Washington to try to iron things out. He succeeded to some extent and the loan when eventually it appeared was not on difficult terms, though some were worried by Jenkins's undertaking in his Letter of Intent to keep down the money supply very firmly indeed. The Commons greeted the news of this further standby with anything but satisfaction. Nor, in July, was there any consolation in the trade figures for the previous month. The deficit for June was £25 million. Invisible earnings probably covered this gap, but in view of the debt incurred, Britain needed more than a bare balance to meet her obligations.

The Parliamentary No. 2 Bill

There were other problems too. The promised but still-born Industrial Relations Bill was by no means the only Parliamentary casualty of the Summer. In what was to prove one of the most diverting Commons exercises for decades, a number of Tory and Labour M.P.s. combined in a remarkable alliance to kill stone dead the Bill, approved by both front benches, to reform the House of Lords. The Parliamentary No. 2 Bill, as this drastic measure was called, was the fruit of long consultations between the three parties on the future of the Upper Chamber.

The general idea looked harmless enough, attractive even. The hereditary peers would be phased out and gradually replaced by Life Peers nominated in proportion to the parties' strength in the Commons. To provide independence, there would be the cross-benchers of no declared party allegiance whose numbers would be calculated according to a careful formula, so that the Opposition in the Lords, plus nearly all the cross-benchers, would form a strong block of votes to keep any really bad Government Bill at bay for some time. And to provide an incentive to join the Upper House there would be a salary of £2,000 a year.

This thoroughly alarmed many of the sprightlier

back-benchers. What a power of patronage for the Party leaders was envisaged here!—a title *plus* £2,000 a year. The Upper House too, with its hereditary principle ended, would be more inclined to assert itself over the elected House.

Some of the best brains and most eloquent tongues in the Commons united to fight this Bill to the death. On the Tory side there were, among the ex-Ministers, Powell, John Boyd-Carpenter, Sir Derek Walker-Smith, Nigel Birch and Hugh Fraser. The first four were certainly among the best debaters that the House could produce. Also in the campaign Michael Foot and Manny Shinwell were among the best Common debaters on the Labour side; and they were ably backed up by younger colleagues.

They were soon tearing the Bill to shreds as it started on its protracted committee stage through the House. What would such patronage do to politics? How were these vital cross-benchers to be chosen?

In a superb amendment, all in legal language and a page long, Birch tabled an amendment to insert a safeguard about the cross-benchers. This would have obliged anyone nominated as a cross bencher to appear before a panel consisting of a bishop (nominated by the Archbishop of Canterbury), a High Court Judge (nominated by the Lord Chief Justice) and a psychologist (nominated by the General Medical Council). This body would have to be satisfied that the proposed cross-bencher did not hold, had never held and was not likely to hold any political views. Satisfaction was not, unfortunately, ever reached. But what *was* to stop cross-benchers shifting their allegiance? How was the required frequency of attendance to be assured?

The opposition to the Bill was made up of about a score of activists and about the same number again of supporters. But this relatively small group employed brilliant tactics. The slightest slip by the Government would lead to points of order being exploited for up to an hour at a time by these Parliamentary old-hands. Debates were often prolonged into the night. Divisions were called on every possible pretext. Government supporters kept up by these guerilla tactics grew restless. Some commented after hearing the critics' speeches that, anyway, the Bill sounded a pretty sloppily drafted if not unworkable measure.

With the prospect of the Bill taking up nearly a month of Parliamentary time at the rate things were going, the Government finally surrendered and abandoned it. It was a triumph for back-bench opinion. It made nonsense too of the assertion by Hogg at about that time that back-benchers counted for little in Parliament these days.

The biggest row at the end of Parliament, however, was on the Government's decision to cheat on the Parliamentary boundaries. The Parliamentary Boundaries Commission had completed its review of the constituencies and put forward recommendations for the redrawing of boundaries to allow for population drifts since the last review in the early '50s. It was estimated that the result of the impartial commission's recommendations would have been an extra 15 or 20 Tory seats after a general election.

The Government coolly announced that it would shelve the proposals. Since the Redcliffe-Maud Committee Report had recently recommended radical changes in local government boundaries, it would be wise, according to ministers, to wait until the resultant changes were made in the 1970s. Parliamentary and local government boundaries were supposed to match where convenient. It was of course a blatant piece of gerrymandering and unprecedented in modern times. The Opposition and a handful of Labour back-benchers attacked the Government with fury. The House of Lords rejected the Government's Bill to implement only changes in London where the balance of power would not be affected. This, and a private High Court action to compel the Home Secretary to fulfil his legal obligations on the Commission's report, led Callaghan to an odd procedure. He tabled all the relevant orders incorporating the Commission's proposals in the House of Commons. But then he promptly urged the Commons to defeat his own propositions. The Government's majority comfortably carried the day. Outside the Commons, particularly in the press, the manoeuvre was described as unusually squalid.

After Parliament rose, Callaghan found himself at the centre of a crisis full of the most alarming implications. The problem was Northern Ireland. Ironically, it was Callaghan who was responsible for retrieving a situation which he, more than any other minister, had been responsible for provoking, though few at the time, however, appreciated the extent of his irresponsibility and involvement. It seemed in retrospect that the Government had rushed to the brink without care, peered into the abyss, shuddered at what it saw, and back-pedalled furiously.

The essential element in the troubles of August 1969 was obviously the hostility between the Catholic and Protestant communities in Ulster. The growth of the Catholic contingent due to free entry from the south, and a higher birth rate, was threatening the Protestants' numerical dominance of the province. In the Ulster of the early 1960s, however, this was not the threat to the province's integrity which more rabid Protestants had proclaimed. Catholic loyalties were no longer automatically to the Republic as they had been in the past. The patent difference in economic prosperity between Ulster and the south was making life harder for the Republican cause. At the same time, a new spirit was abroad in the Unionist Party, which had controlled the Stormont Parliament for over fifty years. The new Prime Minister, Captain Terence O'Neill, set his aim on quiet reconciliation between the two communities. Apart from such gestures as opening Catholic schools and occasionally attending civic Catholic church services—important and unusual gestures in Ulster—he embarked on three reforms to be introduced gradually. The first was an overhaul of local government and in particular of voting. When Great Britain in 1945 had decided to extend the vote in local government from householders to all electors, Ulster had declined to follow suit. Captain O'Neill decided that this method of capitalizing upon the more affluent and usually Protestant vote in municipal affairs must stop. Secondly, he decided that some of the local government boundaries must be redrawn for greater fairness. Thirdly, the allocation of council housing on a community basis, so that there were separate denominational housing estates, must be vigorously discouraged. In some ways Captain O'Neill was an unexpected vehicle for this policy. An ex-military man with a rather supercilious air and a substantial estate, he seemed the epitome of squirearchical conservatism to many. Some of his fellow Unionist M.P.s. found his personality almost as much of a problem as his policies.

There can be little doubt, particularly in retrospect, about the wisdom and diplomacy of his policies. For those who were safely insulated from the reality of Ulster, it was easy to howl for immediate reforms. But those on the spot knew what latent, anti-Catholic hostility could be (and later was) unleashed by the Protestants if the Ulster Government was too precipitous in its changes.

Captain O'Neill however was soon in trouble, particularly with his own right wing. He found himself facing a full scale party revolt. After a dissolution, he was returned to power with a stronger right-wing to handle, but in May 1969 he resigned and was succeeded by Major Chichester-Clark. In a futile but well-meant gesture, he ordered an amnesty for all who had been concerned in recent disturbances. The disturbances themselves were little more than a year old when the newly formed Civil Rights movement had begun to take to the streets in an effort to provoke trouble and, in a few cases, sincerely, to accelerate reforms. By early August, however, a first-rate constitutional crisis seemed imminent.

Though the militants dubbed Northern Ireland 'a police state', its total police force was only 6,000, a lesser number than the Metropolitan Police had mustered for January's anti-American riots in Grosvenor Square in London. Once rioting reached substantial proportions, therefore, it was hard to know how it could be contained by the civil power. It was here that the British Government's behaviour proved grossly irresponsible. Political correspondents of the London papers were explaining how any decision in Stormont to call for British troops would, 'it was thought in Whitehall', probably lead to the imposition of direct rule from London. Desperately anxious to avoid this step, which would probably provoke even greater trouble, the Northern Ireland authorities found themselves pushed further and further into the position of having to call out the B Special Constabulary. This was a predominantly Protestant and inadequately trained force which, anyway, existed mainly to guard key points during IRA raids. Whitehall, of course, was fully aware of the implications for Stormont ministers if they were pushed into calling out the B Specials for riot duties in the now violent Catholic areas of Londonderry and Belfast. Indeed, when the civil power in Northern Ireland finally did ask for military aid in Londonderry, the request was met with a refusal from a senior officer. His instructions from London were plain, he said: the B Specials must be used first. This caused shock and dismay: the deployment of B Specials would incite the Catholics, it was protested. The officer was adamant. In the event, when the situation deteriorated very rapidly, the troops were released shortly after the deployment of the B Specials.

In Belfast, at the end of the same week, violent riots in the

Falls Road area, during which a police station was attacked with petrol bombs, were met by a savage counter attack in the area. It was a night of rioting and shooting. The next day, with the Falls Road and certain neighbouring areas totally in the hands of the mob, the British Government flew in the troops that should have been standing by in Belfast days before, had the Government been serious about wanting to stop any outbreak of disorder.

The troubles were by no means over, though Callaghan now started impressively to retrieve a situation which his own folly had helped to create. A rapid reorganisation of the Royal Ulster Constabulary took place, the B Specials were disbanded and the British Government, for the first time, made it clear that it stood four-square behind the Stormont Government in maintaining law and order. The much argued reforms, as Callaghan told the Commons, were under way and had been for some time; there was no cause for grievance there. He was appalled by the behaviour of some Protestant thugs. But, he said to the dismay of many of his own followers, were the Catholics playing their full part in improving community relations? Was their exclusiveness a good answer to complaints about discrimination by Protestants? Callaghan was at his most impressive. He steered the middle course with consumate skill undeterred by criticisms from Labour left-wingers; and even receiving applause from Ulster Unionist M.P.s. Ironically it was during the same Autumn that he was pushing through his measures to gerrymander the party constituencies.

Towards 1970

Hopes that the economic improvement would lead to relaxation by the Government, were dashed at the end of October. After days of speculation in the Press that the travel allowance was about to end, Jenkins told the Commons that the £50 limit would stay, and so would the import deposit scheme, though with the size of the deposits cut by one-fifth.

At the turn of the year, however, with further good trade figures to hand, Jenkins relented on the travel allowance and scrapped the restriction altogether. This was widely interpreted as the first in a series of announcements which would be carefully timed to lead up to an election in October. That, almost all M.P.s. calculated, was to be the chosen time. The beginning of the autumn is traditionally believed to be a good time for the party in power. Summer weather and holidays, runs the theory, produce an afterglow of satisfaction which inclines at least some electors to believe that the status quo is not so bad after all. The more pessimistic Tories were arguing that this, against the background of an easy budget made possible by the good trade figures, would bring the two parties close in the opinion polls. The long-standing Tory lead in the polls would be reduced by two or three points and then the Prime Minister would make a lunge for it, confident in his ability to make up the required ground in a campaign. On the Government side, this was the view of the more sanguine Labour M.P.s. Certainly, very few expected any substantial swing to Labour in the early summer.

Nagging doubts about the cost to Britain of Common Market entry reappeared in February with the publication of a Government White Paper on possible costs. It was supremely vague. Costs to the balance of payments might, on certain hypotheses, be as high as £1,000 million per year; on others, perhaps as low as £100 million. On the other hand, it was emphasised, the various hypotheses about future Common Market agricultural prices, British industrial costs, sales orientation, continental inflation and so on were all liable to a very wide margin of error. The pro-Marketeers on both sides were annoyed with the White Paper and regretted having pressed for its preparation and publication in the first place. But the anti-Marketeers, were delighted and used the occasion for a fierce attack on the application for membership. Powell, who had by then been an anti-Marketeer for some 18 months, joined in with vigour. This was resented by some of his colleagues who recalled him as a one-time supporter of British entry.

But a more memorable debate was on defence. The Tories were again attacking the Government plans to economise in this field. Healey, whose arrogance the Opposition usually found intolerable anyway, charged the Conservatives with wanting to bring back conscription, provoking the Tories by the end of the debate to uncontrollable rage. They genuinely had no plans for conscription and Healey's visible pleasure in stating otherwise, for obvious electoral reasons, proved unbearable. The row which followed, comparable to feeding time at the zoo, led later to a charge from a Labour M.P. that some Tories were drunk. The dilatoriness of the Speaker in pressing for the withdrawal of this most unparliamentary remark earned a rebuke from Heath. Relations between the Opposition and the Speaker, already far from ideal, were to decline further in other, smaller incidents as the Session proceeded.

Otherwise what happened in the House during that last session was distinctly predictable. An Ulster Unionist used some unparliamentary language about Miss Devlin (Independent Mid-Ulster) and would not apologise. Rhodesia provoked another of those 'dialogue-of-the-deaf' debates and Anthony Wedgwood Benn, Minister of Technology, was intermittently to be observed rushing forward with Treasury cheque book in hand to rescue those shipyards where managerial incompetence and union obduracy had precipitated the real likelihood of closure.

And of course there was the budget. The 'War for Jenkins's ear' was unusually fierce. Labour M.P.s, particularly those then expected to lose their seats at the Election, pressed anxiously for a 'give-away' budget. They found great comfort in a report by the National Institute of Economic and Social Research predicting that the balance of payments surpluses, on current form, would be colossal to the point of folly. But there were voices of caution too. The balance of payments figures were fine but wage inflation seemed to be gathering speed. The success of the dustmen in the previous autumn, in gaining a very substantial wage increase through striking, produced a new phase in industrial bargaining which was to dominate a great deal of discussion in wages right up until the Election itself. 'Give us a dustman's rise' was commonly heard. Even the teachers, who won a rise after a threat to strike, were heard to use the same slogan. Another section of the community, which since the time of the dustmen's strike had gained substantial pay rises, included the miners.

In the light of all this, it was argued that any substantial addition to consumer spending power would turn the existing rate of inflation into a positive gallop.

In the event, Jenkins was cautioned. The budget was reflationary only to the extent of £200 million a year, which was in the lower limits of what economists had thought safe. The benefit was almost entirely concentrated on the two million people in the bottom income tax range, who, by new allowances and changes in the intermediate rates, were exempted from tax altogether.

The reaction of Jenkins's colleagues was glum. His fellow Cabinet Ministers had not been much impressed by this as a 'life saver' and in the Commons itself the Chancellor concluded his speech to near silence from his own side, instead of the usual loyal cheers from the back benches. The Tories treated the budget with disdain. By Heath's calculations, the rise in spending power generated by the budget proposals would be absorbed by one month's price rises. It was, he said in a good phrase, much cheered by his own side, 'a one-month budget' (in fact, the price index was then rising so fast—more than was generally realised—that it proved to be more like a fortnight's than a month's budget in that sense.)

Seen in retrospect, however, the dismay of Labour back-benchers only served to confirm what was emerging as a good rule: the immediate reaction of Labour back-benchers, particularly the left-wingers, was invariably wrong. When Callaghan introduced SET the back-benchers at first thought it was very clever. When he produced his steady-as-you-go Budget in 1967, the reaction of Labour M.P.s was one of relief. When Jenkins brought in his massive taxes in 1968, the left-wingers actually cheered enthusiastically, being overwhelmed at the prospect of the long-sought-after Wealth Tax. It needed an hour or two for the full deflationary picture to sink in. Now the back-benchers were glum but the country, as it later appeared, saw the budget in a much better light. Indeed a Labour recovery seemed to date from that time.

The previous week had seen local government elections for London and for the less important local authorities outside the capital. Labour hopes of regaining control of London were firmly dashed. Some Labour voters seemed to be returning to the fold in certain predominantly Labour areas but the Tories were still doing well on the whole, particularly in the North of England. The only real bright spot in fact had been the South Ayrshire Parliamentary by-election where Labour had done unusually well, keeping the swing to the Tories down. But that was considered to be rather a flash-in-the-pan in a seat with unusually fierce Labour loyalties. It certainly looked this way in view of the subsequent local results. Anyway the Bridgwater by-election which followed South Ayrshire still showed a comfortable swing to the Tories.

The opinion polls were showing a slight move back towards Labour, it was true, but it had to some extent been expected. In early 1969, two of the opinion polls had actually shown a Tory lead of over 25%. Even the most optimistic Tories viewed this as amusing but unrealistic. A lead of around 5 to 10% was what they expected in the early months of 1970, with the gap narrowing towards October. After all, as several Tories reminded their more slap-happy colleagues, the notable feature of British elections since the war was that it was always hard to defeat the Party in power. Sir Winston Churchill had only just scraped home in 1951 and so had Wilson in 1964.

In the early months of the year the Tories still seemed safe if not exactly riding high. In March the Conservative lead, according to Gallup, was 5½%, and down from 7% in February. But that was at least a lead the Tories expected to hold.

Then things started to go wrong. The late April Gallup showed the Tory lead down to 4½% with generally favourable comments being made on the Budget. The same day, to the horror of the Tories, the Harris Poll in the *Daily Express* showed an actual Labour lead: 2%. It was hastily pointed out that the Harris Poll was a relative newcomer. But Labour M.P.s were elated. The miracle, some thought, was actually happening. The next day there was consternation. *The Times* Marplan Poll showed a lead of 0.8% for Labour. In all the polls, moreover, Wilson was showing an increasing lead in personal popularity over Heath.

In early May the polls were put to the test in the local elections for the main boroughs in England and Wales. The results vindicated the polls. Labour was undeniably swinging back into the lead. The Party may not have won back all the seats it lost in 1967 but the vital statistic was that 1,150 Labour Councillors were elected. This compared with 1,200 in 1966, the year of the great Labour victory. Forecasts of a June election were now heard on all sides, with Labour morale rocketing and Tory morale sagging. So long as one or two more Polls showed the right movement, it was argued, the Prime Minister was bound to make a dash for it. Among Labour optimists and Tory pessimists it was said that Wilson was a man who could achieve the impossible. The belief that he could manage miracles was one of the paradoxical legacies of the five-and-a-half years of Labour rule.

Labour M.P.s argued that in an election fight Wilson was bound to make ground against Heath. But Tories countered that in two out of the last four elections the Opposition had made ground during the campaign itself. And with such a wealth of devastating material to use against the Government in an all-out fight, why should not the same happen this time? Anyway, Gallup, which was one of the most reliable polls, still showed a Tory lead. Another Gallup was due out shortly and most, though not all, Tories expected it to show a small Tory lead still. They were in for a shock.

Harold Wilson: Prime Minister

'He is a great master of gibes and flouts and jeers'—DISRAELI, on a colleague.

A reputation for cleverness in politics, once won, is hard to lose. Too many party followers, rivals, lobby correspondents and newspaper editors have publicly committed themselves to the estimate. Apparent subsequent gaffes are, therefore, readily declared to be, in reality, subtle manoeuvres or, at worst, temporary losses of form.

Wilson was by 1970 a politician still very much surviving on the momentum of a reputation for cleverness acquired in Opposition where his undoubted if limited talents impressed many. The remarkable feature of his premiership, however, was not subtlety or real skill, though he had an undoubted talent for fierce in-fighting. Rather it had been a record of amazingly naive errors. A more impetuous and emotional man than many realise, Wilson can easily be pushed into over-committing himself, especially when he knows that a particular remark will raise a loud cheer from his own side. In these circumstances, his undoubted capacity for the memorable phrase became a two-edged weapon.

The number of cases of over-commitment is legion. In early 1966 there was his remark about the Rhodesian rebellion ending in 'weeks rather than months'. Even the average back-bencher would hesitate to commit himself, whatever the advice available, to such a timetable.

In 1967, only two months before devaluation, he took on the 'overlordship' of the Department of Economic Affairs with much trumpeting. In view of some of the expert forecasts at the time on the real balance-of-payments position, this was rash in the extreme. To take over an economy in the belief that it is just about to pick up when, in reality, it is about to crash is about as gratuitous an act of folly as can be imagined in politics.

Again in the case of Rhodesia he committed the Government in the Commons to 'No independence before majority rule', though even the naivest of negotiators knew that such a precondition would have to be dropped in any meaningful attempt to reach a settlement.

In his devaluation broadcast he used the maladroit phrase about the 'pound in your pocket' not being devalued.

In early 1968 he quoted with enthusiasm an obscure foreign economist who speculated that Britain might be 'on the verge of an economic miracle'. In the subsequent recourse to still further borrowing from the International Monetary Fund this phrase was constantly quoted against him.

How, in all these circumstances, did Harold Wilson acquire a reputation for being clever? To maintain such an estimate in the face of such a capacity for being consistently wrong—wrong about Rhodesia, about the economy, about unemployment, about housing—is to make a nonsense of plain English. What the original purveyors of the compliment were, however, able to point to in Harold Wilson was a number of invaluable leadership qualities.

His strengths were really three. The first was sheer physical resilience—an essential quality in any leader, especially in a time of strain. The other two 'strengths', however, stemmed in part from inherent character weaknesses. A remarkable sensitivity to criticism which had existed all his life had led him to cultivate a ferocity of repartee which would have been formidable anywhere and which, in the Commons, was invaluable. In a period when many confuse the art of being disagreeable with the art of debate, this led to Wilson being dubbed a great debater. Indeed, this talent was so developed in Wilson that it enabled him to dominate the House. It was also a talent peculiarly suited to the days of consensus politics. When the policies of rival parties are so close as in some cases to be indistinguishable, the capacity to exploit personalities in argument is of supreme value in Parliament, particularly when the morale of one's own side is low. To be able, however falsely, to make an impressive attack on rivals as incompetent, unintelligent and unreliable is to help convince one's own side that it is, whatever the policy failures, more competent than the Opposition. The regularity with which Heath would keep rising to the Prime Minister's bait was a considerable bonus for Wilson. With a man like Iain Macleod, he would have had a much harder time.

Could Wilson be called a great orator? In some senses, yes. His personality was dominating and aggressive; and he could produce a colourful phrase and an impressive general effect. But in a sense his speeches, particularly those at Party conferences, were like film music—they established a general effect, they stirred, they roused, they soothed. But there was nothing much beyond this sheer effect. There was little argument and no intricate use of logic, no real theme worth recapitulation and no detailed analysis.

Equally important in making him a powerful orator in

this sense was his sincerity. The general picture of Harold Wilson as a twister and a cheat—a favourite theme of the Tories—was really much exaggerated. Certainly he broke promise after promise. But these pledges were not cynically given. On the contrary, such was the basic optimism of the man that he really believed that the whole string of cheering successes which he predicted would take place. He is not of course the first, neither will he be the last, political leader to sound convincing precisely because he is too naive to understand that he is predicting the wildly improbable. But in his case, the streak of maliciousness in his character so evident at times served to convince people that all those broken promises were, in fact, cynically given in the first place. And since most men prefer to be called rogues rather than fools, the Tory tactics of calling him a cheat were not as wounding as some might think.

Notable among the Parliamentary debaters who most visibly discomfited Wilson was Macleod, in his own way quiet and deadly. But even he concentrated too much on the cheating aspect of the broken pledges. More effective was Nigel Birch, the elderly Tory ex-Minister, who treated Wilson with contempt and derision, but who never railed against him. 'To quote the Prime Minister against himself', he once commented in a debate, 'is like shooting at a haystack from two yards'. Adding that he did not therefore propose to waste his time that way, he went on to expose the folly, not the cynicism, of Government policy.

There can be little doubt that Wilson's reputation for cleverness was enhanced rather than diminished by the official Opposition attacks. Barber, in particular, never seemed to tire of calling Wilson 'a twister'. A picture emerged, therefore, not of a man with massive elements of naivity in his character, but of a man of unremitting subtlety. Consequently, when things seemed at the end of 1969 to be coming right economically, few were prepared to accept that the timing of this recovery to fit General Election year was sheer chance. The timing of the wave of prosperity must, some thought, be the result of Machiavellian subtlety but it was surely not due to luck.

There was also an element of sheer cheek about Wilson which the British public did not find altogether disagreeable. Here was the little man who despite every disaster would cheerfully pick himself up at the end of it all and insist that it was all someone else's fault.

So, despite all the disasters of those five-and-a-half years, the British public never acquired quite the dislike for Wilson which the Tories ingenuously hoped for. The Tories were almost doomed from the start in the personal battle between Heath and Wilson to put themselves at a disadvantage. The strategy of turning the campaign into a sort of presidential contest at the outset was not particularly wise. But the Tories had of course all the other factors in their favour. Had the electorate returned Labour in 1970, it would have meant that the voters were returning to power a Government which had been able to produce virtually no fat periods, only lean ones. It would have been against all precedents in British politics.

CHAPTER THREE

THE TORIES IN OPPOSITION

'Those behind cried "Forward"
And those before cried "Back".'—MACAULAY, Lays of Ancient Rome.

Leadership was one of the qualities on which the Tory Party had always prided itself. Many voters instinctively supported the Party precisely because they thought it displayed this quality inherently. To find the Tory Party plunged into a chronic leadership problem in the late 1960s was, therefore, a double blow: it sapped the morale of the Party itself and weakened the Conservative grip on many of its traditional supporters.

It is not difficult to construct a model of an ideal leader for a political party. He will have a political faith which is attractive, distinctive and contagious. He should be a good parliamentarian, sharp and persuasive. This usually, though not always, means that he should be a good debater and speaker. He must at least be able to carry weight in the House. He should be able to select a good team and certainly possess enough self-confidence to be unafraid of potential rivals around him. He should be a good Party manager, ready with little gestures of encouragement for the back-bencher who does well, and, even more important at times, for the back-bencher who does badly. He should be a good diplomat, able to prevent stresses turning into splits. And if he is leading the Party in Opposition, he should of course have a nose for the right issues to exploit. He should be especially able to convince all his audiences that his solutions are distinctive in style and approach.

No Party leader, of course, has all these virtues, but most have a combination of them. The misfortune for the Tory Party in 1965 was that it picked a man who, though he had some impressive talents, seemed to be short of these particular qualities. There was certainly nothing Churchillian about Heath. The little gestures of appreciation to Juniors at which Harold Macmillan excelled were noticeably absent. The affable and reassuring self-confidence of Sir Alec Douglas-Home was replaced with something verging on testiness. There were no Baldwinesque touches to convince people that the Tory leader was as British as roast beef. And his sense of Party diplomacy was almost non-existent. He managed to get on the wrong side of numerous colleagues, both senior and junior, widened splits and ended up, inevitably, having to fire the one man, who, whatever else his faults, was supremely brilliant at Opposition.

The Heath-Powell saga had its origins in 1965. Powell, who had refused to serve under Home in 1963 when the latter had become Party leader rather than Butler, was brought back into the Shadow Cabinet in 1964 to deal with Transport. He played a maverick role from the start which, though it disturbed some, never seemed to unsettle Home, certainly not in the first year or two of Opposition. Home looked on with benevolence and even approval as Powell questioned orthodox beliefs in almost every field of policy. The ex-Premier, at any rate, did not seem to think that iconoclasm was out of place in Opposition.

When Heath became leader he moved Powell from Transport to Defence. The two men had a discussion which provided Powell with the background for a later and often repeated comment that he knew no-one in the Shadow Cabinet closer to him in thinking and outlook than Heath. Powell discerned then in Heath two traits which he also shared: a keen impatience with post-imperial delusions and sharp anti-Americanism. The fact that Heath would not pursue these feelings to the sort of logical conclusion which came naturally to Powell did not then seem to occur readily to the new Shadow Defence Minister.

But at the Party Conference in October Powell made a speech which said, in effect, that Britain should abandon her East of Suez role. The audience, more intent perhaps on the man than interpreting the slightly oblique message of his speech, gave Powell an impressive standing ovation. He had always been a favourite of the rank and file. But Heath, however, soon put it about discreetly that this was definitely *not* Tory policy. Sir Alec did the same, though more mildly, and only in response to queries. Powell was irritated and not surprisingly, having gone to the trouble of sending his speech in advance to both Sir Alec and Christopher Soames, the latter then being Shadow Foreign Secretary. Neither had made any comment in advance. Home was sometimes insensitive to nuances, which was probably why he took little notice of the trend of thinking in the last paragraphs of Powell's 1965 speech. Indeed, at a meeting of the Tory Defence Committee early in 1970 Home said that 'if at the end of the day we decide on a presence East of Suez . . .' and Tory back-benchers who noted the uncertainty raised the matter afterwards but were assured by the leadership that if this really had been said it should not be taken to be significant.

The next point of disagreement between Heath and Powell was an article which the latter wrote in *The Director*. He attacked the Confederation of British Industry for existing at all. Having this 'representative body', Powell argued forcefully, was to offer the Government the very means by which it could coerce and cajole industry. Heath resented this and thought it might annoy the Party's friends in industry.

Still more important in the growing tension between the two men was an incident at the 1966 General Election. Powell, about to make a speech at Falkirk, received an urgent telephone call from an official in Heath's private office. Evidence, said the official, had come to light that the Ministry of Defence had prepared a contingency plan for sending a token British force to Vietnam. Would Powell take the issue up? Powell agreed readily and prepared a speech, even taking the trouble to read the relevant passage back over the telephone. Fine, was the official's comment, perhaps it could even be strengthened a little? The speech was duly delivered with its strong hint that such a plan was being prepared. Denis Healey, the Minister of Defence, reacted furiously, describing the speech as extreme anti-Americanism. That did not worry Powell. But he was sharply taken aback three days later when Heath disowned all knowledge of any such plan. Powell felt double-crossed. It was not until a year later that it transpired that it was a simple matter of bad co-ordination. Heath had never been told about the discovered contingency plan at all. There can be little doubt that the plan existed. In the 1970 Election campaign Wilson admitted that President Johnson had asked for such a force in 1966.

The result of the 1966 Election when it came caused few surprises. The polls had forecast it all clearly enough. The Tories were very disappointed by Heath's personal failure in the opinion polls, but with time, it was argued, Heath would achieve his breakthrough.

A New Tory Front Bench

'*Who? Who?*'*—The Duke of Wellington on hearing the names of Ministers in a new administration.*

One of Heath's early moves was to reconstruct his front bench team. Among the most conspicuous of those he dropped was John Boyd-Carpenter, an ex-Tory Cabinet Minister, conspicuous for his brisk talent in Opposition. Many of those Heath appointed to the front bench were new men, not always very impressive and not particularly sparkling in debate.

Parliament soon provided the new team with plenty of

opportunity for battle. In the main the issues were domestic, though a fierce Parliamentary debate on Vietnam in June had some repercussions in the Shadow Cabinet, where Powell was an almost lone voice in his opposition to the whole American policy. Several other members of the Shadow Cabinet thought that the Opposition ought to be resolute in its backing for the Americans. One or two even wished that a contingency force would be despatched to Vietnam from Britain. There was more than one fierce argument between Heath and Powell on Vietnam. Since their original conversation on East of Suez, Heath had made a tour of the Far East and included a visit to Vietnam, where he had been impressed by the scale and technological efficiency of the U.S. forces. He had come back convinced of the importance of the British role East of Suez and he voiced the view that an American defeat in Vietnam just could not be contemplated or allowed. Rows between Heath and Powell were to be far from uncommon as time went on, with the two drifting steadily towards their ultimate positions of total irreconcilability. (Ironically, however, the biggest row they had in the Shadow Cabinet came later and was over—of all things—Black Rod! Until the change of rule in late 1967 this official was liable to arrive in mid-debate to summon the Commons to the Lords to hear the Royal Assent to Bills. In November 1967 he arrived in the middle of a warm Common Market debate to be greeted to his visible discomfiture with cries ranging from 'Shame' to ' 'Op it!'. In the next Shadow Cabinet, Heath was emphatic that this 'nonsense' must be ended. Not done away with surely, interposed Powell. Didn't Heath realise that even the formula of words used by Black Rod dated back to the 1307 Parliament of Carlisle and was ancient even then? Heath exploded furiously at this, declaring that the British people were tired of this nonsense and ceremonial and mummery. He would not stand for the perpetuation of this ridiculous business etc. etc. etc.)

The announcement in mid-1966 that the Government were going to introduce a mild Prices and Incomes Bill also demonstrated a division of view in the Party. This measure was to establish the Prices and Incomes Board as a statutory body and allow it to defer prices and incomes rises but only while they were investigated. Heath, Maudling, Boyle and, to some extent, Macleod were far from hostile to this limited move. The Tories' National Incomes Commission had been consistently flouted by the Unions. A Prices and Incomes Board with statutory powers to investigate seemed a fair idea to them. They thought that opposition to the Bill could be kept till the Committee Stage. This view was objected to strongly by many Tories at the next weekly meeting of the 1922 Committee, the Committee of all Tory back-benchers. Its elected Executive constituted, as it were, the Shop Stewards Committee for back benchers on the Opposition Side.

Why not a straight hostile vote, many of them demanded, some because they were doctrinally opposed to all such measures and others because they wanted aggressive all-round opposition on principle. This dilemma was resolved by events. It was rumoured, correctly, that the deteriorating economic situation would lead to the Government trying to strengthen the Bill as it went through the House later. So the Opposition was able to unite in opposing, but of course losing, a critical amendment on the Second Reading. Thereafter, much of the session, which ended in mid-August, was taken up with the fight against the later stages of this controversial measure. There was at any rate nothing half-hearted about Tory Opposition at this point, with heavy emphasis laid on the Prime Minister's dishonesty in saying at the Election that such controls were, in effect, out of the question.

But for Heath at that time there was a pressing internal problem: the Party Chairmanship. Edward du Cann, M.P. for Taunton, had been made Chairman by Home in 1964.

It created an awkward situation as soon as Heath took over, since the two men had never got on very well and most M.P.s knew it. Du Cann would last, it was predicted, until shortly after the 1966 Election. Then Heath would ask him to resign and appoint his own man to this important job of running the Party organisation. But visions of graceful letters of resignation and appreciation being exchanged amid a burst of professed mutual admiration faded smartly that summer. Du Cann, quite simply, would not go. The two men had become acutely suspicious of each other. Heath suspected du Cann of having little faith in his capacity for effective leadership. Du Cann suspected Heath of not having backed him up as the Chairman. Both suspicions were justified too. Du Cann wanted to complete certain reforms before he left Central Office. Worse still, he was coolly insisting on having a say in his successor. Heath's embarrassment was acute. A brusque dismissal of du Cann would be unfortunate to say the least. Grumbles about Heath as leader were, after all, already being voiced in the summer of 1966. He was not catching the public's admiration or making much mark in the House. A rumour floated around just before the Party Conference that autumn that the chairman was about to be removed. The reply from the du Cann camp was a 'du Cann must stay' campaign in which various of the Party's leading non-Parliamentary figures made suitable noises of protest. There could be no question for some time of dismissing du Cann in these circumstances. As a successor, Heath wanted Lord Carrington, the leader of the Tory Peers. He was a capable and much liked man in the Party. But he was after all a peer. Du Cann in effect vetoed him. A further possible candidate whose name was mentioned, though not very seriously, was Peter Walker, one of Heath's closest lieutenants. Some indication of the hostility between the Chairman and the Leader is indicated by the fact that they were reduced to negotiating over the successor through an intermediary. Eventually agreement was reached on Anthony Barber, though the final decision to appoint him was taken by Heath only in September 1967 when rumours of the impending change appeared in the press. Du Cann was, by then, ready to go.

The 1966 Conference itself in October passed off satisfactorily enough otherwise. Some of the delegates were in an uneasy mood about the leadership, but Heath made a strong speech, the audience clapped devotedly and the Leader was declared to have made a breakthrough at last. (This comment was to be repeated annually though with diminishing conviction.)

This time too there was no jarring speech from Powell, but it had been a near thing. Powell had shown Home a draft of his speech. The remarks about Australia and New Zealand, in the East of Suez context, might have been interpreted as saying that there was little point in backing nations if it was not in Britain's simple self-interest. Fearing drastic repercussions if the speech were made in that form, Home got Powell to amend the whole passage.

At the turn of the year, however, the enthusiasm of October was waning both in the country and in the Party. Despite the wage freeze, the summer debacle and the continuing atmosphere of economic crisis, Labour had now advanced its lead in the Gallup Poll to $11\frac{1}{2}\%$. A further problem was provided by Ernest Marples, ex-Transport Minister, announcing his resignation from Central Office. In fact, it was not clear what he was resigning from. He had no specific job there, only a general permit to look at possible money-saving schemes in the organisation. The event was more significant for its display of one of Heath's weaknesses: man-management. Marples's grumbles about not being given a proper job to do culminated in a series of exchanges by memorandum between Marples's office in Bridge Street, Westminster, and Heath's office in the House of Commons.

As the distance involved was only about 300 yards, a more sensible approach for Heath would have been to call Marples in and discuss the matter face to face. But as in several other cases, Heath showed that he had no talent for the personal private confrontation, least of all for turning such meetings into reconciliations. Marples was however later put in charge of a research unit dealing with the public sector.

Another such example occurred in one of his periodic rows with Powell. Heath decided in 1967 that a pamphlet which Powell was writing for the Conservative Political Centre as the Party's spokesman on Defence was out of line and must not be published, but he would not confront Powell himself. Eventually Sir Michael Fraser, the Party's Deputy Chairman was deputed to tell Powell it would not do. Fraser was a non-Parliamentary figure who had previously been head of the Research Department. Conservative Political Centre, a department of Central Office intended to stimulate ideas and discussion at all levels of the Party, steadily lost its once powerful influence under Heath. Fraser's Research Department became a steadily increasing power, with the CPC losing the voice it once had in policy.

After Marples's resignation Heath made an attempt to re-establish himself by addressing the 1922 Committee. The Party, he said in effect, had used the new democratic method of electing the Leader; it was now up to all to make a success of the outcome, not to look for any scapegoats. Some interpreted this last remark, wrongly, as a declaration that du Cann was going to be retained. However, daylight was soon in sight, or so it seemed. There were three good by-election results and in April the Tories swept the Greater London Council, winning 82 of the 100 seats. It was an amazing result. There were also further by-election triumphs and sweeping Tory gains too in the May local elections.

There was no arguing with success, so the Party settled

back contentedly. By June, Gallup was showing a 7% Tory lead.

In mid-summer even Powell seemed to be toeing the Party line when he made a stern declaration about the need for Britain to honour its commitments. This put some of those worried about Powell's defence line more at their ease, though not entirely. The officers of the Defence Committee of the Tory Party and its regular attenders knew all too well how far out of line Powell was with the normal Party thinking on defence.

An interesting aspect of this, however, was their personal loyalty to Powell. He differed from the majority of the Defence Committee on about four essential issues: Vietnam, East of Suez commitments generally, the worth of the nuclear deterrent, and the need, as he saw it, for conscription. But Powell had remarkable leadership qualities. As well as being good at handling men, he was indefatigable: he had arranged a weekly meeting for all the officers of the Committee at the abnormally early hour of 9.45 am. There he would be each Wednesday with his marked Hansards ready and his carefully prepared points. He would have a batch of carefully thought out Parliamentary questions and possible supplementaries to farm out among his team and to discuss with them. And, unlike Heath, he had the sort of natural consideration for lieutenants which inspires regard. The personal mention in a speech, the private notes, the word of encouragement—all were there. 'We really felt part of a team' one of them commented.

But by the end of the summer session the old leadership problem had reappeared. There was still no sign of Heath making any serious breakthrough in the opinion polls for his leadership qualities. And in the Commons itself Heath seemed woefully inadequate as a cross-examiner of the Prime Minister, by whom he was consistently and sometimes embarrassingly bested. But one of his speeches did at least appear to rile the Government. Speaking in early July, he attacked ministerial complacency over the balance of payments situation. The surplus in the first quarter, he warned, was largely fortuitous. The outlook was grimmer than people realised. Callaghan took the unusual step of rebuffing this by a statement issued almost at once from the Treasury. Events were to prove Heath all too correct.

At the Autumn Conference, Heath faced some open, and a lot of private, criticism. It was, he felt in retrospect, his most difficult time as leader of the Party. But he made a good off-the-cuff speech; the Chairman of the Conference predicted that Heath 'would emerge very fast indeed as the right man'. And with the repetition of this annual chorus, plus the predictable ovation, Heath emerged secure enough for the moment.

When devaluation took place two months later Heath's standing rose as inevitably as the Prime Minister's fell. He made a particularly effective television broadcast, denouncing the decision, the principles behind it and the likely consequences. As one who had never been suspected of any momentary enthusiasm for devaluation, he was well placed to do this and enthusiastically supported by the Party.

1968 opened on a reasonably easy note for Heath. The Government was trying desperately to defend itself after the steady abandonment of pledges as it imposed the post-devaluation curbs. Opposition in these circumstances was not very difficult.

In fact, the Party was heading for its biggest row yet, but it was not then apparent. The main irritant to the back-benchers, rather, was that they were unimpressed by some of Heath's own front bench colleagues. Few of them, it was said, could mount a convincing attack on the Government. Maudling seemed indolent, even if he was not. He lacked punch. Heath himself still performed poorly against the Prime Minister at question time, often dashing hastily in with poor supplementaries when his own back-benchers had carefully prepared and crushing 'spontaneous supplementaries'—or so they thought—ready for the occasion. Sir Edward Boyle, ran another complaint, lacked bite and when he barked he made the wrong noises. His too favourable attitude towards comprehensive schools was out of tune with about 90% of back-bench opinion. These M.P.s could not extract from him any firm stand against the whole idea, mooted by the Government, of taking over the independent schools and integrating them—the formula was as vague as it was impracticable—into the state sector. Boyle, ran the complaint, seemed to have guilt problems about his inherited wealth. Why should he be allowed to work them off as Tory policy? 'Edward is a dear chap,' complained one of his colleagues in a fairly common view, 'it's a pity he isn't a real Conservative'. One of Heath's earliest acts as leader had been to appoint Boyle as Chairman of the Advisory Committee on Policy, a group made up of M.P.s, Central Office officials and leading Party figures. The Committee is not a powerful group, but the Chairmanship is regarded as carrying considerable prestige. Heath, too, seemed to lean on Boyle heavily as a confidant.

With back-benchers in this difficult mood, an attempt was made to improve relations with the front bench. Sir Arthur Vere Harvey, Chairman of the 1922 Committee, arranged a dinner at St. Stephen's Club for his Committee Executive and the Shadow Cabinet. But face to face across a table, and perhaps inevitably, the critics and the criticised found discussion awkward. There were demands for 'tougher front bench' leadership. Maudling and Boyle were criticised variously for not pulling their weight (though Boyle was in fact one of the most energetic men in making speeches up and down the country). One would-be peacemaker asked why Powell could not stick to making speeches on defence? Powell replied that he had made a speech on defence a week before to a Scottish audience only, and the first question from his listeners had been: why couldn't he talk on something interesting? (Unanswerable replies of this sort are a feature of Powell's conversation, as the following incident illustrates when he met a provincial newspaper editor:

EDITOR: Ah, Mr. Powell, I was wondering incidentally if you would write us a main feature article on denationalisation?

POWELL: How much will you pay?

EDITOR (quailing under that cold stare and doubling the figure he had intended): Er—fifty guineas.

POWELL: I don't work for charity, you know.

EDITOR (suddenly thinking he had a perfect reply): Ah, but your leader wrote us an article last week, and did it for twenty-five guineas!

POWELL (totally unimpressed): I'm sure he did. And he'd have done it for nothing if you'd asked him to.

One of the troubles with this sort of crushing logic, of course, as some have found to their cost, is that it tends to bring conversations with Powell to a total standstill after the exchange of about three of four sentences.)

The St. Stephen's dinner was in fact a complete flop. The two groups went away feeling vaguely dissatisfied and with very little clarified. The only consolation was that the affair was not as much of a flop as a private dinner arranged a year earlier to try and bring Heath and his critics face-to-face. Sir Charles Taylor, the wealthy M.P. for Eastbourne, had entertained a very mixed group of Tories to dinner at the end of January 1967. The conversation turned to Heath's leadership about which almost all present proved fiercely critical. In an attempt at a bridge-building operation, Taylor arranged another dinner at his home a fortnight later so that the critics could confront Heath himself. But when the confrontation took place, the critics became uneasy and there was only some desultory criticism of the front bench in general, Maudling coming in for particular complaint. Only one M.P. cheerfully sailed into Heath and his tactics, with the unfortunate result that the Party leader appeared to lose his temper. News of this incident spread among other M.P.s and did Heath's reputation little good.

The big fight in the Party came soon after the St. Stephen's Dinner. The fuse was the Race Relations Bill, and Powell lit it. This measure to make racial discrimination unlawful in housing and employment sharply divided the Party. Some were for all out opposition, but some on the Left were for all out Support. The Shadow Cabinet debated hard and long. Some wanted an outright vote against the Bill's Second Reading. Some wanted only a reasoned amendment, others were inclined not to oppose the Second Reading at all—in other words not to oppose the principle of the Bill—but to leave any criticism until the later committee stage. Heath inclined to a reasoned amendment, certainly not to letting the Bill go through unscathed. Macleod, Boyle, Carr and Joseph were for not opposing it. Carrington put the view of the waverers succinctly: 'I think we've got to oppose this but I wish we hadn't.' The Chief Whip reported an additional complication. Some Tory back-benchers were preparing their own amendment. They hadn't tabled it yet but the press had got wind of it. A split might be awkward. The outcome was an agreement, but only just, to oppose the Second Reading with a reasoned amendment. Macleod, Maudling and Powell were left to draft it and the Shadow Cabinet meeting broke up. The trio took well over an hour, finally agreeing on this formula.

> This House, reaffirming its condemnation of racial discord and accepting the need for steps designed to improve the situation, nevertheless declines to give a Second Reading to a Bill which, on balance, will not in its practical application contribute to racial harmony.

It was the Wednesday before Easter and M.P.s dispersed

to their constituencies, little knowing that the weekend was to see the Tory Party's biggest crisis yet. Powell was due on the Saturday to address the Midland's Conservative Political Centre branches at Birmingham. It was there he launched into his speech in which he compared the Bill with 'throwing a match on gunpowder' and recalled the Roman who gloomily saw 'the Tiber foaming with much blood'.

This time Powell had gone too far. He had been deliberately practising brinkmanship ever since the 1966 Election, carefully calculating how far he could go without provoking Heath into dismissing him. This time he had miscalculated. Matters were made worse by the suspicion of his colleagues that he had somehow double-crossed them. The normal practice with M.P.s' speeches is to ask Central Office to deal with their distribution in advance to the Press. Had this procedure been followed with the Powell Easter speech, officials would have been able to alert the Leadership to the impending explosion. But Powell had ignored these usual channels this time. He had an excuse, however, though few were prepared to listen to it at the time. The Midlands area branch of Central Office had asked him a fortnight previously if it could have charge of distributing his Easter speech. He agreed to this. It is perhaps some measure of the difference in attitude towards immigration between London and the Midlands that no official there tried to flash a warning message through to Party headquarters about this speech.

The reaction to the speech was explosive. Heath curtly dismissed Powell from the Shadow Cabinet by telephone on Sunday evening—it would have been Sunday morning had not Powell's telephone been jammed by incoming calls. A considerable section of the Press warmly supported Heath and hurled anathemas at Powell. But any feeling of satisfaction Heath may have felt in getting rid of this turbulent colleague at last was short-lived. One of Heath's admirers and staunchest senior colleagues commented sadly later:

'Ted never really recovered from sacking Enoch. M.P.s weren't the trouble, they knew Enoch had gone too far, too often. But the grass roots were different. And, of course, there was the Race Relations Bill itself.'

There was indeed trouble with the Race Relations Bill itself. The battle over that within the Tory Party showed how deep was the division. It was not the Second Reading that was the real trouble. In the same week that the dockers marched to proclaim their support for Powell, the Commons debated the Second Reading with remarkable calm. Quintin Hogg, Shadow Home Secretary, rebuked his dismissed colleague for having been inflammatory and one or two Labour M.P.s made savage attacks on Powell. But the Tories at least had their reasoned amendment behind which they could unite, even if one or two of the Party including Boyle preferred not to vote for it. The later stages were however to provide William Whitelaw, the Tory Chief Whip, with a nightmare.

But no man was better equipped to deal with the crisis. Behind the hugely extrovert exterior of this jolly Border squire there lurked a shrewd mind and a remarkable sense of tact. His language to erring M.P.s would often be picturesque, even crudely Anglo-Saxon. But he was an impossible man to dislike and the easiest of men to approach. He, more than any other man in the Party, held the Conservatives together during difficult times. But all of Whitelaw's talents were to be stretched to the utmost over the Race Relations Bill, especially as M.P.s were daily reporting a massive pro-Powell mail.

The standing committee considering the Bill included two Tory left-wingers, Nicholas Scott and Sir George Sinclair. Their tendency to vote with the Government and not the Opposition during the Committee Stage of the Bill meant that the measure reappeared with scarcely any changes for its Third Reading in the House. Indeed, Hogg told a meeting of the 1922 Committee at that time that, because these two men were supporting the Government so often, he thought he would have to recommend an Opposition vote against the Third Reading.

Whitelaw viewed the outlook with alarm. How could the Party avoid advertising its deep division on the issue? If the Shadow Cabinet decided to vote against the Third Reading, several dozen of the more left-wing Tories would certainly vote for the measure. Whitelaw got the Shadow Cabinet to agree to no opposition on Third Reading. But this angered many Tory back-benchers on the other wing. Here was a Bill, they argued, which the Party had said in its original amendment on Second Reading was likely to do no good. It had been scarcely altered in Committee and now the proposal was to let it through without a protest! The majority of the 1922 Executive marched off to confront Heath and Whitelaw. It was an uneasy meeting to say the least. Heath appeared to take the view that when one had advanced a firm line on Second Reading it was not necessary to express an opinion on Third Reading. This was of course constitutional nonsense and Heath as an ex-Chief Whip should have known this. Certainly it caused mild astonishment among his visitors.

The meeting broke up with nothing settled and the protestors feeling, if anything, more irritated. The dissidents retired and prepared their own amendment with which to oppose the Third Reading. Who should they get to sign it? They contemplated going for just a few senior Privy Councillors to show that some of the most respected old hands disapproved of the Party's tactics. Another possibility was to go simply for numbers. Then, as one of the Executive commented with concern about the publicity effect, the difficulty would be to stop the rush of signatories. In the end the critics on the Executive decided that they alone would put the amendment in (though one Privy Councillor complained of not being asked to sign). Heath would get the message plainly enough in view of the meetings that had recently been held. The general public on the other hand would not be treated to the damaging spectacle of wholesale protest. All in all, the critics thought they were behaving rather responsibly.

Whitelaw played his next card carefully. Commons business each week, including the allocation of a certain number of 'supply' days each Session when the Opposition chooses the topic for debate, is arranged through a meeting between the Leader of the House, the Government Chief Whip and the Opposition Chief Whip. The Government of course has the main control of business, but there is a certain amount of co-operation in these arrangements. These periodic informal meetings between the two Whips are always referred to as 'the usual channels' even though they may strike the outsider, used to Party rivalry, as 'unusual'. It was through these 'usual channels' that he arranged for the Third Reading of the Bill to come on in the small hours of Friday morning. With Fridays normally confined to Private Member's Bills, M.P.s are usually only too anxious on Thursday evenings to get away to their constituencies or to the country. Whitelaw reckoned that in the early hours of Friday, many Tories would have succumbed to the temptation to go home; or if not, at least they would have no wish for an angry debate. And it would all, with luck, be too late for the morning papers to cover it at any length. His plans however were spoilt by Hogg.

The Shadow Home Secretary made an absurd speech when the Third Reading finally came up at 4 a.m. on Friday. His contribution was convoluted, silly and eventually rude. He provoked cries of 'rubbish' from exasperated Tory backbenchers and his speech ended with the following odd exchange.

MR. HOGG: My hon. friends are perfectly at liberty to disagree with me, but I am entitled to express my opinion. I have served my Party for thirty years—

A TORY BACK-BENCHER (and with indignation): So have we.

HOGG: And I have given up what I believe to be a promising professional career and I have abandoned a great hereditary position. I am not now going to be put down for saying what I believe it is my duty to say by unmannerly people who cannot hear views different from their own in silence. I ask my Party to agree with me.

Any doubt about whether the critics of the Bill would divide the House were firmly resolved by that speech. Forty-four Tories marched resolutely into the Noes Lobby. The pianissimo Third Reading which Whitelaw had hoped for had not taken place.

An additional divisive factor in the prolonged dispute over the Race Relations Bill was that Boyle had defied the Tory three-line Whip on the Second Reading amendment and abstained. He was not even rebuked for this. This angered not just the Powellites but also a number of other M.P.s who had for some time been irritated by Boyle's Education views. Boyle in fact was becoming an increasing problem. His lukewarm reception by the Tory rank and file at the Conference each year was a frequent enough reminder of how little the grass roots of the Party esteemed his views. 'Opposition since 1966,' commented one member of the 1922 Executive later, 'seems to have been one long sterile debate about Edward Boyle'.

In a typically subtle move, Macleod had urged, supported by Carrington, that Boyle should be moved up to become the opposite member to Richard Crossman, who was Secretary for the Social Services. It was a job he would have done well. As an ex-Treasury Minister, he would have had expertise which Crossman could not match. And of course it would remove him from the awkward field of Education. But Heath resisted the idea. The only open move to get rid of

Boyle came in April when Sir Gerald Nabarro announced at a 1922 meeting that he was going to ask for the removal of Boyle. He had, he said, with that supreme lack of tact uniquely his own, already told the Press that he was going to make this demand. Two Tory Knights-of-the-Shires promptly leapt down his throat, demanding how dare he behave in this fashion, using the meeting as a vehicle for personal publicity? With this, the affair was over in a few minutes, with the merits or demerits of Boyle himself hardly being reached.

The inevitable question after the Heath-Powell split with its long-term damaging effects at all levels of the Party was: could Heath have kept Powell in the Shadow Cabinet? Very few thought he could, after what had happened in April, coming as it did at the end of a whole series of speeches which questioned the official Party line. Nor, of course, was Powell unaware of the risks he ran. His air of injured innocence after his dismissal was totally unconvincing. He had been deliberately provocative, picking out issue after issue on which to challenge the Leadership's line. But that in itself of course was partly Heath's fault. He seemed to have no talent for reconciliation, only a capacity for irritating colleagues and not just Powell. He was a good man of business, a tireless administrator, a stubborn fighter. But he had a manner which on occasions, could make 'good morning' sound like a rebuke. And far from entering into policy discussions with enthusiasm or zest, he seemed to have a talent for seeing any deviation from his own views as a challenge to him personally. He was, too, running the Shadow Cabinet on a strangely tight rein. No intellectual himself and far more interested, it often seemed, in the machinery of Government than the purpose of Government, he appeared to think that his Cabinet *in posse* should behave like a Cabinet *in esse*. And here his instincts as an ex-Chief Whip seemed to reinforce his other convictions. He had little or no appreciation of the freedom which Opposition conferred on politicians—the chance to argue a bit more openly, debate publicly, fly kites and so on. Opposition gives politicians, as it were, the chance for 'a bit of fun', the more valuable after the constraints of Government and collective responsibilities. But under Heath the Shadow Cabinet was seen rather like the real Cabinet with portfolios shared out carefully and colleagues urged not to trespass in each other's territory. Hogg used to get particularly irritated by others' excursions into his Home Affairs department, even though he was never reluctant, as his colleagues commented, to charge pell-mell into everyone else's territory. An interesting contrast between the style of Opposition under Heath and under Churchill in 1945 to '51 is drawn in George Hutchinson's *Edward Heath—A Personal and Political Biography* (Longmans 1970). There it is pointed out that in Churchill's time all Conservative Privy Councillors sat on the front bench, the division of responsibility was much more vague, and the 'Leaders Committee' only met once a fortnight for lunch, not twice a week as under Heath. The style of Opposition was much freer and possibly because of it the style was also more aggressive.

Heath also suffered from a considerable lack of self-confidence. Men of ideas or marked personality seemed to upset him. He had to have some in his Shadow Cabinet, but otherwise the tendency was to choose easy-going and non-combative men and the pattern was largely repeated in the second rank of Party spokesmen, the Shadow Junior Ministers. The result, not surprisingly, was too much easy-going, non-combative opposition in the House, which only served to make many of the back benchers restless. Men whom Heath fell out with included Angus Maude, Shadow Colonial Secretary in 1966, Edward du Cann, Ernest Marples and Enoch Powell. In his Shadow Cabinet reconstructions, he dropped John Boyd-Carpenter, whereby hangs an interesting tale. During the 1945-51 Parliament, Boyd-Carpenter was so quick off the mark with the awkward question to ministers that he acquired the nickname of 'spring-heeled Jack'. He was, undoubtedly, superb at Opposition. A number of Tory M.P.s after 1966 pressed again and again for 'spring-heeled Jack' to be brought back into the Shadow Cabinet to strengthen the front bench. The answer that came back (amazingly) was, 'Ah, but he argued in Shadow Cabinet'.

An Opposition Leader who turned down combative men on these grounds seemed almost bound to produce unforceful Opposition. In short the atmosphere in the Shadow Cabinet, though enlivened occasionally by fierce argument from Mrs. Thatcher—who was once said to have given Heath an almost embarrassing reprimand for backsliding on nationalisation —and the occasional snort of disagreement from Geoffrey Rippon, was far too somnolent.

But not all the fault for poor Opposition lay with the Leadership. Arranging a full-scale attack in the Commons on a particular Government measure was only worthwhile if the Whips could be certain that there were back-benchers ready, willing and able to sit through the debate and deliver well-prepared speeches. But here the Opposition had allowed itself to be partially emasculated by the Government's so-called Parliamentary reforms. The manning of all the new Select Committees on matters ranging from Education to Technology, with numerous sub-committee off-shoots, involved drawing back-benchers away from the main Chamber and into the committee Rooms, frequently during important debates. There had been warnings to the House at the time from senior M.P.s that this might happen, warnings from experienced Parliamentarians like Michael Foot and Nigel Birch. But the Tory Leadership had rather ignored these points and Heath particularly was ready to listen to the younger Tories who saw these committees as a splendid reform to Parliament's supposedly creaking machinery. The back-benchers were foolish to fall for this new 'reform'. The Leadership, however, with its greater experience of Parliament must shoulder most of the blame for not foreseeing the consequences—though that extreme fellow Powell had of course, in his irritating way, issued various warnings about what might happen.

It was not hard to see why the Tory zealots outside Parliament were warming more and more to Powell. In the Commons, the Opposition seemed to lack both bark and bite. For example, one of the Government's Bills in mid-July that year to raise the now nationalised steel industry's borrowing powers involved the revelation that the Government had been £100 million out in its estimate of the overdraft and trade liabilities of the company that took over. Yet what happened? The Government's request was acceded to without even a vote, there were hardly any Tories present and only two of them seemed to want to understand the scale and nature of what had gone wrong. It was all a far cry from the days of 1945 to '51 when the Tory Opposition would raise the roof about small Government wastage. By far the most effective opposition in the House seemed to come not from the official Opposition but from the small group of Labour left-wingers consistently fighting the Government over its policies.

The Tory Conference that autumn was a worrying prospect for the Leader. As he and his friends feared, it was dominated by the Powell question. The man himself spoke in the debate on immigration, the very mention of his name as a prospective speaker being enough to spark off a roar of applause intermingled with some boos as well. The speech itself, calling for aided-repatriation, but moderate enough on the whole, was greeted with a prolonged standing ovation which Powell himself felt obliged to subdue in the end. The motion for that debate of course was carefully chosen for its woolliness and was passed without difficulty. Heath, who spoke very well, had no great problem in provoking the familiar standing ovation for his final speech. And to familiar assurances that Heath was now really emerging at last, the Tories went back to Westminster and to the constituencies.

One of the first events there was the election of the 1922 Executive. Now some of the Party loyalists were able to wreak a mild revenge on the Right as they had promised. Two of the signatories of the Race Relations Bill Third Reading amendment were voted off the Committee and one did not stand. In some of the other committees, right-wingers were also removed in the ballot for officers. It looked like a demonstration of solidarity for Heath. Powell delivered another blockbuster of a speech on immigration some weeks later, provoking 100 Labour M.P.s into signing a motion attacking him. Some Tories were only just dissuaded from following suit by the intervention of some of the older of their colleagues. Not the least interesting outcome was a subsequent speech in which Heath attacked Powell's views by implication and in remarkable language. It included the comment:

'That way lies tyranny. It must be fought wherever it raises its ugly presence. It had to be fought in Germany in the 1930s, in America in the 1950s. Wherever it happens today it must be fought.'

A politician who can mention Hitler's Germany and Eisenhower's America in the same breath in a condemnation of 'tyranny' must either be strangely insensitive to words or strangely anti-American.

At the end of November the Government launched into yet another draconian emergency budget. It further improved the Tories' standing in the opinion polls and made the problem of Heath's suitability as Leader still more academic. Few in the Party then believed that Labour could ever catch up again, no matter how hard it tried. In any case, and this was the crucial factor throughout all the rows about the Leadership, there was no obvious alternative. Maudling had been defeated in 1965 because he seemed too easy-going and not sufficiently dedicated to politics, least of all to the battle of political opposition. The impression grew rather than declined after the 1966 defeat. Powell had many admirers, but also many enemies. And even most of his admirers were a bit uneasy about the idea of Powell as the actual Leader—it would carry excitement in politics just a little too far. Home of course was much admired and universally liked. Many Labour M.P.s were among his personal admirers. 'What a mistake you made dropping Alec for Ted' was the sort of comment frequently made by Labour M.P.s to Tories during the 1966 to 1970 period. But loyalty was a very strong feature of Home's character. One word from him would have rocked the boat with a vengeance. But it never came. He kept his critical views of Heath to himself.

Heath of course was still highly sensitive about Powell, watching his every pronouncement with anxiety. Just as Maudling was inclined to overreact in the Commons to allegations that current difficulties stemmed from the 1964 deficit—he thus helped keep the issue alive, much to Labour's satisfaction—so Heath was inclined to overreact to Powell.

In November Powell had made a speech advocating more denationalisation. He even went to the trouble of quoting Heath's comment at the Party conference: 'We will begin to reintroduce private ownership into nationalised industries.' And how it was applauded, said Powell approvingly. But he also had a private bet with another Tory that Heath would instinctively rebut his view publicly. He had only a few weeks to wait. Heath made a speech including the comment that widespread denationalisation was not of course possible It was not very wise of the Leader. Many Tory M.P.s wanted more extensive denationalisation than the Party was committed to. So the report from a group of Tories who had at the

Shadow Cabinet's request been studying denationalisation was promptly leaked to the Press. It suggested that rather more was possible than Heath had implied in his speech. ('We will call a halt to further nationalisation' was one of the phrases which had kept appearing in Heath's speech. As one Tory M.P. commented with increasing anger, each time this phrase appeared, 'What the hell does that mean coming from a Tory?')

Arguments about denationalisation and the return to full-blooded capitalism were frequent in the Party Committees. On steel, the Shadow Cabinet had back pedalled. When the Bill to nationalise the industry first appeared, the front bench line had been quite plain: the Tories would denationalise steel when returned. Later the formula was watered down to an undertaking to 'put steel back into a competitive framework'. (This non-committal formula was Barber's.) Originally the Shadow Cabinet said it would abolish the Industrial Reorganisation Corporation. Later this was watered down to an undertaking that a Tory Government would 'take away the IRC's funds.' Heath himself had long favoured the idea of some sort of state merchant bank. Maudling, among senior colleagues, had always disliked the idea.

By the time of the Party Manifesto, the undertaking had become even vaguer: 'to drastically modify the Industrial Reorganisation Corporation Act'. Joseph, as the spokesman on trade and industry, was far from unsympathetic to the more radical attitude of those on the back-bench Trade and Industry Committee, but as one of them commented: 'Old Joseph would have good ideas, but so often he would trail back a week later from his Shadow Cabinet to say that he had been overruled.'

Though Joseph had split from Powell on the immigration issue, he admired much of the latter's economic thinking. And in a television interview in mid-January 1969, he insisted that he was proud to be a colleague of Powell's. There was even some speculation shortly afterwards that Heath intended to take Powell back into the Shadow Cabinet. It was hopelessly wide of the mark. The thought never crossed Heath's mind. Indeed he found the very idea repugnant. Some leading Tories long hoped that Powell and Heath would be reconciled. Boyle entertained the idea of making peace between the two as late as mid-1969. His hope was to be able to get Heath and the Powells, plus one or two friends of both, to a weekend at his country house in Sussex. But the idea was eventually abandoned. Lord Aldington, an ex-Deputy Chairman of the Tory Party and a friend of both, had also wanted to try to conciliate. But the gap was unbridgeable.

In any case, it was not just Heath who was annoyed with Powell. Macleod reacted angrily to a speech in which Powell attacked the 'myth' that savings were especially virtuous or deflationary. And Maudling assailed Powell's constantly reiterated call for a floating pound. (This was an interesting about-turn on Maudling's part. In 1965 he had publicly said he was far from hostile to the idea of floating exchange rates.) Strong reaction to Powell's speeches by Tory colleagues tempting as it always was, was not a particularly good tactic from the point of view of closing the Party ranks. For every one pleased to see Powell rebutted, there was at least one—and often a Party worker at that—who was displeased. And to the outsider, the process was a reminder of the deep split in the Party. Controversy on policy would not have been too bad, stimulating even. It could suggest that the Tory Party, for a change, was a ferment of ideas. But the division now was blatant, too personal and anguished to convey anything but bitterness to the outside world.

The leadership's own version of fermenting ideas was unimpressive. A number of policy groups had been set up in 1966 to keep ideas up to date. But they were not always a source of strength to the Party or of unity either. For one thing, they were not particularly productive in new or interesting ideas. There seemed to be too much in any case about the machinery of Government rather than the application of Conservatism. Another problem was that some of the outsiders on the Committee were so nervous about having their names connected with the Tory Party that their identities were kept very secret. It was a source of irritation to some of the elected officers on various back-bench committees to find that policy proposals were being sent to the Leader from a group containing men whose identities they could not even discover.

The problem of bad communications or poor contact between the Leader and the led was by no means confined to Parliament. Heath's forays into constituencies were all too often stiff, uneasy affairs, with Heath putting nobody at their ease. His platform manner was often harsh and awkward and the speeches lacked flair or perception; M.P.s' wives were sometimes introduced two or three times within a short space without Heath remembering them. Committing to memory the faces of all colleagues and their wives is of course a murderously difficult task for every party leader, but Heath's particular trouble was that a massive memory for detail was supposed to be one of his greatest strengths. The fact that he was bad at applying this strong point to faces and names did not go down well. It added to the impression of remoteness. He was often insensitive too about candidates. The Party Leader saying '. . . and I look forward to your candidate John Bloggs joining us as a colleague at Westminster soon . . .' is a ritual which means a lot to Bloggs and the local Party workers. Forgetting this was a mark of insensitivity which was often resented after Heath's tours. There was also a constant problem with his television appearances. One or two set-piece Party broadcasts showing him relaxing with his constituents went down very well. If caught at the right moment Heath could be seen as relaxed and amiable. But in television interviews, as one of his colleagues commented, he came across as 'incredibly uncosy'. Before these appearances, Heath and his colleagues would sit around discussing the probable questions which might come. They were not hard to guess. But Heath, when he appeared, showed little finesse in answering. His replies were always fluent and unhesitating, but usually banal too. And his taut, sometimes hectoring manner, suggested constantly that he was on the defensive. He wrongly gave the impression, almost the worst possible in a Party Leader, of being the sort of man who could be panicked, a man who might lose his head at a pinch. Wilson usually managed to convey an impression of unflapability by contrast. Nor had Heath a flair for simple language which is essential in the effective television interview. Where he should talk about 'price cutting', which all understand, he would refer to 'the abolition of resale price maintenance'. Some TV experts were called in to coach Heath. The results, however, were only a marginal, and not a sustained, improvement.

But in one respect at any rate Heath was making progress. His House of Commons style was improving quite strikingly. As with so many other things, Heath was not a man of great natural talent but his pertinacity was tremendous. He became by the end of the 1966-70 Parliament a first-class Parliamentary performer. Originally he had been a bit stiff and his real forte in the Commons as a Minister was mastery of detail. Now he was at last mastering the act of dealing with Wilson in the House. 'What happens', he asked the Prime Minister after his announcement of the abandonment of the Industrial Relations Bill in 1969, 'when the Unions ignore the Prime Minister and go on striking?' The Prime Minister, waiting for a blast of indignant protest from which he could choose convenient points for his answer, was stumped. Was that the best the Leader of the Opposition could do, he asked scornfully? 'Answer, Answer,' came the roar from the Tory benches. Again and again Heath pressed the point with the

Prime Minister unable to find the convincing answer. This was in fact the right way to deal with Wilson and Heath seemed to be finding it at last.

He followed this up with an impressive speech in the subsequent debate on the Bill's non-appearance. From about this time in fact he became a consistently good Parliamentary performer, getting to the heart of issues, detailing the Government's shortcomings in simple and striking phrases and giving Wilson a number of highly uncomfortable moments.

And when the row over the Boundaries Commission reached its height, Heath put on one of his best performances ever. Late at night the Government announced that it would guillotine the Boundaries Bill then going through the Committee Stage with the Opposition trying hard to delay it. Heath blasted the Socialists savagely. So this was Labour's view of democracy, was it? Fiddling the boundaries and then trying to cut short the debate? Michael Foot tried to intervene and earned the rebuke from Heath that, of course, Foot was a good crusader about democracy—in Northern Ireland or in South Africa. But in Great Britain, where Labour stood to lose by democracy—ah, then it was all very different. Heath soon had Labour M.P.s howling with rage.

On one issue, however, Heath constantly had difficulty: Rhodesia. He would often let that issue pass in silence. Labour M.P.s often taunted him on this. But Heath was all too well aware of the strains in his own Parliamentary Party. The issue had split his followers' ranks several times. Indeed it was dividing his own Shadow Cabinet even then. Sir Alec, it was thought, saw little point in trying to pretend that Rhodesian independence was much less than a *fait accompli*. Others were strongly for the maintenance of stern disapproval with no British recognition of anything less than a Constitution which guaranteed substantial African political advancement. Boyle was among this group. But it was becoming clear that Boyle, though not on this issue, was a liability to Heath and the Party. Back-bench pressure for his removal had been growing steadily. Rumours that he would take an academic post somewhere grew towards the end of the summer. In October it was to be announced that Boyle would become Vice-Chancellor of Leeds University. It was a highly satisfactory formula; and Mrs. Thatcher was switched to become Shadow Education Minister. That met with general approval in the Party.

More or less at the same time as the row over the boundaries, Heath's personal popularity in the polls showed a slight rise. To Gallup's question 'Do you think Heath is a good leader of the Conservative Party?' the answer was Yes: 40%, No: 35%. It was at least an improvement. One of the most worrying aspects of public opinion for the Opposition had been that Heath's personal standing was consistently low, not only in absolute terms but also very low in relation to the popularity of the Party itself. Huge Tory leads in the polls had been recorded in the earlier part of the year. In January, for example, the Tory lead had been a massive 22%. A month before, the lead had been over 25%. But to the question asking whether Heath was a good leader, the answers were:

	December	January
	%	%
Is a good Leader?	30	31
Is not a good Leader	49	44

The balance 'did not know'.

By April the proportions were fractionally worse. Wilson of course also stood very low in the public esteem at that time. But experience had shown that it was rare for a Party Leader actually to stand lower in public esteem than his party. Wilson's rating fell as the popularity of Labour fell, though not so fast. Heath's rating was consistently lower than that of his Party and, ominously, lower than that of the Prime Minister's. The July jump to 40% approval for Heath showed a swing in the opinion of Tory voters particularly, most now agreeing that he was a good Leader. But the mood did not last. By September, Heath was back at 32% approval only, with little more than half of the Tory supporters agreeing that he was a good Leader.

No small part of this was due to his public speeches. Except for his conference speeches, they were remarkably unimpressive. Content, presentation and language alike were unimpressive. In mid-1968, for example, it was announced that Heath was going to make three major policy speeches on the economic situation, culminating at Wembley in mid-July. The press, duly appraised, provided appropriate trailers. But when the speeches themselves appeared, they turned out to be little more than a reiteration of familiar points he had made many times, with only one or two new points added. The fairly small space and prominence given to the speeches in the press irritated Heath, but it did not result in any improvement in his speeches.

But at least the Tory Conference in October 1969 promised few difficulties for Heath personally. It was generally expected that it would be the last Conference before the election and the feeling of the rank and file was that it wanted to close the ranks. The Tory lead, though reduced, was still a comfortable $9\frac{1}{2}\%$. Perhaps even more important, the polls showed that the electors still disapproved of the Government's record by a massive majority and was confident that the Tories would handle better nearly all the major issues ranging from inflation to strikes and even including unemployment.

The only serious difficulty for Heath at the Conference was the familiar immigration issue. A motion to approve the official Party policy was strongly opposed, with the clear implication that those against the motion thought the policy not restrictive enough. The official line was approved but only by a majority of 395 out of a total vote of 2,300. This discouraging result was, however, partly the personal fault of Hogg. His speech was confused and, worse still, flippant in places. The motion to approve the Party's policy towards the Common Market was passed by a ratio of 3:1. The test for Heath came on the last day and here he was in powerful form. So the delegates left Brighton in a heartened mood, ready for the coming election more or less happy about the Leadership. They were certainly spoiling for the General Election.

But the Tories got a nasty shock only a few days later. Gallup showed their lead down to a mere 2%. And though two other polls presented a very confused position, a lurch towards Labour seemed in progress. The sharp improvement in the balance of payments seemed to be taking its toll. A Cabinet Minister had commented in 1968: 'Our only hope is to get the country so neurotic about the balance of payments that when it finally does come right, the relief will be overwhelming.' Events seemed to be proving his view correct. The Leadership ratings were discouraging for Heath too. He was rated as a good Leader by 33% and not a good leader by 44%. In November the Party's lead crept up to 3½%. But the Leader's position remained unchanged. However, opinion polls, as the Party leaders kept saying, were only opinion polls. When it came to the Ballot Box itself, it was a different matter. Certainly, when it came to by-elections, it did seem to be a different matter. A series of five by-elections at the end of October produced an average swing to the Tories of over 10%. This was a slight improvement for Labour compared with some previous by-elections. But it was a fairly drastic swing against the Government just the same. Tory M.P.s were on the whole content with the outlook; the Government could hardly recover in the time left to it, most reckoned. One slight problem worrying some back-benchers, however, was the way in which the Opposition's specific proposals had been spelt out. Hogg and Home as old political hands had often voiced doubts about announcing policies in much detail until very close to the Election time.

A whole series of promises had now been made to spend more and more on the social services, coupled with promises to abolish SET and cut income tax too. In the Shadow Cabinet itself the voices of Maudling, Joseph and Mrs. Thatcher were occasionally raised in doubt. Among the backbenchers there were some doubts as well. Ministers were having some fun, jeering at the arithmetic of the Opposition. Macleod was invited to talk to the 1922 Committee on this matter and it was suggested that he should try to convince supporters of the feasibility of the Opposition's plans financially. He tried, but did not convince many of the doubters.

Powell became once more the centre of a storm in the New Year. Speaking at a Young Conservative meeting at Scarborough in January, he spoke derisively of the notion that Commonwealth immigration would be solved by the programme of Special Aid for the Social Services in the areas of high immigrant population. His actual words were:

'Except in connection with and as an integral part of a policy of voluntary repatriation, measures of finance and others to alleviate the problem of the areas especially affected and, still more, measures to promote and facilitate the absorption or integration of that part of the coloured population which will eventually make a permanent home here and become a part of the national life, are worse than merely neutral. They are positively harmful in their net effect, because they encourage all concerned to deceive themselves for longer and longer as to the true magnitude and nature of the prospect and to squander these few remaining precious years when it might still be possible to avert disaster.'

This was immediately interpreted by the Press as a demand

that the Special Aid to these areas should be stopped. Powell did not *exactly* say that, though it is easy to see how the inference was drawn. But Heath adopted an even harsher interpretation at once and promptly declared in a radio interview:

'The conclusion as I understand it is that—certainly the implication of it is—we should do nothing to help the cities and boroughs like Birmingham and Wolverhampton which have got these problems, in the hope that if only we left the housing to get bad enough and the Health Service to get burdened enough, the immigrants will go away of their own accord and the problem will disappear.'

For good measure, Heath added that Powell's views were unchristian and an example of 'man's inhumanity to man'. Powell was incensed. But anxious not to protract the personal battle which was emerging, he sought out Whitelaw with a proposed correspondence. Powell suggested that the matter could be closed by two letters. There would be, first, a 'Dear Ted . . . Yours ever, Enoch' letter, saying that Powell enclosed the full text of his speech and hoped that the Leader would note that it did not in fact bear the interpretation which he had placed upon it. Then this would be followed by a 'Dear Enoch . . . Yours ever, Ted' reply, saying 'Thank you for your letter. I note what you have said.' Whitelaw, anxious as ever to keep the peace, endorsed the suggestion and took the proposal to Heath, Powell meanwhile releasing the text of his letter to the Press. But one of Heath's colleagues immediately objected. It was a trap! Whitelaw was being taken in! Powell, when he got the letter back, would counter with something like 'Dear Ted, thank you for your letter. Since you note what I have said, will you not now agree that my speech does not in any way bear the interpretation you put upon it?' The upshot was, though it seems unlikely that Whitelaw was convinced of Powell's plotting inclinations, that Heath's reply was a curt 'Dear Enoch, thank you for your letter. I have nothing to alter or add to what I have said'.

An irritant about this incident for the Tory leadership was that it came on the very eve of the weekend conference of the Shadow Cabinet at the Selsdon Park Hotel, Croydon. The exercise was essentially a public-relations affair. To 'get over' to the public the Opposition's plans for government, the paraphernalia of a conference was arranged, with officials of the Party's Research Department in attendance. For a moment it did catch the public attention. It reminded the public about the various issues which the new Tory government wished to treat. It was even vaguely if convincingly hinted that the Tory Party had enough legislation now planned to last for a five-year period.

One matter left in some doubt was the Value Added Tax. Macleod had been advocating this for some two years, even announcing at the 1969 Conference that he had asked a Tax expert to prepare a draft Bill on the matter. The essence of VAT is that it would replace Corporation Tax, Purchase Tax, Duties and SET with a tax which would add so much to the value of a product or service at each stage of 'production'. If Britain joined the Common Market she would have to copy the Six and have some form of such a tax. If she did not, argued Macleod, it would still be a good idea.

The Socialists had frequently taunted the Tories over VAT. The Conservative Party line was that food would not be affected by the Tax and small shops would not have to meet it either. A Government report on the vast number of extra civil servants required for such a tax was produced. Ministers warned about a VAT raising the cost of some things not now taxed. It was not all that long before the Tories began to get cold feet. At Selsdon Park it was announced that the VAT proposals were tentative. Macleod had lost round one. A more promising field, however, was law and order which was emphasised at Selsdon Park. The impending South African cricket tour was threatened by the 'Stop the '70s Tour' group which promised violence to get the visit called off. Polls showed the public 2:1 in favour of the tour going on. Labour M.P.s fought fiercely to have it called off. Wilson himself said on television 'every one should be free to demonstrate against apartheid. I hope people will feel free to do so'. But they would not, he hoped, turn to violence or anything of that sort.

This was promptly declared by many Tories to be an open encouragement to demonstrations which it was known were intended to end in violence. In due course, with the Home Secretary leaning heavily upon the Cricket Council, the tour was called off on May 22, less than four weeks from polling day. It might have provided a resounding theme for the election itself. But after one or two preliminary noises it was scarcely mentioned by the Conservative Party Leader himself. Other candidates took up the theme with far more enthusiasm however. If it was a serious factor in the result it certainly provided the ironic thought that white South Africans had played a large part in getting Harold Wilson out of Downing Street.

The Greater London Council Elections in April and the Budget almost immediately afterwards convinced most Tory M.P.s that at least there was little likelihood of a summer election. Central Office had, of course, its contingency plans but October was still the favourite.

The shift that began to show in the opinion polls in late April took Tory M.P.s unawares. At that rate, they reckoned, Wilson might just chance his arm on a summer contest—not that they much doubted its outcome. Then came the local government elections in early May with widespread Labour successes. With two of the newer polls showing small Labour leads now, Tories waited uneasily for the Gallup due out on May 13 in the *Daily Telegraph*. That had shown a Tory lead of $4\frac{1}{2}\%$ in late April. Other polls even suggested a very small Labour lead. Gallup, the Party feared, might endorse the increasingly pessimistic view that perhaps the two sides were running neck-and-neck. But even this speculation was to prove optimistic when the poll came to be published.

The Tory Errors

The cry was already being heard by early May: 'What has gone wrong?' Was it policies or men—or the man? Few Tories had many doubts on the last score. Heath was a crucial factor. Many of his own followers, after all, had found him even more difficult to warm to than the general public.

But it was not so easy to pin the blame at that point on one man. There was the matter, not to be underrated, of Tory opposition tactics generally. Parliamentary Opposition had rarely been impressive since 1964. It is very easy to dismiss what goes on in debates in the House as relatively unimportant. The votes are predictable, the speeches too in so many cases. But the essence of the Commons is that it highlights issues. Reports of individual debates in the Press and on television and on the radio will scarcely sway voters one way or another. But the cumulative effect over a number of years is important. How the Parties feel about issues, which side makes out a convincing case, what is a positive scandal, what is a side issue, what particular politicians set as their priorities—all these come through in the long term. In the House, the Tories were not impressive. 'Just suppose,' said one of the younger Tory M.P.s in early 1970 'that unemployment had reached the present sort of level under us; the row in the House would just about have brought the place to a standstill!' He was right. The undramatic protests the Tories had made in the House on this issue, for example, had certainly not caught the public imagination. The conclusion of many voters must have been that high unemployment was inevitable or that the Tories would not seek to make considerable change when in office themselves. The failure to catch the public imagination through Commons debates was notable on several issues. One of the more notable was the rigging of the Parliamentary Boundaries. Certainly there was a considerable row at the time. But was it a big enough one and was it as protracted as it should have been? Some Tories certainly thought not and said so at the time. There had been suggestions from Tories ranging from Shadow Cabinet Ministers downwards that this measure was so monstrous that it deserved the ultimate deterrent: co-operation through 'the usual channels' (see page 96) should have been ended. Pairing arrangements should have been dropped. Votes should have been forced on every conceivable issue, procedural and otherwise. Such guerilla tactics would have made life hell for Labour M.P.s. The bulk of them would have had to be kept within a stone's throw of the Chamber for most of the Parliamentary day. Otherwise whole periods of Government business might have been lost. Many Labour M.P.s would have been unable to perform jobs outside the House or attend functions. It would all have been very unusual and perhaps 'ungentlemanly' for the Tories. But it would at least have conveyed to the public that the Boundaries procedure was really quite extraordinarily irregular. It might even have persuaded the Government to drop their scheme: improbable perhaps but just a chance of it.

The idea of such tactics was overruled however. The Tories, it was countered, did not do that sort of thing!

Nor of course was the skill of Labour's ministers as debaters to be underrated. In times when Parliamentary reports tend to consist of the summaries of the main points by the front bench speakers only, the Tories were foolish to let some of their best debaters languish on the back benches. But that was Heath's style. He saw Opposition more in an administrative than a political light. The Opposition front bench was for the training of the men he intended to make ministers rather than a place for the star brains and star performers on his own side.

Certainly the Opposition managed to convince the public that it was better at handling many vital issues than the Government. But this happened largely by default. The Government convinced the public of its own incompetence. Were the advantages of the Tories as a Party enough to outweigh the public misgivings about Heath himself? Evidently not. Here the Party chiefs made the mistake of over-exposing Heath without managing to correct those faults in him which apparently unsettled the public. The four men who were cloest to Heath in the Shadow Cabinet were Whitelaw, Carrington, Home and Barber. Whitelaw saw his essential job as peacekeeping. Home was loyal and helpful but reserved. Carrington was unquestionably one of the most popular men in the Party. But he had never been an M.P. himself and the rough-and-tumble of politics slightly pained him. Barber viewed his role as that of supporting and promoting the Leader. The four men made up a loyal quartet. But what Heath really needed was cruelly candid friends.

Du Cann had always doubted whether Heath would ever 'get across' as a popular political figure. The arrival of Barber at Central Office therefore saw a switch in tactics. The emphasis in Party propaganda thereafter was predominantly on Heath, almost to the exclusion altogether of his team, several of whom were much more likely to impress the public than Heath himself.

The Opposition's tactics towards Wilson personally were also wrong. The pugnacious approach particularly favoured by Barber was widely adopted. There was a sustained and furious attack on Wilson as a twister, a cheat, a fraud, and a con-man. It was almost certainly a mistaken assessment of the man and of the public mood. The Opposition seemed to imply that Wilson had about the worst record of treachery since Judas Iscariot. In fact the man's real fault was that his capacity for foresight compared unfavourably with that of Ethelred the Unready. Every eventuality caught him unawares. But the Opposition, instead of treating him with derision, reviled him as a twister. The sentiment was genuine enough, but the expectation that the country would recoil from Wilson with the same horror as the Tories was naive. For one thing, the epithets all suggested extraordinary cunning in the man; and not a few among the public thought that such a characteristic in a politician was almost a necessity. The Tory Leadership in fact seemed to suffer from an overdose of Christopher Robin, forgetting that the British public's heroes are more often Pistol, Bardolf and Nym.

The concentration of maximum exposure on Heath and maximum denigration of Wilson meant inevitably that the contest would be more presidential than ever. It was liable to play into Labour's hands. The Tory approach could have been different. Heath could have been kept in the background as a slightly Olympian figure, the great expert on details, on administration, on international matters like the Common Market. The cosier and more easily understood leaders like Maudling and Macleod could have been used more. But that strategy was not chosen. Heath was determined to be exposed; the machine backed up that strategy and so the Party came close to playing its weakest not its strongest card. It would in fact have been easy to make a virtue of necessity by adopting as a Tory theme: we are not a one-man-band like the Socialists, but a team. Instead, the Tories appeared ready to cry that they too were a one-man-band.

Another problem stemming from Heath's own personality was his lack of a decisive political philosophy.

What did Heath stand for? Of all the figures in the Shadow Cabinet, he was probably the one with the least definable political position. In its outstanding coverage of the Election, the *Guardian* carried a fascinating interview with Heath on June 9, which showed his position unequivocally.

Terry Coleman, the interviewer, wrote:

> He had said: 'The key to everything is the creating of more national wealth.' Was this the key to everything?—'Yes'.
>
> Without exception?
>
> 'Without exception.'
>
> What about things such as freedom? Did that depend on wealth?
>
> At this, he came alive and spoke with a direct strength I had not seen the previous two days. 'If you've ever been poor you will know that.'

To want everyone to be better-off is commendable of course. But it is hardly a political philosophy. Nor could this train of thought, which marked Heath's speeches so emphatically, be said to differentiate the Tory cause from the Labour cause. After all, Labour too wanted most people to be better-off. It was no surprise therefore that the Tory campaign seemed to revolve around one argument, almost to the exclusion of all others, that a Conservative Britain would grow faster economically than a Labour Britain.

Other Shadow Cabinet Ministers could argue with eloquence and conviction about the value of freedom and opportunity and the menace of Government interference, not just in detail but as a principle. Heath, a *dirigiste* by inclination, could strike no such convincing note. And it is an established political fact that a politician who cannot assail his opponent's policies in principle will tend to concentrate on detail and personalities. The approach is liable to make for repetition and dullness, to produce speeches which lack a ring. The problem for the Tories as the election loomed up was whether Heath could turn relatively narrow differences in politics into a convincing campaign.

CHAPTER FOUR

THE LABOUR PARTY

'How matters press upon me, what stubborn things are facts'—
WILLIAM HAZLITT.

FOR the first time ever, the Labour side of the House of Commons in 1966 comprised more university-educated Members than the Conservative: the ratio was 189 to 170, though the Labour figures included 103 from non-Oxbridge universities. In terms of occupation the pattern set in 1964 was accentuated, though not markedly: for instance, there were 56 teachers or lecturers, compared to 46 in 1964; while the number of journalists, publishers and public relations men remained constant at around 40. Perhaps the more significant change lay not in the number of university lecturers but in the influx of a group of managers, executives and administrators. But in appearance the 1966 intake did not differ greatly from that of 1964: there were just rather more of them.

Iain Macleod looked at the entry and wrote that their talent had been much exaggerated: the really outstanding Labour group, he believed, were those who had won in 1964. No doubt Macleod is romantic about those who come into the House after a closely fought election: he himself won in 1950. Still, there does seem to be some tendency (which has to be gauged subjectively because it depends on one's own estimate of ability) for the abler Members on both sides to represent marginal constituencies. But there is no need to make too much of this one way or the other. By any standard the Labour side after the 1966 election were vigorous, well informed and independent-minded.

And they expected, not great things—they were too worldly for that—but something from Harold Wilson and his new Government. Here it is necessary to stray slightly beyond the time-limit set for this chapter. A myth has grown up that between 1964 and 1966 everything had gone remarkably well for the Government, give or take a few setbacks such as the non-nationalisation of steel (owing mainly to Desmond Donnelly and Woodrow Wyatt) and the loss of the Leyton by-election (owing at least partly to Patrick Gordon Walker). But in reality things had not gone well at all. The only thing that had gone well was the 1966 election.

In 1965 the deficit on the balance of payments had been £265 million. The Rhodesia affair had not been settled and looked no nearer to settlement. James Callaghan had introduced several 'crisis' budgets, in particular a remarkably severe set of deflationary measures in August 1965. George Brown had, it is true, secured a 'Declaration of Intent' from the employers and the unions; and he had produced a National Plan. But Brown had also rushed panting down to the TUC's gathering at Brighton to demand a wage-vetting procedure. After some confusion, and with some reluctance, the unions had agreed to go along with Brown. Later, in 1966, it was made clear that a statutory incomes policy (though not a wage freeze) was also to be part of the Government's plans. On the whole, the left wing of the Party was opposed to this policy: 'on the whole' because Members such as Michael Foot believed in an incomes policy as part of a Socialist society, but were unwilling to accept Brown's because he had originally introduced it in order to impress foreign opinion.

Nor was this the only subject about which there was dissatisfaction immediately following the 1966 election. Both wings of the Parliamentary Party were uneasy about the

Common Market: broadly the Left wanted the Government to take up a more hostile position, the Right a more friendly one. Then there was defence policy East of Suez. With the ending of 'confrontation' between Indonesia and Malaysia both wings of the Party looked forward to reduced defence expenditure in the Far East, but of this there was little sign. Then again there was support for American policy in Vietnam. Michael Stewart, the Foreign Secretary, refused to give an inch; and Wilson's dissociation from the bombing of Hanoi and Haiphong did only a little to mollify the Government's critics.

On the whole the Party was happy enough, however, about the Government's handling of the economy. Devaluation was not, nor did it ever become, a popular demand in the Party as such. It was somehow thought of as the capitalist remedy. Its principal supporters were Ministers such as Anthony Crosland and Roy Jenkins (the former having been a consistent devaluer since 1964) and back-benchers such as David Marquand, Brian Walden, Joel Barnett, and Robert Sheldon. The revision of sterling's boundaries as an international reserve currency was urged occasionally by members of the Left such as James Dickens: but the demand was not very insistent. The Left's prescription remained virtually the same at this time and later: salvation lay in cutting defence expenditure and mobilising the dollar portfolio.

But if, immediately after the 1966 election, the Parliamentary Party was broadly happy about the Government's handling of the economy, the City and the financial commentators were not. The favourite remedy was a severe budget by Callaghan. As things turned out, he was not as severe as he had been urged to be, and as the Parliamentary Party expected him to be. His budget inaugurated the Selective Employment Tax, designed by Dr. Nicholas Kaldor and intended to force workers into productive industry from service industry, about which Dr. Kaldor had particularly strong moral feelings. The Parliamentary Party breathed again: Jim had not been exactly generous, but he had been remarkably imaginative.

Not that the Parliamentary Party was happy. Wilson, fresh from his triumph, seemed to be becoming more and more remote from both his Ministers and back-bench M.P.s. There was no sign of a change in his attitude either to East of Suez or to the Anglo-American alliance. Then there occurred two events which were to have a profound effect on the position of the Government in the months ahead. Frank Cousins resigned from the Cabinet; and the seamen went on strike.

Cousins's union, the Transport and General Workers, had from the beginning opposed the Incomes Policy. He himself had pointedly refrained from saying anything in its favour. The strain proved too great for him; at last he decided to go. Now it would have been possible to interpret his departure as a sign that the Labour Government was resolved to carry out its Incomes Policy come what might. The foreign bankers interpreted it differently. To them it was a sign that Wilson had lost control of the unions, whose representative Cousins was supposed by them to be. It contributed to the run on sterling which was to end with the July measures.

The seamen's strike was a worse example of bad luck or miscalculation (it depends how you look at it) by the Government. For months and months, even prior to the 1966 election, Ministers had been saying privately that they would like to take on a Trade Union in order to prove their sincerity over the Incomes Policy. Finally a candidate presented itself: the Seamen's Union. Wilson immediately made the Government a party to the dispute. He went on television to denounce the seamen as enemies of the State. The seamen were unmoved. The Parliamentary Labour Party were disappointed at this rapid move over to the other side. They were still more disappointed when Wilson denounced the strike as being the work of a 'tightly knit group of politically motivated men', some of whom he proceeded to name in the House of Commons. The strike ended. In this, Wilson had been successful. But the whole episode left a nasty taste in the mouth. After this, the militant unions were never able to come to terms with Wilson, nor he with the militant unions.

And this was not all. If Wilson had been successful in ending the strike, he had not been at all successful in impressing international financial opinion. Indeed the Government's attitude had precisely the opposite effect. The Gnomes, instead of saying: 'Look how tough he is' said: 'Look, he cannot control the unions. They are on strike.' And this was undoubtedly an important factor in the run on sterling. The sterling crisis of 1966, then, came to an already disappointed Labour Party. The response to Wilson was as much one of bewilderment as of anger. Foot had used his influence in 1964-66 to keep the Left friendly: Harold Wilson, said one Minister, will never know the debt he owes to Michael Foot. At that previous time, when Labour's majority was so small, Foot confided that Harold's heart was really in the right, or left, place. After the 1966 election, the proposition became increasingly difficult for anyone, even of Foot's powers of persuasion, to maintain. The July measures made it well-nigh impossible.

The particular measure which aroused the most anger was the wage freeze. At any rate, because it formed a part (Part Four) of the Prices and Incomes Legislation, it was the simplest against which to stage a demonstration. In the division on the Bill 26 Labour Members abstained. (Figures for abstentions are always questionable, known not even by the Whips, owing to absences that may be accounted for by illness, transport difficulties or plain idleness.) What should be done about these abstainers, or 'rebels' as they were called? The Trade Union Members and some others—who came to be known as the tea-room set—were in favour of the sternest action. The consensus seemed to involve boiling oil. The Left, said those Members who had loyally supported the Government, were not the only ones with consciences. Others had them as well, hidden away in corners of their lockers. Why should the Left be the only ones to be allowed to gain credit with their constituency parties? Discipline was clearly necessary.

Wilson had recently re-shuffled his Cabinet (see page 23). In collaboration with the new Chief Whip, who was John Silkin, Crossman, the Leader of the House, set about the reform of party discipline. He had long held that Labour's intolerance, its tendency to withdraw the Whip, was a source of weakness rather than strength. (Expulsion from the Party is much rarer than withdrawal of the Whip, and is carried out by the National Executive, not as in the latter case, by the Liaison Committee of the Party.) He would therefore make a bargain: abstention would be allowed in 'matters of conscience', which would be interpreted to include all political topics, not merely drink, sex, religion and hanging, provided the Whips were allowed to attend meetings of unofficial groups; provided also the privilege was exercised responsibly. And there was more to the Crossman/Silkin bargain with the back-benchers. They would be allowed more say in policy-making, both in Parliamentary and in purely Party committees, provided Government business went through more expeditiously. The influence of the reforms was two-way. They derived from Crossman's perception of the younger, more middle-class character of the Parliamentary Labour Party; and the reforms, in turn, affected the nature of the Party, making it more tolerant than it had been in the past.

The revolt, then, had taken place, and nothing more would be done about it. It remained for Wilson to square the TUC and the Labour Party Conference. At Blackpool the Prime Minister, who was not on his best form, as he rarely is when dealing with Trade Unionists, first baffled the delegates with talk of illiquidity and the Eurodollar market, and then went on to frighten them with talk of deflation (which was in fact taking place) and unemployment (which was also taking place under the more emollient name of redeployment).

The Labour Conference at Brighton was more difficult. Wilson decided to brazen it out. He did not mention devaluation, bankers or the role of sterling as a reserve currency. Callaghan went even further and denied that the July 1966 measure had had anything to do with bankers: the measures were a simple consequence of our living beyond our means. Most of the delegates—bullied and bewildered as they were—accepted the Government's economic arguments. They even approved the wage freeze. They did, however, refuse to accept the Government's line on redeployment, on military expenditure and on Vietnam. The Attlee Government had been defeated only once at a Party Conference, on tied cottages. Wilson's administration had been beaten three times. 'What would he do?' he was asked. He replied that he would continue to govern.

At Brighton something else happened. News leaked out—Crossman was suspected by some of being the source—of the 'July plot' against Wilson. There had, it appeared, been two plots: one among a few of the younger Labour M.P.s to replace the Prime Minister with Jenkins, or in some versions, Callaghan; the other, a separate plot by Conservative Central Office and the City to form a national Government, though it was never wholly clear whether Wilson was in this event to stay Prime Minister. It was only this last plot that the Prime Minister took at all seriously: he resolved to have nothing whatever to do with national Governments.

At this stage (that is, the latter part of 1966 and early 1967) there was no threat to Wilson's position inside the Parliamentary Party. For one thing, Labour was still, astonishingly enough, ahead in the opinion polls; and, for another, it was felt that it was only fair for the 1966 measures to be given time to 'work'. But there was nevertheless both disappointment and unrest. Wilson came down to a special meeting of the Parliamentary Party and won a vote of confidence in his East of Suez policy, which was almost inevitable because Ministers were allowed to, indeed forced to, vote; and then, following large-scale abstentions, in the defence debate, he made his famous dog-licence speech (see page 32) to the Party meeting. This speech was released to the Press by Silkin, and frightened the journalists more than it had the M.P.s to whom it was originally addressed. He also threatened a dissolution of Parliament and a General Election if the indiscipline continued—a favourite device, never put into practice, of all Prime Ministers when confronted with trouble on their own side.

Not that Wilson wished to restore Party discipline in its old form. He was a strong supporter of the regime presided over by Silkin and Crossman. Indeed it was claimed that Wilson came down to the Party meeting and made his dog-licence speech not so much because he was worried by the down-the-line rebels as because he was afraid that the Party loyalists might themselves rebel in protest against the rebels. There had been signs of this happening at the time the wage freeze was inaugurated in 1966. Now Frank Tomney and Tom Steele, for instance, were abstaining in the defence debate as a protest against the lenient treatment accorded to Stanley Orme (the most insistent rebel, in terms of votes lost against the Government, of the entire 1966/70 period) and his friends.

And Tomney and Steele were not alone. There was also the Chairman of the Parliamentary Party, Emanuel Shinwell. Shinwell had always practised rebellion himself (even though this seldom extended to voting against the Government), while preaching loyalty in others. He was joined by the Paymaster-General, George Wigg, whose duties were mysterious and who, though like Shinwell a bit of a rebel, believed in the military virtues for other people. Shinwell was an old ally of Wigg's and neither was well disposed towards Crossman.

The animosity between Shinwell and Crossman first became outward and visible at a meeting of the Parliamentary Party which was discussing the Common Market—entry to which had slowly become part of Government policy. Orme asked whether it was in order for Brown, as Foreign Secretary, to be a leading member of a pro-European pressure group. Then Shinwell began to speak. It seemed as if he was going to go on for a long time. Crossman moved next business. Shinwell said that he was not going to be told what to do by 'you, Crossman'.

Later, when the Party Liaison Committee (which includes the Chief Whip, the Leader of the House and the Chairman and Deputy Chairman of the Parliamentary Party) was considering what to do with the abstainers in the defence debate, Crossman said he would 'never put the clock back' as far as discipline was concerned. Shinwell said publicly that Crossman had prejudged the question: privately, that he could not work with Crossman. Crossman retaliated by saying to the Prime Minister, among others, that he could not work with Shinwell. Shinwell resigned and was replaced by the former Minister, Douglas Houghton, who had been 'overlord' of Social Security and had been asked to resign from the Cabinet in January 1967 on account of his age (which was 68). He was to turn out to be possibly the most influential Chairman in the Party's history.

There were numerous grumbles at this time, but the Party remained basically trustful of Wilson. Or, if it was not trustful, it was prepared to allow him the benefit of any doubts, and there were many, which existed. For instance, when the Government rejected the report of Lord Radcliffe, Shinwell and Selwyn Lloyd on the D-Notice affair, it would have been possible for those Members who were critical of

Wilson's 'style', and there were many, to use the episode against him; hatred of the Press (particularly of the *Daily Express*) combined with loyalty to the Government to send the entire Parliamentary Party united through the Lobbies in support of Wilson. Generally, the position was that the Government was trying to carry out various laudable reforms simultaneously with a conservative economic and foreign policy; and inevitably there were tensions.

We should not exaggerate the conservatism of Brown's foreign policy. He had, with Wilson's encouragement, taken the Party closer to Europe; though whether one describes this as conservative or not is a matter of choice. More important, the Government decided to disengage from its role East of Suez. Early in 1967 Herbert Bowden made a tour of the Far East to discuss troop reductions. In July the Government announced Britain's departure from East of Suez by 1973-5. What crystallised this decision was the Arab-Israeli war. Wilson, Brown and Stewart were in favour of some form of British action to keep open the Gulf of Aqaba. They were opposed by Callaghan, Crosland and Jenkins. Callaghan in particular was concerned about the effect of any British initiative on the balance of payments. To this extent the gloss put upon Gordon Walker's gnomic reference in his book *The Cabinet* is justified. If Britain was powerless in the Middle East (and also, by the way, in Rhodesia), was she not equally powerless in the Far East as well? To this extent Gordon Walker is perfectly right to say in his book that the decision to withdraw East of Suez was a gradual one, and not taken, even though the time scale was revised, simply as a hurried consequence of devaluation.

Nevertheless, the displeasure caused in the Party by Brown's continuing support for the Americans in Vietnam, about which he had proved much less independent-minded than originally expected, more than balanced the satisfaction over the projected withdrawal East of Suez. Indeed the latter decision did not gain much publicity at the time. Still, there were compensations for those who chose to look for them. There was Barbara Castle and her Transport Bill. There was Crosland, persuading the local authorities to go comprehensive. Above all, there was Jenkins's reign at the Home Office. All three were doing things to which M.Ps. could point when asked by supporters: 'Well, what's the Government doing?'

Jenkins's achievements were broadly two. First, he saw the need to extend the scope of the original Race Relations legislation to cover discrimination in jobs and housing; he gave the State a more positive function, the function of working to improve Race Relations. And secondly, he presided over the greatest period of libertarian reforms known in this century. Hanging had already been suspended for a trial period of five years (which was later confirmed) before he took office. He gave every encouragement to Bills to legalise homosexual conduct between consenting adults and to extend the circumstances in which abortions could legally be performed.

The Homosexual Bill was introduced by Leo Abse, after preliminary work in previous Parliaments by Humphry Berkeley and the Earl of Arran. The Abortion Bill was introduced by the Liberal, David Steel. On both, the Government's attitude was one of benevolent neutrality: but there is very little doubt that they would not have been passed if Jenkins had not been at the Home Office. And here something should also be said about the Labour M.P., Peter Jackson, who acted as an unofficial Whip for the measures. He was that rare political combination, a left-wing Socialist and an extreme liberal as far as personal conduct was concerned; and he deserves almost as much credit as Jenkins.

The Government did not boast of these measures. After all, they were not strictly speaking the Government's. No doubt Wilson and his colleagues saw some possibility of a loss of votes—though opinion polls, contrary to what the Cyril

Blacks of politics frequently asserted, tended to favour libertarian reforms. The opinion polls on other subjects were much less satisfactory. The Government had lost the lead which it had retained in the worst days of the freeze. There had been disastrous results in local and by-elections. Wilson did not elect to address the TUC at Brighton. He went to Scarborough, the scene of his famous speech of 1963 on science and Socialism, to face an even more bewildered conference than that of the previous year. Once again he was unapologetic. He quoted figures, using a pre-1964 base of £100, to show how great an increase there had been in social spending. (That, said a horrified Treasury Minister, was exactly what foreign opinion did *not* want to hear.) He developed the theme of Government intervention in industry: we heard about the computer industry and about aluminium smelters, subsequently one of the Prime Minister's favourite conference-props.

Callaghan directed himself more to economics, as was only suitable. He dismissed devaluation as 'a gimmick'. He said that the country could pay itself only what it earned. He easily knocked down opposition with his combination of flattery, cajolery and genial bullying: 'Come off it, Clive' (referring to Clive Jenkins of ASSET) . . . 'You know as well as I do, Terry' (referring to Terry Parry of the Fire Brigades Union). The conference believed Callaghan, as they believed Wilson. One delegate, it is true, went so far as to say that Labour would never win with Wilson as Prime Minister, but he was booed perfunctorily and called to order by the Chairman. While Christopher Mayhew, who had earlier in the year resigned from the Government over its East of Suez policy, said in a more significant intervention that, as far as his colleagues in the Parliamentary Party were concerned, Wilson and his Government were on trial.

But devaluation was shortly to be proven not a gimmick at all; or, if it was, one that the Government could not very well do without. Once again the proximate cause was a strike, this time a strike of dockers in London and Liverpool. Another cause, much relied upon by the Government, was the Middle East war. In the weeks before the decision was announced the fear in the Parliamentary Party was not of devaluation but of a massive loan. When the decision was announced the Party breathed an almost audible sigh of relief. Foot rose from his seat on the front bench below the gangway and said that at last Britain had cut herself free of the bankers. He was echoed by the majority of the party, one of the few dubious members being Mrs. Anne Kerr, who believed that the standard of living of the poor would be depressed. In Party political terms, the consequences of devaluation were not to turn out nearly so well either for Wilson or for his colleagues as one might have expected from this preliminary response; yet before turning to these consequences we must have a look at another episode, the one involving the sale of arms to South Africa.

The Labour Government had continued its predecessor's practice of selling arms to South Africa. Its sole claim to have taken a moral stand was that no new contract had been entered into; but previous contracts had been extended by every imaginable means open to the lawyers. At the end of 1967 the practice could be continued no longer: the Government had to make up its mind about whether the new contracts should be re-negotiated. An assembly of the Defence and Overseas Policy Committee of the Cabinet, over which Wilson presided without, it appears, committing himself one way or the other, asked to be given until the end of January 1968 to make up its mind. Callaghan was not a member of the DOP Committee; certainly he was not present when it decided to ask the South African Government for time. But at a social meeting of young M.P.s he said, in answer to a question, that he was fully in favour of selling arms to South Africa, or to anyone else who would buy them.

There was consternation in the Party. Jackson and Dickens were round at the Chief Whip's door in an instant. Silkin, the Chief Whip, informed Wilson. Wilson told him to go ahead and encourage signatures to a motion opposing the sale of arms to South Africa. One Member was quietly told that if he signed he would be doing the Prime Minister a personal favour. He replied that he was against the sale of arms to South Africa, but also against doing the Prime Minister personal favours. Nevertheless Silkin collected 136 signatures. The Cabinet, however, was unimpressed. It re-affirmed the original decision of the DOP Committee. The Prime Minister said that his position was impossible and the decision would have to be reversed. And the Cabinet agreed to do so.

The significance of the episode is that the Prime Minister used the Parliamentary Party against his colleagues. It is possible that even at this time he suspected a plot against him: what is certain is that in the months that followed, the dissatisfaction about Wilson inside the Cabinet itself attained its highest level. It was not an edifying beginning to 1968.

Worse was to come. For a matter of weeks the whole atmosphere on the Labour benches changed. Twenty-six Members abstained in the division on the post-devaluation cuts in expenditure. Foot said to a friend that the abstainers were doing no more than their patriotic duty: if they had voted with the Government, the foreign bankers would have concluded that there must be something wrong with the Government's measures.

The middle-of-the-road Members, who had always been suspicious of Silkin's regime, were not disposed to treat the business quite so humorously. There were demands for Silkin's resignation. These were not new. What was new was the level of dissatisfaction with Wilson personally; and also the source of that dissatisfaction. For the Left was not anxious to replace Wilson with someone else. The younger, Right-inclined M.P.s, though they were no more favourably disposed to the Prime Minister than they had been in the past, were, as people with an intellectual vested interest in devaluation, anxious not to rock the boat: for the time being they were prepared to put up with Wilson. It was the loss of faith of the Centre which was more worrying: more so than either the behaviour of the Left (who remained loyal to the Prime Minister) or the coolness of the younger devaluation-supporters towards Wilson. For years they, the less articulate members of the Parliamentary Party, had loyally defended the Government's economic policy, the policy of not devaluing. Now it was all changed. They resented the change. In particular, they resented the behaviour of the Left. The Left had opposed the Government's previous economic policy: now they were opposing this one too. And the Left were—apart from an attempt to bar them from Party meetings—getting away with it.

At this period the Government was undoubtedly at fault in its handling of the Parliamentary Party. It was a fault not so much of lax discipline as of leadership. Of course, this was understandable enough. Wilson was at his most depressed. Jenkins, the new Chancellor, somehow failed to convince the Party that a fresh start was being made. The series of Cabinet meetings to discuss where the cuts in expenditure should be made seemed to go on and on. This was certainly healthier, in terms of proper Cabinet Government, than the situation that had obtained in 1966, when Ministers had been virtually presented with a set of measures put together by the Civil Service over the weekend, and given the opportunity only to say yes or no. But it added to the depression.

It was left to Jenkins, in his Budget, to put some heart into the back-benchers. He did so, not only by the jaunty tone he adopted, but by the Capital Levy he introduced. In fact the budget took about £900 million 'out of purchasing power': the Socialist measures, such as the attack on the payment of school fees by grandparents, were peripheral. But the joy, such as it was, was of short duration. At Whitsun the Parliamentary Party became thoroughly bad-tempered. The Finance Bill following the Budget was, by virtue of the Crossman reforms, being taken in Committee upstairs, and not on the floor of the House. At the same time the Transport Bill, one of the longest measures ever to be passed by a British Parliament, was being taken in Committee; while morning sittings of the House, which had also been inaugurated by Crossman, were hardly fulfilling their original function, for Members found themselves in the House early in the morning and late at night. There were complaints that the same old people were being exploited while the lawyers and the journalists turned up late and left early.

The Party sustained two further blows, though some M.P.s thought they were blessings. George Brown, the Foreign Secretary, and Ray Gunter, the Minister of Labour, both resigned. Brown's departure was caused by pique, combined with a more generalised dissatisfaction about 'the way this Government is run'; by which he meant that he was excluded from the more important decisions, particularly those relating to the economy. As referred to, the proximate cause was the visit by Shore, Jenkins and Wilson to Buckingham Palace to make up the necessary quota of Privy Councillors for a closing of the Stock Exchange. This was made necessary because of the gold crisis. Shore was taken along simply because he happened to be around at the right time: there was not, it seemed, any deliberate attempt to slight Brown. Nevertheless, he felt his omission to be a slight, and he resigned.

With Ray Gunter the case was slightly different. Having been shifted from the Ministry of Labour to the Ministry of Power, he felt somewhat lost. Power was not his kind of

Ministry. It involved too many figures, too much detail, not enough human contact. Gunter resigned, saying in his letter of resignation that 'I no longer wish to be a Member of your Government'.

Neither of the resigning Ministers had a large following in the Party as a whole. Nevertheless, their departure was a sign that the Government was hardly a band of brothers. At this period the Party was exercised by three matters. There were the Kenyan Asians—those Asians, chiefly of Indian extraction, who lived in Kenya and retained British passports, which they had been allowed to retain because they might at some time wish to come to Britain. By 1968 the time had arrived: the Kenyan Government was carrying through a policy of 'Africanisation'. The Kenyan Asians wished to come to Britain. The Conservative Duncan Sandys, supported by Powell, forecast that too many would come; something, he said, should be done about it. As a consequence of Sandys' advocacy, even more started to arrive. The Government gave way. Callaghan, the Home Secretary, maintained privately that his predecessor Jenkins had put work in hand to produce a similar Bill of exclusion. The Bill was passed with 31/40 abstentions and 35 Labour M.P.s voting against it.

Then there was the legislation on Prices and Incomes. In 1967 the Government, under pressure from the unions, had allowed the compulsory provisions of 1966 to lapse. Their revival was part of the post-devaluation package. In May 1968 there were 32 abstentions on the Second Reading of the Bill; 20 on the Report Stage; 29/32 on the Third Reading. Looking back, it is perhaps necessary to emphasise that statutory control of prices and incomes, however effective it may or may not have turned out to be, was quite different from the proposals produced later to which the unions objected so strongly.

Again there was Rhodesia. Wilson had begun by saying

in 1965 that his Government would never use force to come to a settlement. This continued to be the Government's position. It was broadly accepted by the Parliamentary Party, who were prepared to content themselves with crying 'treason' when anyone on the Opposition benches made observations vaguely sympathetic to Rhodesia. The Government's intention was to settle the matter without appearing to betray its principles. On several occasions Barbara Castle murmured about resignation if there were a 'sell-out': Ministers such as Healey and Crossman, on the other hand, were anxious to get rid of the problem on almost any terms. Wilson made his first attempt at a settlement in December 1966 on board *HMS Tiger*. Moves towards a second attempt were going on during the Labour Party Conference of 1968. Joan Lestor, Frank Judd and other Labour M.P.s were active in lobbying against any concessions. The agreement which Wilson reached, or nearly reached, with Smith would have given the Rhodesian Government effective sovereignty. In a division in the House, the Opposition abstained: up to 75 Labour Members also abstained, while 58 voted against. If Smith had accepted the terms, the revolt would have been even more serious.

Rhodesia was also the indirect cause of what turned out to be another defeat for the Government. In the summer of 1968 the House of Lords rejected the Rhodesian Sanctions Order: those making up the majority were predominantly Conservative and hereditary peers. Prior to this vote, discussions had been going on about the Reform of the Lords. They had involved Crossman, Lord Shackleton (the Labour Peers' Leader), Lord Carrington (the Tory Peers' Leader), and other representatives of the front benches. Wilson answered that, in retribution for the Tory Peers' action, the talks would be broken off and the Government would put forward its own non-agreed solution. Crossman was perhaps the only Minister, Lord Shackleton aside, to perceive the dangers of this course. The advantages of all-Party agreement were being lost merely in order to satisfy Wilson's need to make a gesture.

In the event, the Government's proposals for Lords Reform differed in no significant way from those which had previously been agreed. They provided for the elimination of the hereditary peers' right to vote; and vastly increased the Prime Minister's powers of patronage. M.P.s started to make claims, in writing, for consideration for a peerage when the measure was finally passed. The Government's White Paper was approved by 272 votes to 161, with about 50 abstentions: 47 Labour M.P.s voted against. The Government decided to persevere with the Bill. The Committee stage was taken on the floor of the House. It was not taken 'upstairs', so Ministers subsequently claimed, because the Bill was a constitutional one. This argument was specious: constitutional measures have occasionally been taken in Committee upstairs; just as the guillotine has sometimes been applied to them. But this time there was no guillotine, and no upstairs Committee. The result was that the sharpest debating talents in the House were set free to oppose the Bill. The Opposition took up an attitude of lofty neutrality. The Government Whips could not guarantee to deliver the vote. After some months of this, the Government stated it was abandoning the Lords' Reform measures to make way for the Merchant Shipping Bill and, dread words, an Industrial Relations Bill.

The genesis of the Industrial Relations Bill lay in Wilson's conviction that strikes were an electoral liability; and in Barbara Castle's compulsive activism. Not that they were totally without reasons for 'wanting to do something about the unions'. In the autumn of 1968 there had occurred the Ford and Girling strikes. Mrs. Castle's Ministry, the Department of Employment and Productivity, produced proposals for a secret ballot before strike action was taken, and for a 'cooling-off' period of 28 days. These proposals were embodied, together with numerous others more acceptable to the unions, in the White Paper, *In Place of Strife*.

Richard Crossman objected to these because, in his view, there had been inadequate Cabinet consultation and because he thought it dangerous to divide the Party in the year before an election. Anthony Crosland agreed: moreover he supported the proposals for union reform embodied in the minority recommendations (written by the former journalist Andrew Shonfield) of the *Donovan Report*; though he did not favour taking any action until after the General Election. Richard Marsh and, above all, Callaghan were also opposed to the White Paper. Callaghan had, he said, no objection to Trade Union reforms in principle: but, as Party Treasurer, he did not want to see the flow of funds dry up. (In fact the unions continue to subscribe at their usual rate even though there is disagreement between them and the Party, as there was for most of the 1966-70 period.)

And in March 1969 Callaghan, at a meeting of the National Executive Committee, carried his opposition further than any other Minister had done. He voted against the Government. Joe Gormley of the Miners' Union first proposed a motion rejecting 'any' legislation based on 'all' the White Paper, *In Place of Strife*. Callaghan then proposed an amendment, which was carried, deleting the word 'any'. It is difficult to see what difference this made: but it was intended as an exercise in bridge-building. Mrs. Castle, who was also a member of the Executive, then proposed a blanket amendment endorsing the White Paper. This was lost, and Callaghan voted against it. He claimed that he was doing no more than trying to prevent the Party causing itself damage. He also maintained that it was possible to make a separation between a politician's position as a member of the Cabinet and his position as a member of the Executive. Even those Cabinet Ministers who were sympathetic to his attitude towards *In*

Place of Strife refused to accept this distinction. Certainly the Prime Minister refused to accept it.

At this stage the camera, so to speak, speeded up: the politicians began to move faster and more jerkily, like the Keystone Cops. In March, a Commons motion approving the White Paper had been carried by 226 votes to 64, which included 55 Labour Members. There were about 42 abstentions. It would have been possible for the Government to postpone legislation based on the White Paper until 1970 or 1971. Instead the Government decided, or rather Wilson decided, to hurry up the legislation, and in the form most unpalatable to the unions. Jenkins announced in his Budget speech that the statutory Incomes Policy would lapse, and the 28-day pause and so-called penal sanctions be incorporated in a short Bill. This course was decided on, it seems, in order to get a messy business done with as soon as possible.

Callaghan remained obdurate. Wilson retaliated by dismissing him from the Inner Cabinet, and considered dismissal from the Outer Cabinet as well. Callaghan also contemplated resignation, though he cast it rapidly from his mind. Wilson, for his part, sacked his Chief Whip, John Silkin. Discipline in the Party, so the Prime Minister considered, was becoming too lax. In some ways Silkin's sacking was surprising. Of all the Members of the Government there was no one man more personally devoted to the Prime Minister, always excepting the ever-loyal George Thomas. It was Silkin, after all, who had personally supervised the collection of signatures in defence of the Prime Minister's position on South Africa arms. For this reason he was disapproved of by the younger, more 'realistic' members of the Cabinet. He was also disapproved of by the younger, Gaitskellite M.P.s. His supporters in the Parliamentary Party remained the Left. And yet Silkin subsequently claimed that he could have forced the Industrial Relations Bill through Parliament; and he was probably right.

His successor was Robert Mellish. Ironically enough, it was he, more than anyone else, who was responsible for the defeat (though Downing Street did not like the word) sustained by Wilson and Mrs. Castle. Three other people played parts that were almost as important: Douglas Houghton (the Chairman of the Parliamentary Party), William Hamilton (of the Party's Liaison Committee) and Victor Feather (the General Secretary of the TUC). There was talk of replacing Wilson unless he dropped the Bill. The Prime Minister's strength was that the Left, who were most passionately opposed to the Bill, were nevertheless prepared to put up with Wilson. The only dilemma in the Left's attitude towards the Leadership was that they were now in no circumstances prepared to put up with Mrs. Castle, who during 1968 had been touted as a possible successor.

Houghton, while opposed to the Bill, was nevertheless concerned to safeguard Wilson. He refused to state clearly the circumstances in which he would feel it right to confront the Prime Minister with a demand for a new election for the leadership. (This would have happened by virtue of a memorandum by the then Labour Shadow Cabinet in January 1957, following the choice of Harold Macmillan in preference to R. A. Butler. The author of the memorandum was Patrick Gordon Walker.) Fifty signatures on a petition? A hundred? Houghton would not say. He was clear only that the number would have to be 'large'. Hamilton, however, was less charitably disposed towards the Prime Minister. He did indeed collect some signatures calling for a change in the leadership.

Victor Feather was not concerned about the leadership. If anything, he rather approved of his fellow-Yorkshireman Wilson. He was, however, concerned about the Bill. His principle was not so much to produce the TUC's interventionist solution as to persuade the Government to enter into negotiations with the TUC. From the moment the talks started, it was clear that some kind of compromise was going to emerge. An emergency conference of the TUC, held in the modern setting of the new Fairfields Hall, Croydon, overwhelmingly endorsed Feather's proposals for intervention by the TUC in strikes. Astonishingly, a statement put out by Mrs. Castle's Department of Employment and Productivity said that the proposals were not satisfactory.

Then was there a rebellion in the Cabinet. Ministers such as Callaghan, Crossman, Crosland, Mason and Marsh were joined by such figures as Peter Shore and Mrs. Judith Hart. Mellish informed the Cabinet, on his own initiative, that he would not guarantee the passage of the Bill. The Cabinet accepted what was, in effect, though with a little top dressing, Feather's original solution.

There was a little skirmishing afterwards, but it was the last great fight. The skirmishing occurred at the Labour Party Conference at Brighton, when Mrs. Castle insisted that she would have to 'reactivate' Part Two of the Prices and Incomes legislation, which provided for delays of up to four months in wage rises. Earlier, at the TUC at Portsmouth, Wilson had adopted a cool tone to the delegates, and had been still more coolly received. Hugh Scanlon of the Engineers' Union and Jack Jones of the Transport Workers' made a determined effort to have Mrs. Castle removed, but Mrs. Castle obstinately stayed. In Parliament the imminence of an Election, and the improvement in the trade figures, did more than anything else to produce relative peace and concord.

And what conclusions can be drawn? First, the Left produced figures such as Stanley Orme, Eric Heffer and Norman Atkinson, who were not only attractive characters but had first-hand experience of industry. Moreover, they often turned out to be correct in their judgements. East of Suez was perhaps the outstanding example; devaluation less so. The Left were by no means a negligible force: the

Government had continually to pay attention to their views Secondly, the Party as a whole became more rebellious. Sometimes, the rebellions succeeded, as they did over the House of Lords and Industrial Relations. More often, as over Vietnam and Biafra, they did not. With the change in the law on hanging, abortions, homosexuality and divorce, Labour M.P.s, aided by the Government, forced the most substantial libertarian reforms of the century.

Despite the presence of valuable Members such as Orme, Heffer and Atkinson, the Party became more middle-class. Back-benchers not only dressed the same as the Tories; more, they frequently (as academics, journalists and writers tend to do) looked down on the managers, the advertising men and the representatives of the unit trusts who sat on the benches opposite. The impetus for Parliamentary reform came not from those who wanted to harass the Executive—they were happy enough with the opportunities already provided on the floor of the House—but from those who wished to prepare themselves for Government. Wilson was frequently criticised by these men; they sometimes made half-hearted efforts to remove him; yet in himself, he embodied many of their virtues, and more of their faults.

PART TWO

THE CAMPAIGNS

CHAPTER FIVE

THE LABOUR CAMPAIGN

' "I has a go, ladies and gentlemen, I has a go." '—JOHN OSBORNE, 'The Entertainer'.

In the later sixties the fashion developed of juxtaposing a number of small objects and then photographing them in order to symbolise or illustrate a desired theme. The device was used on book-jackets; more frequently, in coloured advertisements in magazines. Thus, for example, a white carnation, a cigarette lighter, a wrist watch, a quantity of five pound notes and a cigarette packet (of the brand being advertised) were used to symbolise an expensive evening out. What collection of objects, one wonders, could be assembled to illustrate the Labour campaign in the General Election of 1970?

At least two sets would have to be put together. Harold Wilson's objects would include a pearl tie-pin, recently given to him by his wife to mark their pearl wedding; two ties, one bright green and the other elaborately floral; an egg; a pipe, for smoking in public; and a cigar, for smoking in more relaxed moments. The journalist's objects might perhaps include an expensive fountain pen; a cheap propelling pencil for use if the pen ran out of ink; a green notebook; a yellow card saying 'Press: Admit one to all the Rt. Hon. Harold Wilson's Election meetings and news conferences'; a quantity of five pound notes; numerous hotel bills, for the Albany at Nottingham, the Midland at Manchester, the Albany at Birmingham; and a sheaf of Transport

House news releases, explaining, expanding, guiding, clarifying, now making a point, now avoiding one, all designed to help Labour win the Election and all, even so recently after the event, acquiring a faded, forgotten, rubbish-like aspect.

And yet, let us disinter one dog-eared sheet and use it to refresh the memory, supplement the notes and act as a starting point to our enquiry into what must have been one of the strangest Election campaigns in the post-war era. It is entitled 'Schedule for Rt. Hon. Harold Wilson, OBE. Tuesday, June 16 1970', and goes as follows:—

4.00 Depart Euston.

6.37 Arrive Manchester.

7.00 Leave Piccadilly Hotel. Proceed to Oldham via the A62—via Newton Heath, Sailsworth, Hallinworth to Oldham. On reaching the Town Centre proceed along Yorkshire Street for approximately ¼ mile to Horsedge Street on the left (by Hope Bros. the tailors). Turn left into Horsedge Street and Bartlam Place is on the first turning, left-hand side.

7.35 Arrive Oldham sub-area Committee Rooms, Weavers Offices, Bartlam Place, Oldham. OLDHAM EAST CONSTITUENCY. OLDHAM WEST CONSTITUENCY.

7.50 Depart for Middleton. Follow the A665 Oldham to Middleton until you reach the roundabout at Middleton (approx. 3 miles) follow the sign to Town Centre and proceed to the traffic lights at the corner of Wood Street—turn left into Wood Street and proceed until Bowness Road is reached on the left-hand side (approx 400 yds).

8.10 Arrive Middleton and Prestwich sub area Committee Rooms, 195 Bowness Road, Middleton. MIDDLETON AND PRESTWICH CONSTITUENCY.

8.25 Depart for Crumpsall. Go back along Bowness Road to Wood Street, turn right until the traffic lights are reached. Go across the roundabout and on leaving the roundabout bear left into Manchester Old Road. Go past road works with Heaton Park on right-hand side (approx. 1 mile). Approximately 300 yards after passing under the railway bridge turn left into Witton Road.

The Committee Rooms are on the right-hand side of the road.

8.40 Arrive Manchester Blackley sub-area Committee Rooms. Witton Road, Crumpsall. MANCHESTER BLACKLEY CONSTITUENCY.

8.55 Depart for Radcliffe. Proceed forward from Committee Room to junction of Bank Road and Crumpsall Lane (approx. 400 yds), turn left and proceed forward to junction of Crumpsall Lane and Middleton Road (approx. 300 yds). turn left at Halfway House traffic lights, then turn right and follow the main Bury Old Road to the traffic lights at the junction of Bury Old Road and Bury New Road. Proceed on and 400 yds past the Besses-o'-the Barn railway bridge bear left into Higher Lane and proceed across traffic lights at the corner of Church Lane and Ringley Road into Dales Lane. Proceed until you come to the 'T' junction with Radcliffe New Road, turn left into Radcliffe New Road down the hill for about half a mile into the Town Centre. Proceed through the Town Centre to Ainsworth Road. Turn right into Ainsworth Road, and Red Bank Road is approximately half a mile on the left-hand side of the road. (There is enough car parking space at the rear.)

9.15 Arrive Bury and Radcliffe sub-area Committee Rooms. 21, Red Bank Road, Radcliffe. BURY AND RADCLIFFE CONSTITUENCY.

9.35 Depart for Piccadilly Hotel, Manchester, via the A58 (this is the main road to Manchester).

10.05 Arrive Piccadilly Hotel, Manchester. Stay overnight in Piccadilly Hotel, Manchester.

And what was it really like? On the platform at Euston there is the Stationmaster, not wearing a top hat but his ordinary uniform. Wilson's party takes up only three first-class compartments: one for himself and Mrs. Wilson, another for two detectives and his aides, another for two girl secretaries from No. 10 who skim lightly over a typewriter that has been installed. Wilson's aides deserve further description. There is Mrs. Marcia Williams, his political secretary. She advises him on whom he ought and ought not to see, and sometimes her advice is accepted. She is even rumoured to have successfully recommended for junior office an M.P. who was at school with her brother, although obviously he must have possessed other qualities as well. She is tall, calm, efficient, unaffected, long-faced and attractive in a serious kind of way. Above all, she knows the Labour Party. Then there is John Allen, in his mid-thirties, perhaps slightly solemn, a Cambridge graduate, a former member of the Transport House staff. He specialises in what politicians call research.

But on this occasion neither Mrs. Williams nor Mr. Allen is on the train. Alfred Richman, however, is. He is a journalist by trade, a former member of the *Daily Herald's* staff, now employed by the IPC. He is a Londoner who slaps your back, smokes cigars and makes jokes. He is extremely kind-hearted. His function is not so much to deal with the Press as to deal with Wilson; Sancho Panza and Jeeves. He advises Wilson on such matters as whether to be photographed and, if so, with or without his pipe. Gerald Kaufman, Wilson's former link with the Parliamentary journalists, is also on the train. He is not, however, a member of Wilson's group. He is going up to his new constituency of Ardwick, Manchester (which he is to win). Kaufman's successor for the purposes of the campaign is William Camp; and to him we must now turn.

Camp is big, balding and languid, though capable of moving with speed when the occasion demands. In the opinion of many working journalists he is the best public relations officer in Britain today: which is to say that, though he may not tell the whole truth, he does not tell lies. When he promises to telephone you, he keeps his word. He does not refer you to White Paper XYZ, but tries to arrange an interview with whomever it is you want to see. He is very hospitable. He is also a Socialist with a stirring belief in the nationalised industries, having been PRO to the Gas Council and the inventor of the slogan 'high speed gas'. He is currently on three weeks' loan to Wilson from the British Steel Corporation. He is regarded as something of an interloper by the more securely established members of Wilson's retinue, but Wilson nevertheless consults him frequently.

In the first-class compartment adjoining Wilson's are the journalists. Others are scattered throughout the train, though at a convenient distance from Wilson's carriage: Ian Aitken and Peter Jenkins, both of the *Guardian*, Nora Beloff of the *Observer*, Nicholas Tomalin of the *Sunday Times*, Cyril Aynsley of the *Daily Express*, Gordon Greig of the *Daily Mail*, George Scott who is attached to the *Economist*, Hedley Donovan of *Time* Magazine, and many more besides. 'The best turn-out so far,' says someone. Some of these have been following Wilson throughout his tour; others have joined him as the inclination, or the demands of their newspapers, took them. The only notable absentee is George Gale, who writes for the *Evening Standard* and the *Spectator*. 'Where's George?' somebody asks. 'He said he was coming', says somebody else.

Picture, then, the scene as the train evades the Chilterns and makes for Manchester. The businessmen, the soldiers going on or off leave, the young women with crying babies: all may have, and as we now know did have, their reservations about Wilson. But in the first-class carriage at the rear of the train there are no doubts at all as to the outcome of the election to be held in 48 hours' time. The journalists, the aides, even, one suspects, the secretaries and the detectives: everyone believes that Labour is to win the Election. They are on the triumphant lap: first to Manchester, then a tour of some of the Lancashire marginals, then the traditional eve-of-poll factory gate meeting at the Metro-Vick/AEI works at Manchester (home of such stalwarts as Hugh Scanlon, Stanley Orme and Norman Atkinson: 'A veritable nest of vipers', as one Gaitskellite M.P. put it), then the progress to Huyton, and then the return to Downing Street.

Such, at any rate, is the scenario as the express goes north.

And is Wilson as confident as the men and women who accompany him? If he is not, he does not show it. First he has a short sleep, then a cup of tea, then a large cigar. Camp ushers groups of journalists, six, seven or eight at a time, into his carriage. Wilson's greatest virtue, next to his kindness to individuals, is his complete lack of pomposity. He talks easily, confidently, as if he expects to stay Prime Minister. The Conservatives' greatest error was the Selsdon Park Conference at the beginning of the year. The enemy were delivered to him. They were a sitting target, like a stationary train stopped in the snow. There is some talk, which Wilson does not encourage, about the composition of his next Government. He wishes he had managed to visit more Tory marginals instead of predominantly Labour ones. He has clearly come to believe that Labour may increase its majority. No, he did not want a quiet campaign: on the contrary, he wanted to enliven it. And the next batch of newspapermen is shown in to talk to this pleasant, confident man in grey suit, white shirt and green tie.

Later that day, in Oldham, he reads out a statement attacking Heath for his whispered prediction of another devaluation under Labour. 'I'm going to hit him hard', he had said earlier, without malice, as if it was a painful Prime Ministerial duty. After he has finished, Camp appears as distressed as he ever allows himself to be. 'ITN missed it', he says. 'They were in the wrong place.' Afterwards Wilson makes a more relaxed speech, or rather he exchanges badinage with Oldham, and the motorcade moves off; Wilson in a Daimler; the *Daily Express* in a Jaguar; six cars in all, the journalists having sorted themselves into twos, threes and fours for the purpose of following Wilson, with winks and nudges and embarrassed excuses about being committed to others as far as transport is concerned, like schoolgirls at a dance.

There is a symbolic contrast between the folk-humour of

the meetings and the brutal efficiency of the motorcade. It bowls along at fifty miles an hour, with an escort of two policemen on motor-bikes. One policeman stays at the front with his headlamp flashing aggressively. The other stops at the traffic crossings, which are numerous, and waves the cars through the red lights. 'My sister was born at Crumpsall', confides Wilson to the crowds. 'You're too young to know anything', he says to a heckler with long hair. Later, at Radcliffe, a section of the crowd of about a thousand begins to sing something hostile. 'That's right, sing,' says Wilson, 'you've got to keep your spirits up somehow.' He attacks, or appears to pity, Heath, with his 'dreary indoor meetings . . . that lonely figure with the Dr. Who apparatus behind him. The reference to Dr. Who always gets a laugh. Indeed in private conversation Wilson recurs to the Conservative symbol of concentric circles. His conceit, in both senses of the word, is that the Conservative leader will slowly be sucked into it.

The sun goes down over Radcliffe, but Wilson is not finished. 'Don't think you can do better than Robin Day,' he says to a persistent heckler, and there is an appreciative laugh, for references to television or television 'personalities', like references to branded consumer goods, are highly popular with audiences. 'I suppose you were one of the ones who sent a postcard', he goes on, referring to the *Election Forum* television programme in which he was treated with some hostility by Day. The crowd pick up the allusion without his having to explain it. They laugh once again more confidently. 'Well, put a stamp on it next time,' says Wilson, and the house collapses. The journalists turn to one another and smile and feel slightly ill at ease and say: 'You've got to hand it to him, haven't you?'

These meetings began more quietly two or more weeks previously. The way they were conducted demonstrated (as other aspects of the campaign demonstrated also) that the last thing Wilson was doing was fighting the Election as a

Prime Ministerial figure. A Prime Minister should surely be restrained, sober, statesmanlike. Wilson was not this. Indeed his performances were exaggerated versions of those he gave as Leader of the Opposition in 1963-4. He spent much of his time pitying Heath and attacking the Conservatives. Therefore the common description of the campaign, which is to the effect that Wilson was fighting it as a near-presidential candidate, is not quite accurate. Still less so is the second limb of the common description: that Heath fought a uniquely lofty and principled campaign. As the chapter on the Tory campaign demonstrates, he concentrated, after a brief flirtation with Wilson's 'style', on high prices and high taxation.

An issue can be defined as a political area or topic where, (i) there is an objectively perceived difference between the Parties, (ii) at least one of the Parties wishes to publicise that difference and (iii) the difference elicits some response from the voters. (This definition differs slightly from the one given in David Butler's and Donald Stokes's *Political Change in Britain.*) According to the first definition, there were few issues between the Parties. It is true that Anthony Crosland, in a little-reported speech at York in the middle of the campaign, and later in even less-reported speeches in the East Midlands, tried to place some emphasis on Labour's commitment to high social expenditure and therefore, presumably, to high taxation. But his approach was not followed by the majority of Ministers and candidates, with the exception of Richard Crossman. He said on June 12 to a joint meeting of the Oxford City Labour Party and University Labour Club:

'What amazes me most about this election, is how little attention has been given by the Press and television to some of the vital issues which will be decided on June 18. I want to talk about one such issue—social policy. What we have done, what we shall do, and why the Tories are determined to halt the greatest reform of the Welfare State since Beveridge if they get the chance.'

Crossman was being understandably tactful. His speech was intended to act as a corrective not so much of the Press and television as of Wilson. It was the fruit of an informal meeting between Crossman and Wilson on June 9, ostensibly to discuss the dispute on doctors' pay. Crossman asked for television confrontations, if not between Wilson and Heath, then at least between Ministers and their Shadows. Wilson said: 'We don't want confrontations', or words to this effect.

Crossman accepted this, but went on to ask whether he could make a speech about the Pensions Policy, which was a clear difference between the Parties. Wilson agreed, though without, it seems, any great enthusiasm. It may be that, as far as pensions were concerned, Wilson was broadly right. From the evidence of the polls, for what it is worth, there was no great enthusiasm for Labour's pensions proposals, though Crossman naturally looked upon them with the eyes of a fond parent. This was hardly the case, however, with other Labour policies. The most outstanding examples were the policies on comprehensive schools and defence East of Suez. Whenever Labour education policy was mentioned, in a little meeting in Derbyshire, at the eve-of-poll meeting in All Saints, Birmingham, even at the Metro-Vick meeting at Manchester, there was an answering cheer from the audience. And yet education policy was scarcely emphasised. No attempt was made by the central directorate of the campaign to convert it into an issue. Indeed one supporter tried to obtain a poster about comprehensives from Transport House, only to be told that none had been printed. In a sad little interview after the Election had been lost, Wilson even went so far as to admit that he might have laid more emphasis on education.

One talks of the 'central directorate' of the campaign. But of whom exactly did it consist? In the months before the

Election there was a Campaign Committee consisting of representatives from the Government and the National Executive Committee. There was also a smaller committee concerned with posters and advertising on which sat David Kingsley, the Party's Advertising expert, and Percy Clark, the Party's Press Officer at Transport House. During the campaign itself a group would meet at Transport House which included Benn, Healey, Wilson, Camp, Michael Miller, Miss Doreen Stainforth, Harry Nicholas and Gwyn Morgan. (The latter four were employees of Party Headquarters, Miss Stainforth being the Party's Broadcasting Officer, Nicholas the General Secretary and Morgan his Assistant.)

This group, or members of it—for there were many occasions when all were not present—would meet in the mornings before the daily Press Conference. This was held not, as at previous elections, in Transport House but in a little hall, redolent of amateur dramatics, in a lane off Great Peter Street. Healey was always present, and sometimes took the Press Conference himself; next to him sat Wilson; then Nicholas; then Morgan. They sat, like the preacher, four feet above contradiction, and Nicholas acted as a firm but fair Chairman. Heath, by contrast, had a much more modernistic backcloth at Central Office: not only did he sit almost on a level with his questioners, but he allowed himself to be surrounded on three sides, and moreover acted as his own Chairman. Journalists shook their heads sadly at one another and concluded that, despite the village hall setting of the Labour Conferences, Wilson was really handling them much better.

It was at these gatherings that Wilson appeared at his most Prime Ministerial. They may have given rise to the impression, disputed above, that he was conducting a uniquely presidential kind of campaign. In a way the Conferences opened badly, with the exclusion of the foreign press. Wilson believed they took up valuable time, asking questions to which he had given the answers years or months previously. Perhaps the overseas correspondents did waste time, though not in the sense that Wilson indicated: they tended to ask questions about NATO and the Common Market and the Middle East and the Anglo-American alliance—all subjects which Wilson was anxious to keep out of the campaign, not because they were necessarily embarrassing to him, but because there were no votes in them. (To be fair to Wilson, for let us have no humbug about the high-mindedness of the Conservative campaign, Heath was similarly reluctant to bring up foreign affairs.) Several aides opposed the decision to exclude the foreign press, who were to be given their own Conference later in the morning and presided over by Healey. 'Isn't it a bit xenophobic?' asked one of them.

Wilson probably believed that there were a lot of votes in xenophobia. Certainly he kept coming back to the theme of Heath's 'alien' ideas, particularly in relation to the Conservative proposals for Union Reform. After a few days, however, the foreign journalists were re-admitted, and they wrote as admiringly as anyone about Wilson's Prime Ministerial style. He gave the impression that he was merely looking in on the morning gathering as a diversion from the more serious business of running the country.

Of course there were flashes of that combativeness which was to appear more strongly later in the day, at the evening meetings and walk-abouts. On one occasion he advanced the psephological law that, contrary to the generally accepted idea, the movement during the course of any campaign was not towards the Government as such but towards the Labour Party. At the same time he asked with apparent innocence what political party had ever won an Election when its Leader was 'trailing' it as badly as Heath was. On another occasion he suddenly appeared from behind the red curtains at the back of the stage and said: 'I expect you'll all want to know what I've been doing'; and no-one contradicted him. Indeed, in contrast to Heath, he was treated with near-reverence by the Press.

It has already been said that, outside his morning conferences, Wilson hardly conducted himself in what one would have thought was approved Prime Ministerial fashion. In one sense, however, the campaign was undoubtedly Prime Ministerial, or presidential, or personalised, or whatever one chooses to call it. He insisted on running his own campaign, and he insisted that he be the centre of it. To this basic position there was no real opposition inside the Party. Crossman, for instance, believed that 'issues' should be raised more frequently; he also wanted Ministers (including himself) to be given more prominent roles to play, especially on television; but at no time was he an advocate of any kind of collective leadership. Other Ministers, and other back-bench M.P.s, liked Wilson's style in the campaign no more than they had liked his style in the previous years: but, as long as he appeared to be succeeding (that is, until about 11 pm on Thursday, June 18), so long were they prepared to give him their warmest approval.

And he appeared to be succeeding not merely on account of the near-Stalinesque unity of the opinion polls but on account of his ability to get on with journalists. Here Camp played his part: the campaign was a triumph for Camp, but in another sense a disaster, for unwittingly he concealed the real political truth. It was not public relations that led to Wilson's unusually favourable press, but anti-public relations. Perhaps art was concealing art: Heath distributed some free gin-and-tonics and travelled by aeroplane; Wilson travelled by train, and the newspapermen made their own arrangements and bought their own drinks (though occasional parties were held late at night in Wilson's hotel rooms). This was part of an engaging amateurishness, a happy, carefree quality, about the whole Labour campaign. Wilson was proceeding, as usual, by political instinct, and most of us took his instinct to be infallible.

Why, then, did it prove so fragile? The obvious answer is that he was talking about something abstract, the balance of payments, though both he and Jenkins tried to make it sound as solid as Nelson's Column. Heath, on the other hand, was talking for much of the time about something which could be more easily understood, the rise in prices. His solutions, it is true, did not sound particularly impressive: an increase in the volume of savings, price control applied only to the nationalised industries, general pressures ('what I want to know is: Who the hell's this General Pressures?' became one of Wilson's favourite evening-meeting taunts) and the wide claim of 'we have done it before, and will do it again'. But he had managed to put the Government on to the defensive.

If Labour's campaign needed anything, it was some specific commitment on price control. Wilson refused to give it. He was arguably too honest. Time and again he said that rising prices were a phenomenon throughout the western world. Britain had done less badly than most countries. Was he worried? Of course, he would say, he was worried. It was left to Jenkins, in his final television broadcast, to promise that price rises would be referred to the new Commission on Industry and Manpower.

Then there was the question of the Wage Freeze. At Labour meetings up and down the country the rises in wages being demanded were the subject of denunciation by the audiences. Here again Labour speakers were arguably too honest. They refused to exclude a wage freeze, and yet they said that they did not want one, that incomes policy was not a panacea. Heath was less straightforward. He gave a firm commitment not to introduce a wage freeze: at the same time he promised to stop wage-inflation.

Finally, there was the political effect of Enoch Powell. For years Wilson had used Powell as a bogey in order to keep his own supporters more united than they might otherwise have proved. Labour speakers now brought in Powell's name, rather as Conservatives had once cited Aneurin Bevan as evidence of disunity in the Labour Party. But Powell, by the simple fact of his being a Conservative, may well have gained his Party more votes than he lost.

All these facets to the campaign (the balance of payments, wage inflation, price rises and Powell) together with one other (Trade Union reform) were brought out in a series of unforeseen incidents; and to these we must now turn.

First, in a *Panorama* television programme on June 1, Lord Cromer, the former Governor of the Bank of England, said that 'there's no question that any Government that comes into power is going to find a very much more difficult financial situation than the new (Labour) Government found in 1964'. Lord Kearton, the Chairman of Courtaulds and one of Wilson's favourite industrialists, agreed, even if a little half-heartedly, with Lord Cromer. 'The very large debts which are still outstanding—', Lord Cromer went on, 'there seems to be some idea abroad that they have been completely paid off. This is very far from the case. The debts which were taken on for balance of payments reasons will stand at just under $4,000 million, and this in comparison with the position in 1964 makes for a very adverse start'.

Lord Cromer's warnings were not taken up immediately by the Conservatives. Indeed in private Wilson was astonished at Heath's failure to exploit the former Governor's words. A week went by before Wilson, leaning out of a window at Nottingham—he was annoyed that the facilities provided were not more conducive to good television—attacked Lord Cromer and emphasised that Britain's economy was perfectly sound. And for the rest of that second week of the campaign, the message was reiterated by Ministers, led by Jenkins.

Secondly, on June 3, Benn, speaking at a students' meeting at Westminster, said that the flag of racialism which had been hoised over Wolverhampton was beginning to look like the one that fluttered over Dachau and Belsen. Wilson was angry. Benn was, after all, a member of the Campaign Committee. He had not shown the speech to Wilson, though Transport House assumed this had been done. The effect of the speech must have been not only to draw attention to Powell but to give him sympathy.

Thirdly, on June 4, the Kindersley Committee on doctors' pay resigned. They did so in protest against the Government's refusal to implement their report in full. It recommended a 30% rise for all doctors: the Government was prepared to accept 30% for junior doctors, and 15% for the rest. Originally Wilson and Crossman had wanted to keep the report unpublished during the Election campaign. The doctors, clearly calculating that publication during the campaign would help to get the award accepted in full, threatened strike action. The Government gave in over the date of publication, though not over the acceptance of the award. The doctors leaked to the *Sunday Express* Crossman's alleged statement that the award could not be implemented in full because of the country's condition of economic crisis. What Crossman says he said is that the settlement would have been inflationary: in particular it would have disturbed the arrangements on forces' pay.

But no matter: the damage was done, and on the following Monday the doctors, the wage freeze, price rises and wage inflation were subsumed under the general cry of 'economic crisis' from Heath. Perhaps it can be said in favour of both Wilson and Jenkins that they behaved with dignity and restraint. They contented themselves with quietly saying that there was no economic crisis. It might have been better if at this stage they had shouted slightly louder. But if they had done so, they would not have been heard as clearly as they might have been. For there was another misfortune.

Fourthly, there was a national Press strike lasting inclusively from Wednesday, June 10 to Saturday, June 13. Some thought that the absence of pro-Conservative newspapers would help the Labour case. Wilson was not so hopeful. Strikes, he believed, always harmed Labour. Besides, he had intervened in the strike and had failed either to prevent it or, after it had begun, to persuade the printing unions to go back. Above all, the strike showed that the Government's industrial policy—which consisted in a reliance on God and Victor Feather, in approximately equal proportions—was hardly working perfectly.

The polls continued to show Labour as comfortably ahead. But on June 15 there fell a fifth blow. A deficit of £31 million was announced on the visible trade balance. Jenkins explained that £18.5 million of the deficit was accounted for by the purchase of two Boeing 747 aircraft, referred to more racily by Wilson in a public meeting at Hammersmith as 'jumbo-jets'. Wilson was at his most confident at this meeting, the biggest West London had known for years. Michael Stewart was on the platform, with Ivor Richard, and Frank Tomney. The heckling was persistent but good-natured. Wilson dealt with it like a man who knew he was going to win. Professor Samuel Beer, the American academic, said it was the finest political performance he had ever witnessed.

Afterwards, the Wilsons stood on the steps of Hammersmith Town Hall, and Wilson said a few words to the noisy crowd below: 'The Tories are getting rattled,' he said as he turned away, to go down behind the stage for drinks with local Councillors and Labour Party dignitaries. 'I hope,' he said to a journalist, 'you noticed that wasn't an all-ticket meeting'. This was a reference both to Heath's meetings and to Wilson's previous encounters with the people, when he had spoken in the Committee Rooms only to Labour Party stalwarts. And so, from here, and after a night's sleep,

Wilson went to Euston to begin that last, doomed journey to Manchester, with everyone concerned in the campaign, the journalists included, behaving like the passengers on the *Titanic*.

If this chapter has a bias, and it may be anti-Conservative and anti-Heath, it is certainly not pro-Wilson. He has frequently and rightly been accused of triviality in his manoeuvres over the past six years and more. Today the proposed explanation is that Labour was defeated by a Conservative campaign of staggering boldness and persistence, assisted by a remarkable display of character on the part of Heath. Most psephological evidence is to the effect that the Election campaign is ritualistic, staged for the benefit of Fleet Street and the television cameras. However, Butler's and Stokes's *Political Change in Britain* points to a remarkable volatility in the electorate; and this is borne out by the evidence of Humphrey Taylor of the Opinion Research Centre, the only polling organisation which finally predicted a Conservative lead.

Taylor says that on the weekend before polling day, he and his associates had the feeling that, in his own words, 'something funny was going on'. He discarded a poll which showed a Labour lead of about 4% and then embarked on another one. This showed a Conservative lead of 1%. In Taylor's opinion what turned the balance was the publication of the trade figures on the Monday before polling day. And perhaps—one cannot be sure about this—the effect of the Conservatives' propaganda was not so much to convince people that there really was a crisis as to remind them of what had happened in 1966-9. Wilson was vulnerable to Conservative attack because of the promises he had given on the Wage Freeze and, by implication, on devaluation, in the General Election of 1966.

There remains the question of differential turn-out. In a sense all elections are won or lost by differential turn-out.

But was there, in 1970, a marked failure by Labour to get out the vote? And did this failure increase the swing to the Conservatives? Anthony King has shown that there was no pronounced pro-Conservative swing in those seats which had a low percentage turn-out; if anything, the reverse was the case. But this, with the greatest respect to Professor King, is hardly conclusive: a drop in turn-out tells us nothing about the proportions, in Party terms, of the abstainers. The opinion of those actively involved in the campaign is that on the day 'our people' stayed at home.

Wilson ran a campaign which was every bit as principled as Heath's. This admittedly is not to say very much, but it is something. The odd thing is that, a year previously, a number of Labour M.P.s would have been pleasantly astonished to be told that the Conservatives would win with a majority of only 30. Wilson claimed, both on television and in private, that he fixed the 1970 election date in 1966. Privately he told the story of how he had instructed his staff at Downing Street to get out *Whitaker's Almanack*, which provided a calendar for 1970. He had ringed May 14 and June 25: but finally he decided on June 18. Transport House and the majority of the Parliamentary Party were always against this date and preferred October instead: the Cabinet started off by being against it, but Wilson took the precaution of gaining its endorsement. 'Ah well,' said one Minister afterwards, 'we didn't deserve to win. And at least we weren't massacred.'

CHAPTER SIX

FROM ALBANY TO DOWNING STREET

'He struck me much like a steam engine in Trousers'—SYDNEY SMITH, on Daniel Webster.

At 7.00 on the evening of May 12, Whitelaw was quietly working in his office at the Commons. The 'phone rang. It was Barber with the latest Gallup Poll result, to be published in the *Daily Telegraph* the next day.

'Good God ... What? ... Do you mean it?' exploded Whitelaw. Labour, Barber was insisting, was ahead by 7½%. Whitelaw hastened across to Heath's office. But the Leader was not there; he had gone back to his flat at the Albany to change for dinner. He was to be the principal guest that evening at a dinner in the House of the Unionist Club, a club of Tory ex-Ministers. Visions of Heath returning to the House unprepared for this shock flickered uneasily across the minds of those in Heath's office; and an urgent call was made to the Albany. Fortunately Heath was still there and the news could be broken to him in advance. As soon as he got back to the House, he conferred with four of his senior colleagues. The discussion made him forty minutes late for the dinner that night. He seemed shaken when he arrived but warmed up as the evening wore on, though his speech itself was not particularly inspiring. Whitelaw, meanwhile, was due at a dinner of his old Regiment, the Scots Guards. He decided that it must be business as usual and went. From the dinner he later rang his deputy Francis Pym. He did not intend to return to the House, he said. There was, reported Pym, a lot of gloom around of course. Some Labour M.P.s, he added significantly, were finding the Gallup results almost incredible.

The consensus of opinion at the Shadow Cabinet meeting on the next day was that the figures must be an exaggeration. The swing was too violent to be true. The probability was that the Parties were neck and neck. As to the likely date, Whitelaw had already told Central Office his views at the Meeting of the Departmental Heads that morning. The papers were tipping any Thursday between June 11 and July 2. Whitelaw ruled out the 11th altogether and confidently plumped for the 18th.

One other Committee Meeting that day deserves to be recorded. The Party's Business Committee, consisting of the officers of the back-bench groups, met briefly in the evening to hear the Parliamentary business timetable. Heath rose briskly from his chair to leave at the end and turning to the subject in all minds said: 'Well, we've been in worse corners than this before and we've fought our way out before.' He made this declaration with a cheerfulness and confidence which provoked a spontaneous cheer from his audience as he marched out of the room.

The planning for the campaign had begun in early 1969. The Committee known as 'The Thursday Group'—for the good reason that it met every Thursday morning—consisted initially of Barber, Whitelaw, Geoffrey Johnson-Smith, M.P., Brendon Sewill, Head of the Research Department, Geoffrey Tucker, head of publicity, Jim Garrett, a commercial film producer, and John Lindsay, Head of Central Office Television Department.

Planning was intensely detailed and very much—some thought too much—as if for launching a soap powder. There was even to be a theme tune for the Party broadcasts and to precede the Leaders' platform appearances. Barber later went to Soho to hear this new composition tinkled out on a piano. It was approved and orchestrated, though it cannot be said to have been a great compliment to the Party's musical taste. It sounded like a cross between the Forsyte Saga theme and the opening of a travelogue.

Nothing would be left to chance at public meetings either. Central Office officials already had a fierce distrust of news cameramen who, they thought, often shot Heath from deliberately unflattering angles. In the campaign no less than three advisors were permanently on tour taking with them the new Party emblem and its screens for re-erection in each hall the leader visited. The team consisted of a senior man from the Rank Organisation, borrowed for the campaign, a professional lighting cameraman and the designer of those screens. Their job was to try and see that the setting, lighting and other details were as favourable as possible.

In late March, an unpublicised but immensely important meeting took place between Fraser, Tucker and representatives of the different opinion polls. The two officials cross-examined their visitors on their methods of sampling and analysis. Tucker firmly concluded that there was an error involved understating the Conservative vote, particularly where the housewife was concerned. As a man with a degree in psychology, which had involved a considerable study of statistics, Tucker was able during the campaign to explain this impressively with details and diagrams. It was to be a factor in keeping up morale at the top under a deluge of adverse polls.

As for the Party's theme, Central Office was utterly certain it must be the economy. The Party had arranged for its own opinion poll almost monthly. Voters were asked what worried them most. For the last two years the answer had been consistent, first, the cost of living, second, taxation—except in one month when the order had been reversed.

By May 1970 the manifesto was almost ready. A first

draft had been hurriedly prepared by the Research Department almost a year before when it seemed possible, to the Research Department at any rate, that the Government might be defeated over its Industrial Relations Bill. What was in effect the seventh draft of this document had been before the Policy Advisory Committee at its meeting earlier that month. It had got a mixed reception. Some liked it, some described it as far too woolly. One description was that it was 'uninspiring'. Much had been cut out of the earlier drafts in fact, unfortunately including one or two of the more ringing passages such as, from the Education section: 'The independent schools are the only safeguard against State monopoly over the minds of our children.' The excuse was lack of space but the sentiment itself was not wholly attractive to some of the persistent middle-grounders. Another criticism at the PAC was that the emphasis on economic growth reduced the differences between the Parties to 'we can grow faster than you can'. Another Member of the Committee unkindly suggested that it might at least have proper syntax. On the watering down of the Value Added Tax proposal, it was commented that the Party had now got the worst of both worlds. There was enough commitment to the Tax in principle to give Labour scope for attack; but not enough commitment to justify the all-out defence of a VAT.

The preparation for the final draft was left to the Shadow Cabinet 'Steering Committee', consisting of Maudling, Barber, Macleod, Whitelaw and Home, with Fraser as a sort of Permanent-Under-Secretary.

Confirmation of the Election date came on Monday, May 18. After duly despatching the appropriate private note to Heath earlier in the afternoon, Wilson drove to Buckingham Palace to ask for the poll on June 18.

Heath's closest colleagues sighed with relief that the uncertainty was over. 'The Tory Party, you know' one of those closest to Heath commented, 'sometimes shows a backbone of jelly.' Already some Tory M.P.s were baring their teeth and declaring that 'Ted was the trouble'. A prolonged delay before the contest got under way—and worst of all, a delay until October—would have resulted in frantic, if fruitless, demands from some for rapid change of Leader. And the voices would have been heard at all levels in the Party from the grass roots upwards. It would have provided an unedifying spectacle of dissension.

The question of the role Heath should play in the contest was immediately discussed at the top of the Party. Whitelaw and Barber, who were left to deal with television, decided quite firmly at the outset that there would be no question of masking Heath. Barber suggested to Heath that he should take all the Press Conferences. He instantly agreed. If he was away from London, it was agreed also, there would be no Press Conference at Smith Square to distract attention from the Leader. It was all in sharp contrast to Home's campaign in 1964. Then the Leader of the Party had left nearly all the London Press Conferences to colleagues and concentrated on touring the country. Heath had tried to do both in 1966 using a light aircraft. This time he decided he would use a fifty-seater. Some forty round-trip tickets were sold off to the Press.

Journalists quailed at the timetable involved. Why fly to Portsmouth, they asked, or Norwich and other places which could be reached quicker by train? Some of the towns to be visited had no late trains back to London, it was countered. So why not go by train and come back by plane? But no, Heath and his party would go both ways by plane in almost every case. The strategy in Central Office's mind was that Heath would have a permanent captive audience of journalists wherever he went. Thus, it was hopefully argued, he would get the publicity which he had 'failed to capture' in 1966 (and rushing everywhere by aeroplane was of course technologically 'with it'). The belief seemed to be that the very attendance of the Press would generate favourable publicity. Had Heath used each flight to talk at length with his passengers, it might have been different. But he remained generally a remote figure at the front of the aircraft, dealing with paper work, preparing his speeches and relaxing occasionally by listening to music on earphones. It was not long before comments were appearing in the Press about the sheer futility of flying to cities which could be reached faster by train. The one town to which Heath did not fly was Birmingham, but disconcerted journalists found that a coach had been laid on for their return. The reason for this was soon explained. A stop was scheduled at the motorway cafe at Newport Pagnell. Here they were able to observe the Party Leader eating egg-and-chips with Sir Edward Boyle.

Within hours of the announcement of the Election, Wilson was demonstrating his own particular flair for public relations. A television interview? Of course. He insisted that he should talk to Hardiman Scott, the mild-mannered BBC political correspondent in the garden of No. 10. Heath was asked for an interview, Robin Day from *Panorama* being suggested. He agreed without hesitation. The outcome was that the Wilson interview was a quiet, unaggressive affair, with the Prime Minister being allowed to claim that he planned the Election for June 1970 ever since 1966. It was a wild claim even by Wilson's Falstaffian standards. Heath's interview by contrast came over like a cross-examination of a hostile witness.

Heath, strange to relate, was happy enough with the result and so were most of his advisers. One of their problems was to get him to forget the television cameras. The more aggressive the interviewer, the less inhibited Heath became. And anyway he liked aggressive interviews himself. The result was not necessarily successful, however. All too often it led again to that shrill note of protest from the Leader of the Opposition. One of Heath's own associates was later to describe his reaction in one television interview as 'ranting'.

The propensity of many Tories for confusing aggression with strength had persisted for a long time. Thus, while the Tories for so long prided themselves on having a strong leader, the public took an opposite view. By February 1967 for example, when Heath had at least become well-known to the public, a Gallup poll showed that 51% thought Wilson a 'strong forceful personality'. Only 17% thought that of Heath. Nearly a year before, 28% had been prepared to think him strong.

The *Sunday Times* aptly wrote of the opening of the campaign a week later:

> 'It is a rum election. There in the garden of No. 10 is Harold Baldwin, puffing slowly at his pipe in the sunshine and ruminating on the British people's preference for quiet Government. . . . There outside is apparently the wild radical Ramsey Heath going on about unemployment and the poor.'

Heath was also tactless in the Day interview on the subject of Powell. He declared very forcibly that Powell would not be in the Shadow Cabinet. Some M.P.s were later to report hostile reactions among Tory voters to this. Why, asked these M.P.s, could Heath not at least have sounded less hostile towards Powell personally? Little were they to know how much worse things would get later on.

For Heath, of course, the statement by Wilson that he had planned the election as far back as 1966, was money for jam. The theme of the Leader of the Opposition's speech the next day was inevitable. So the Prime Minister had planned it all? Had he planned everything in 1966—devaluation, unemployment, inflation?

The Shadow Cabinet approved the Manifesto at its last meeting before dissolution. All the polls now showed a Labour lead varying between 1 and 7%. The Tories decided to hold a rally of all candidates to start the campaign. Heath addressed them in Church House, Westminster, emphasising that the issues would be strikes, taxation, unemployment and, above all, prices. To emphasise the last point, candidates were all handed a lengthy brief on prices as they left. And throughout the campaign they continued to be inundated with background material of this sort. Heath, if he was downhearted by the polls, certainly did not show it. Barber, in mock vein, had confessed to the meeting that the Leader had shortcomings compared to Wilson. He was, alas, honest and straightforward! The audience cheered rapturously. Straightforward, honest Heath against wily Wilson was to be the theme of many speeches in almost every constituency. The candidates dispersed in a cheerful mood, many of them saying that an issue they would certainly add to the list was the calling off of the South African cricket tour—'giving in to the mob'.

Officially the Election campaign itself did not start until Parliament was prorogued on Friday, May 28. In the meantime, Parliament had to clear up remaining unfinished business. Conveniently, the Government found that this included the need to make several announcements about public spending. One was that £76 million would be spent on modernising the Royal Dockyards, another was that the Government's plans for roads were ready. These showed a predicted expenditure of £3,400 million on the construction of enormous lengths of motorways. Another was that £40 million would be available for the urban programme which concentrated on areas of high immigration. The announcements were received in the Commons with irreverent jeers from the Tories.

That weekend Heath was going sailing in his yacht. Here at any rate was a chance for the Tory publicity machine to try and deal with the 'remote bachelor' aspect of Heath's public *persona*, for the crew that day included a girl and a very attractive one at that. She had been taken on board as a cook. But the incident, if not exactly counter-productive, proved what an uphill task image-building would be. Ask him why she's there, was one hint, and he would say that the crew was fed up with his saying that they could have only apples and Mars bars for lunch—a very human touch, it was thought. The Press duly asked. Heath merely replied that she was there to cook. Nor was there much more success with the romantic aspect. Was there a romance, asked reporters, hopeful that they might at least get a humorous 'we are just good friends'. But 'ridiculous' was Heath's reply. She was, insisted Heath crisply if ungallantly, 'only the cook'.

Rather more important in the campaign were the opening blows on television. In *Panorama's 'Election Forum'*, viewers' questions were put to all three Party Leaders. Heath, unlike Wilson, did not have to face a barrage of extremely hostile questions, so he emerged from that round looking in distinctly happier shape than the Prime Minister. It made a very encouraging start for Heath and for his senior colleagues who were delighted to see the Prime Minister discomfited.

Publication day for the Tory manifesto was the 26th. It was launched at Central Office by Heath, flanked by Maudling and Barber, both of whom, however, remained mute throughout. And behind the trio was the Party's new and rather mystifying emblem: a device of concentric blue circles with the slogan 'a better tomorrow'. It made Heath look rather as if he was viewed through a gun barrel. It was a device of dubious advantage. For one thing it provoked inevitable ribaldry in the Press about Heath's appearing about to disappear down a plughole. For another, the constant reappearance of that screen behind Heath, wherever he was speaking, made it look, on television at least, as if he was always speaking from the same place. So while Wilson was seen on platforms surrounded by ordinary, breathing people, Heath's impression of remoteness from people was exaggerated. The Tory Manifesto got a reasonably good, although not exactly rapturous, reception. One of the criticisms made at the Policy Advisory Committee meeting earlier that month had been that the main body of the Manifesto was proceeded by an introduction which was a summary of the Manifesto; then there was a preface which was no more than a summary of the introduction. This at least had been changed by the time the document appeared. Heath wrote his own preface, pungent and forceful. It was a crisp condemnation of triviality and dishonesty in politics. (It is also noteworthy that Heath left the subject of 'policies' after a mere four opening sentences and spent the remaining thirty sentences emphasising the different 'style' he would introduce in Government.)

Parliament was prorogued officially on the Friday. Heath, after dropping plans to attend the ceremony, spent the day in his Albany flat polishing up some details and entertaining a Fleet Street editor to lunch. His mood was completely relaxed. That mood seemed to persist at Bexley the next day where he launched into the first of his constituency speeches. He talked almost entirely about the economy, a theme he was to reproduce with depressingly few variations night after night. The lack of impact or variation in Heath's speeches was surprising. He had a staff of three assisting him in this work. The formula was that Heath picked the topic and then a brief on facts and figures was produced from which he could select material. Michael Wolff of Heath's personal staff, would then produce a draft speech which Heath would push and pull into the shape he wanted. 'There is no secret of what is needed to get a good speech out of him,' said one of his staff: 'it's simply a matter of giving him enough time.' Perhaps it was. At any rate, he never seemed to find enough time during the campaign, to judge by the results.

More important at Bexley, perhaps, were the questions. Hardly any at all were about the economy. There was a tricky one too about Powell's election address which had been published that afternoon. 'The great dangers facing Britain' and, Powell had said, 'were Commonwealth immigration, the Common Market, and Socialism, in that order.' On immigration, his comment was that it 'was a threat of division and bloodshed of American dimensions and adds a powerful new weapon to the armoury of anarchy.'

What, demanded the questioner, had Heath to say about that? 'It doesn't seem to me that Mr. Powell is saying anything he had not said before.' The answer was given with an easy smile. Unfortunately it was to be almost the only time that Heath handled the Powell issue with wisdom. Later remarks by Powell, though not really so strikingly different from those in that Manifesto passage, were to throw Heath and some of his colleagues completely off balance.

The poll news in the papers on Sunday, May 1, showed the first encouraging signs for the Tories for weeks. Gallup, in the *Sunday Telegraph*, reported the Labour lead down from 7 to 5.5%. More encouraging was the *Sunday Times*. This declared in a banner headline that the last-minute polls showed the Tories in the lead by 2%. Less encouraging was Heath's poor personal showing in the ratings. But he was not cast down by that. And it was certainly not a novelty.

The next day saw the beginning of the campaign proper with its ritual of daily Press Conferences. Heath's routine for the day was to read the papers over breakfast in his dressing gown. Robert Allan the ex-Tory M.P. for Paddington North, and now a businessman in the Cowdray Empire, was acting as his Personal Assistant for the campaign. Allan would arrive at the Albany soon after 9.30, Heath would change and they would then travel to Central Office arriving at about 10.00. At that time, the Heads of Departments of Central Office would be meeting for a briefing under Fraser. At 10.15, Heath and his personal staff and any Ministers would join with most of those at the briefing to discuss what needed to be said at the Press Conference. Miles Hudson, from the

Research Department would start with a report on the Press for the previous 24 hours. 'Usually' commented one of the group 'it was a matter of agreeing to what Ted had already decided he wanted to say.' At about 10.45, Heath would be left to prepare details of whatever statement he wanted to make to the Press.

The Press Conferences of the main Parties opened in a flurry of rhetorical questions for the Party Leaders.

Would Mr. Wilson deny that . . .?

Would Mr. Heath explain how . . .?

The questions were duly relayed to their targets by the core of journalists trailing from one Press Conference to another. Heath, at one point during the week, declined to answer Wilson's questions until he (Wilson) gave some proper answers to his (Heath's) vital challenges. The proceedings had an air of quiet futility. The public was hardly likely to be wildly roused by many of Heath's points since they were so packed with figures.

That night, the Tories put on the first of their new-style Party political broadcasts. Moving right away from the standard Party political piece, it turned out to be a skit on ITV's *News at Ten* with M.P.s Geoffrey Johnson-Smith and Christopher Chataway playing the two newscasters briskly putting over critical items about Labour's record in rapid alternation. There was even a 'commercial break' in which Labour promises were recalled and their outcome recorded. Each ended with a reminder of the rate of inflation, showing a pound note being cut away and forecasting that by 1975 Labour would be offering (compared with 1964) 'the ten-bob pound'. It was unquestionably one of the points which stuck most in people's minds. At the end a senior Party spokesman would appear to give a short straight-to-camera talk. Heath appeared on the first one and made one of his best showings yet. The technique used was to film him in close-up. This meant, among other things, that he talked quietly into the camera. It was just what was needed and gave him that appearance of quiet thoughtfulness which his other appearances were all too often to belie.

Another and certainly more controversial possibility in broadcasting had been suggested from another source, particularly for use on the final night. The idea had been, bearing in mind that Wilson would probably again be offering false promises, to exhume television film of Wilson making his various pledges ('500,000 houses by 1970' and so on). These would be played back as Tory party political broadcasts. But it proved impracticable because the film was the copyright of the TV companies and they were nervous of putting the material into the hands of one party to use against another.

Heath's theme remained the economy. A considerable amount of election fodder had been provided by the controversial television programme (see Chapter 5) in which Lords Cromer and Kearton had criticised the economic situation. Heath had no intention of ignoring this nor, later on, a comment of Callaghan's at Cardiff that wage inflation would have to be dealt with soon. So all was not rosy? Would the Government deny that a freeze was on the way? What would Heath do, came the demand from the Press. He replied that the whole package of Tory measures showed the way to get inflation under control in due course. He promised that there would be no statutory freeze at any price. The same promise was not so easily extracted from Labour leaders.

What was Heath's reaction to Wilson being hit two-days-running by eggs, was one question. Heath became solemn. It was a grave matter, Heath said, the more so because Wilson's tour itinerary was a secret. What the situation really meant was 'that there are men and women in this country walking around with eggs in their pockets on the off-chance of seeing the Prime Minister'. It was an excellent joke, received with a roar of laughter, and it was in fact entirely

Heath's own. More dubious in some eyes were his remarks in a speech during which he commented on the fact that the end of the Department of Economic Affairs was commemorated in a Westminster pub with a humorous plaque. Suitable, he said, since George Brown was the DEA's founder.

One point at least was quickly settled that week. Some senior Tories had privately expressed the fear that Wilson would, if he started to trail in the polls, announce just before Election day that a referendum would be held under Labour prior to any irrevocable step in joining the Common Market. Heath had never thought that there was much mileage in that idea, even though some of his colleagues disagreed. But at any rate, the problem was not going to arise now, for Wilson told a questioner that Parliament only would take the final decision. Nor, unfortunately for Heath, did it now look as if Wilson would face the prospect of trailing in the polls. They showed considerable variation in the size and nature of the Labour lead, but they all agreed that there was a clear and continuing trend to Labour.

It was on Wednesday night, during this first utterly unexciting week of electioneering, that Anthony Wedgwood Benn dropped his bombshell. In what might have been described as an outburst, had it not been delivered at dictation speed from a prepared script, Benn accused Powell of hoisting over Wolverhampton the flag that was 'beginning to look suspiciously like the one that fluttered over Dachau and Belsen'. There were also comments about Powell's policy as 'evil', 'filthy', 'obscene' and an attack on the Tories for distributing his speeches.

The reaction of Benn's own colleagues was instant horror at this language. Powell's own reaction was prompt, because a TV reporter read out the text of Benn's comments to him at the public meeting at Smethwick within minutes of the attack.

'I will reply briefly to that' he barked snatching up the

microphone: 'All that I will say is that, for myself, in 1939 I voluntarily returned from Australia to this country to serve as a private soldier in the war against Germany and against Naziism. I am the same man today.' It was a brilliant answer. It was only two sentences long, it contained no counter slanging, it was dignified, it may even have reminded the audience of Powell's brilliant military career (he had risen from private to brigadier). No speech writer, with weeks of preparation, could have produced anything more effective.

The Benn attack was inevitably the main topic of Heath's Press Conference the next day. And what an odd performance the Tory Leader gave. Here was a politician's dream. Here was a chance to reconcile Powellites by springing to their hero's defence, here indeed was a chance to please the millions of Labour voters who also regarded Powell as a hero, here was an attack so odious that even Powell's critics wished for it to be rebutted. But Heath's pathological hatred of Powell prevented him from handling the situation sensibly. He muffed the operation. He rose too easily to the Benn jibe that 'Mr. Heath dare not speak his mind about Mr. Powell.'

Heath raged against Benn's attack as 'an attempt to smear the *whole* Conservative Party with Naziism and anti-semitism.' His own views on Powell, he went out of his way to remind his audience, were perfectly clear. He had sacked him from the Shadow Cabinet. He had disowned his views on immigration unhesitatingly. There was, significantly, no defence of Powell personally.

Several Party officials were appalled. So too were some of Heath's Parliamentary colleagues when they later heard the text of his comments. The emphasis on attacking Benn for 'smearing the *whole* Conservative Party' seemed, in the context of the other remarks, an implication that it was all right to smear Powell that way but not the whole Party.

The point was not lost on the public or on Powell's Parliamentary colleagues.

Powell's own postbag for the next fortnight was to be an amazing 500 letters a day. Only about 1% were hostile to him and many were furious protests of sympathy from Party workers.

There were protests to Heath as soon as he left the conference to prepare for his trip to Birmingham later that day. His advisers complained that, among other things, Benn's tactics would divert attention from what they still saw as the main topic—the economy. If Heath did not kill the whole matter off quickly, this diversion would damage the strategy as they saw it. Heath agreed to put in a stronger attack on Benn that night. But again the emphasis was on the 'whole of the Party' aspect of Benn's remarks. Heath went on to say that he had sacked Powell, now Wilson should sack Benn. It was not quite what his advisers meant. Heath's colleagues were readier to spring to Powell's defence. Sir Alec Douglas-Home reacted at once by describing Powell as a man of wide human sympathies. Maudling, campaigning in Devon, commented in a remark of calculated contempt: 'Well, I do not share his (Powell's) views in many ways, but in others I do. I won't say that Mr. Benn has made a big boob last night because Mr. Benn is not big enough to make a big boob.'

It was with some relief that Heath found himself able to turn the next day to a different topic: Doctors' Pay. The Government had been anxious not to publish, or to announce a decision on, the Kindersley proposals for 30% pay rises for doctors until after the Election. But under threats from the profession, Crossman, as Secretary for the Social Services, announced that the Government would pay the full increase to junior doctors, half the proposed increase to senior men and refer the balance to the Prices and Incomes Board. The Kindersley Review Body resigned en bloc; and

Crossman had the task of explaining his decision to BMA representatives. The explanation according to Dr. Stevenson, included the fact that a claim of such magnitude threatened the country, which was in 'extreme economic peril'. The Tories jumped on this. What sort of condition was the economy really in? Would the Prime Minister come clean, demanded Heath? The Government reaction was twofold, first Crossman denied having uttered the celebrated words, despite the testimony of four dentists and six doctors to the contrary—and Wilson said that the Kindersley Review Body had misunderstood its role.

But the Conservative fire had been given the fuel it needed and demands for explanations increased. Would the Government confirm or deny that there was no economic problem facing Britain? Was another freeze or squeeze and another emergency budget, to be expected if Labour returned to office? Government responses were evasive. Crossman had added to the Prime Minister's difficulties by giving an interview in a Medical newspaper saying that he would find more money for the Health Services by cutting agricultural subsidies and industrial grants. Maudling confronted Crossman on television and the latter sidestepped all relevant questions completely. Doubts grew. The Conservative Leaders refused to make a firm statement about what they would do about the doctors' pay on the grounds that they and the country were obviously not in full possession of the facts. It was a convenient if not entirely convincing answer.

This was all good ammunition but when fired off it still seemed to make little impression on the public. By the weekend, Heath's spirits were beginning to sag, though he scarcely ever showed it outside his private office or his flat. He had decided that the meeting he had arranged at the Albany the following Sunday—Maudling, Macleod, Hogg, Barber, Carr and Carrington had better be enlarged to a full-scale council of war. Senior Shadow Ministers near London were phoned up by Fraser and asked to come. This brought in Joseph, Balniel, Jellicoe (Deputy Leader of the Lords), Mrs. Thatcher and Sir Peter Rawlinson, the Shadow Attorney General. Jim Prior was also there as Heath's Parliamentary Private Secretary. So was the ubiquitous Fraser.

After a pause for coffee and Press photographs, the group got down to business. Rather to the surprise of his colleagues Macleod said he thought the Party was coming across as credible and honest. Honest, yes, but not 'getting across as credible', insisted Carrington. People did not seem ready to believe in the reduced-tax and higher-benefit programme. The real need, according to Hogg and Thatcher, was to raise the tone of the Party campaign. The main part of Heath's speeches which the Press and TV seemed to pick out—sometimes the only parts—was his sniping at Wilson. (It was not altogether surprising, because the rest was repetitive and dull.) Barber agreed that the message was not getting across. 'You are the only one getting the publicity, Ted' he said. So it was the Leader who would have to get the message across to the public. 'Put the fear of God into them' as one put it. (In fact Heath had been urged at the outset by some to use the word 'crisis' about the economy, but he had refused.) But was it right, to concentrate just on economics? Prior pointed out that he was getting plenty of questions from constituencies which had nothing to do with the economy.

It was all rather inconclusive and the meeting broke up after one and a half hours with the feeling that what had been said before had to be said even more forcibly from now on, and better too.

Heath appeared at his morning Press Conference the next day flanked by Maudling and Carr. Barber had received comments that the Press Conferences were not a great success and were too much one-man-band affairs. These conferences were unusually important because nearly all Heath's public meetings were ticket-only affairs without questions. At the morning conferences, the public could see him facing questioners. And with so many of Heath's speeches throughout the country being repetitive, TV as well as the Press, gave particular prominence to these morning question-and-answer sessions.

Heath was in an aggressive mood that day, demanding once again Wilson should 'come clean' about the economic situation. Was there a crisis or was there not? What did he intend to do about wages? Journalists pressed Heath to know what he too would do about wages but were not able to get very clear answers. Heath inisisted that Wilson must say whether there was a crisis. Would Heath use the word crisis? It was for Wilson to make the point plain. 'Well, I am asking you if there is' snapped one correspondent back at Heath, a little tired at the Leader's hectoring manner. Heath's reply to this and other questions was a reiteration of Tory policies and a demand for Wilson to come clean.

It was in many ways surprising that Heath was able to convince a number of people that he was fighting an exceptionally straight campaign. Indeed, there were times when it was scarcely possible to dignify Heath's answers with the title 'evasive'. He would keep replying to difficult questions 'my position is absolutely plain . . .' and follow this with a jumble of remarks which were anything but plain. He seemed at times hardly to take in the questions. There would be a key word in the question which he would pick out —the economy, inflation, wages, unemployment—and he would promptly bark back some stereotyped and unimpressive answer. Monday's proceedings were hardly helped by the fact that Maudling and Carr could not get a word in edgeways, though both at certain moments looked as if they wanted to speak. But the worst moment of this singularly unfortunate opening of the penultimate week of the campaign came at the end. The Prime Minister had said an hour before that the misery-bound Tories were even glad that Britain had just lost to Brazil in the world cup. This sparked off a tirade from Heath who demanded: 'Is there no triviality to which that man would not descend?' Getting steadily angrier, he snapped out comments about patriotism and how he had, in winning the Sydney to Hobart yacht race, been determined to do well for Britain and, moreover, . . .

'God, that was embarrassing,' commented a Central Office official afterwards. Undignified too, might have been a suitable if cruel comment for this and some other of Heath's appearances.

But at least there was material at hand for Heath's economic message. As soon as the campaign opened, an economist in the Research Department had looked up the newspapers of a year ago and various other documents. Apart from producing some useful anniversary material—it was on June 18, 1969 that Wilson had capitulated over the union reforms—the exercise enabled Central Office to plan for the likely economic indicators which would be published. There would be, for example, the balance of payments results for the first quarter published on the 10th. That would certainly show a big surplus, so comments in advance about the importance of looking forward rather than back could at least be carefully prepared. There would also come the unemployment and retail prices figures and probably something from the Bank for International Settlements. The BIS report was certainly a help to the Tories. It severely criticised the pace of wage settlements in Britain. There was too an unexpected bonus in the Annual Report of the Government-sponsored Industrial Reorganisation Corporation. That too warned about the danger of Britain losing its competitiveness in world markets. There was a similar message from the Confederation of British Industries. And the Bank of England quarterly out that week, carried another warning about inflation. The Ministry of Labour Gazette, too, was due to publish the latest strike figures on the 15th. The Tories knew that they were bad and were able to prepare accordingly. The Tory leaders hammered away at their theme, about the precariousness of the economic situation, though not with demonstrable success according to the opinion polls.

Heath maintained the economic theme in his nightly speeches. The present prosperity, he kept on saying, was 'phoney' and then there would follow an exhaustive list of Labour failures. His audiences cheered, loyally if nothing else.

Heath's lack of eloquence or flair was made worse by the fact that nearly all his colleagues could put things better than he could. Thus, while TV showed him, one day, making unconvincing attempts to corner the Government, his own Shadow Education Minister, Margaret Thatcher, was declaring at a meeting in Finchley: 'Either the present inflation is deliberate, in which case it is a trick and a mean fraud; or the Government is helpless in the face of it—in which case we really are in a crisis.' It was neat and professional.

Had Heath not hogged the limelight so determinedly, some of his colleagues might have got more succinct messages like this through to larger audiences earlier in the campaign.

The second Heath Press Conference of the week showed a marked improvement. Maudling and Carr were again present and this time Heath diverted questions to them having realised that hogging all the questions the previous day was a mistake. Both the Shadow Ministers were fluent and competent and for the first time the atmosphere in the Conference became relaxed. With Heath away in Edinburgh on Wednesday, it was decided that Maudling should have a Central Office Press Conference himself. Again, the atmosphere was easy, calm and confident. The theme of course was still the economy. With the newspaper strike now on, television and radio and the provincial Press became more important. Carr on the Tuesday had been fluent and impressive on the Tories'

Industrial Relations proposals which included the possible imposition of a cooling off period before a threatened strike. Few disputes could have illustrated his point better. Here was a threatened strike in which a union had demanded 25% rise and allowed only a fortnight for discussions. Precisely the sort of situation, said Carr, in which a cooling-off period should be available for imposition. But what would happen if the unions disobeyed the court, came the question. That rarely happened, said Carr. Nearly all Court Orders in the past had been obeyed by the unions. To press the point home, Central Office had a duplicated pile of examples of Court Orders obeyed by unions in the past available as soon as journalists arrived for the daily conference the next day.

For Heath, the disappearance of the national Press robbed him of coverage of one of the happiest incidents of his campaign. Alighting from his aircraft at Edinburgh airport, he was promptly confronted by a Board of Trade interviewer, who was interviewing every 30th passenger arriving at the terminal. It was a public relations man's dream as this attractive blonde read out her questions.

What was the last country you lived in?—England.

What is the reason for your visit?—Politics, winning the Election.

What organisation do you belong to and how long has it been operating in the region?—Since the time of Disraeli.

('Ah,' she said, 'that comes under the heading "more than ten years".')

What is your final destination in the United Kingdom?—10 Downing Street.

How many people do you expect to meet you at the airport?—Hundreds and hundreds.

('That must go under "more than five" ' she replied.)

What is your occupation?—Unemployed (replied Heath, adding that he was having a row with the Treasury about whether he should receive his salary as Leader of the Opposition after prorogation).

Heath began his tour of the city with a 'meet the people' stroll through the city centre. Since the week-end, in fact, he had decided that he must appear less aloof. So he followed the technique of Wilson, plunging into crowds, shaking hands, signing autographs and making conversation. It did not always come off well. Heath had no capacity for small talk and, as one newspaper later put it, sounded rather like an orderly officer asking for complaints from the other ranks. But at least the general impression it gave was an improvement on the aloofness which had emerged the previous week.

The effect in Edinburgh was very nearly spoiled entirely by his final remark after he had walked some way down the street. Gracelessly, and what was worse, loudly, he turned to one of his officials and commented: 'I think that's enough for them, don't you?' He then got into a car and drove away.

Thursday found Heath back at London for his Press Conference and then it was off to Norwich for his evening meeting. It was a happy enough occasion, with Heath warming up as the evening progressed. It was not a particularly good speech but the ticket-only meeting cheered him to the echo. Later that night he strolled into the dining room of the nearby hotel where 16 journalists from his plane party were still eating despite the fact that the coach was anxious to leave for the airport. 'I'm told,' he said with a guffaw 'that I should make a speech to you—it's the only way to make you all get up and go.' Alas, there was almost a painful element of truth in this.

Two hours later, when Heath got into the car waiting to collect him at London Airport, the mood of cheerfulness evaporated suddenly. Powell's latest speech was shown to him. He had queried the figures provided over a long period on immigration and now he was asking if it could be that the Foreign Office was not the only Department which had been penetrated by 'enemies of our country'.

Heath was furious, and so was his entourage. Something

would have to be done to refute the speech, he decided. In any case, he was certain to be questioned about it at the Press Conference the next day. The obvious quandary was how to deal with it? The night before on television, Hogg had been asked about it and had been inclined to deal with the matter briefly. The point had also been put to Wilson who angrily demanded that any evidence Powell had should be shown to him and it would then be referred to the Security Commission. But he did not push the matter much further than that.

Clearly Heath could have adopted the same approach. Alternatively, he might have brushed Powell's speech aside lightheartedly. Inaccurate statistics suggesting spies? Well, the Board of Trade had come up last year with a discovery that it had underestimated exports for about three years. It was hardly grounds for suspecting the Civil Servants involved. Anyway, most Government departments made wrong statistical forecasts from time to time—and had made a strikingly large number of inaccurate forecasts under this Government.

Clearly the scope for brushing aside this incident with a touch of humour was immense. It was, in short, a problem which most politicians could easily have sidestepped. Anyway, there was less than a week to go to polling day, all Heath needed to do was to invite Powell to let him have any evidence as soon as he could (it certainly would not have to be dealt with before Thursday) and leave it at that.

But no! Heath, the next morning, marched unerringly into the minefield detonating every booby trap in sight. After the 10.15 conference at which no-one seems to have counselled caution, he was left at 10.45 to prepare his own statement, which he duly delivered fifteen minutes later. There was to be no sidestepping; on the contrary, he chose to make the occasion a direct confrontation with Powell's views. He attacked his familiar views on immigrants' dependants.

Areas of high immigration, Heath went out of his way to emphasise, must have special help. As for the Civil Service, Heath leapt to the defence as if he was the Head of a Government department under attack. If there was any evidence of spies, Powell must place it before the Home Secretary. (At least he might have said the incoming Tory Home Secretary). He did not share the views of Powell about the numbers that might return under schemes of financially assisted repatriation. Above all, he said with rising indignation, he did not share Powell's pessimism about the prospects of racial disharmony.

This fierce denunciation of Powell's views was the more striking because of the obvious, fierce, personal antipathy which Heath felt towards the man and which seemed to exude from him that morning.

After such a starter, there was clearly only one subject for the day. So the questions poured in thick and fast. Would he expel Powell from the Party? No, he was the official candidate. Heath acknowledged, but with apparent reluctance, that Powell did not believe in racial discrimination. Was Heath asking for the voters of Wolverhampton to support Powell? Heath sought desperately to avoid having to say a simple 'Yes' to that. Powell was the official candidate, he replied. The Tory Party did not disown any adopted candidates. The voters of Wolverhampton were free to make up their minds. Did Heath want to see Powell in Parliament? 'Er . . . Yes.' Twice Heath tried to change the subject. He wanted to get back to the economy, for one of his complaints was that Powell was diverting attention from the economy. But it was naive in the extreme, once he had opened on that note, to have expected the Press to let go so easily.

The message that went out from Smith Square that day was unequivocal. The Leadership was in a state of war with Powell.

The row rumbled on the next day at the Press Conference

and on the next day (Saturday). This was the day on which Powell was intended to make another major speech. He was circulating them himself at this time, so when the Press Conference came, the text was not in Heath's own hands though some of his staff had obtained copies. The Leader of the Opposition was clearly in an impatient not to say irritated mood. He made a long statement demanding that people should get back to the real issues of the campaign, but choosing himself to bring up the subject of immigration! Some people, he said, were obsessed by it. (It was true in more senses than one.) The real debate he declared in a resounding but banal declaration was 'which Party is going to make Britain strong?' He concluded with equal resonance (and equal banality):

> 'The kind of Britain we want to live in reflects the kind of world we want to build. We in Britain cannot hope to make the world richer if we as a nation become poorer. We cannot work for harmony among the races if we are at loggerheads amongst ourselves; we cannot help to create a united world if we ourselves are divided. We will not be able to defend the liberty of others if we abuse our own freedom. We will not restore pride in our nation if we have lost respect for ourselves.'

A rather bored Australian journalist eventually commented languidly: 'Mr. Heath, to say that the issue is which Party will make Britain strong is not to say very much more than that an Election is being held.'

The journalist received a glare for his pains and a long, if not very helpful, answer about the importance of a strong economy.

Barber, who was with Heath that morning, was questioned about the opinion polls, which still showed a strong Labour lead, even a rising one. Heath himself, in Manchester the previous night, had been told on the steps of the Midland Hotel by journalists, that the latest National Opinion Poll the next day would show no less than a 12% Labour lead. He had flinched visibly at the news. Barber, who had visited scores of marginal constituencies, insisted that what he had seen did not bear out the polls, particularly the canvassing results. Little notice was taken of this however. Most political journalists are inclined to the view that there are lies, damned lies and canvassing returns.

One inevitable question to the Leader that morning: Had Heath seen Powell's speech for the day? No, he snapped. There was a chuckle from several journalists which was greeted by another scowl from Heath. It was not a good day for the Tory Leader. Immediately after the Conference, one of Heath's aides took a journalist aside and told him that the Powell speech for that day, which he had read, was 'real fascism'!

Shortly after that the evening papers were on the streets declaring that Powell was about to make a speech of such impact that it clearly constituted 'a bid for the Party Leadership'.

In fact the 'real fascism' speech turned out to be an attack on anarchists, rioters and all those determined to overthrow existing society. Powell said the danger to Britain from these groups was greater than when the Nazis were re-arming. The prospect of civil strife lay ahead. In the past three or four years they had seen the universities of America being destroyed. The same enemy in his student manifestation had not only terrorised one European city after another but even brought down one of the strongest European governments (France). Civil Government itself had been made to tremble by the mob—in its modern form, the demonstration. The nation had suffered a disastrous defeat when the Home Secretary surrendered to the mob over the South African tour. That was not the end, it was just the beginning.

'Race', he insisted, was billed to play a major, perhaps a

decisive part, in the battle of Britain. The immigrant population would be exploited by 'this evil force'. He went on to attack those who had been brainwashed and mesmerised by all the organs of communication. A Party leader could be mesmerised into describing a lifelong colleague as 'unchristian' and 'racialist' for raising the subject of immigration. People could be mesmerised into believing that, in Ulster, arson and riot stemmed from dissatisfaction over council houses and employment opportunities. People could be mesmerised into believing that the Western world should be ashamed of its own achievements and should go on its knees before the underdeveloped nations to offer them taxpayers' money as a guilt offering. It was clearly implied in his speech that Heath and other Conservative Leaders would not recognise the serious problems facing Britain as he, Powell, saw it.

It was a fierce speech but hardly 'facism'. The very fact that one of Heath's aides had made this comment suggested that the brainwashing had gone just as far as Powell contended. Powell's comment that these enemies of society, in their battle to overthrow the British system, would do their damndest to exploit race, was really a gift for Heath. The *Observer* the next day, in otherwise stiff criticism, commented that this was a most welcome sentiment to hear from Powell.

But the speech caught Heath and most of his colleagues totally off balance. Heath's paranoia about Powell seemed to have spread to several of his colleagues. He was furious and had started to prepare a reply that day. He spoke to several of his closest colleagues mainly by telephone, and a whole range of possibilities, from withdrawal of support for Powell as a candidate to silence, was discussed. Both extremes were quickly discarded. Heath soon drafted his statement and later it was released to the Press.

It declared that the Tory Party had been the Party of one nation since the time of Disraeli and that those who tried to be divisive rendered a disservice. The statement, it was announced, had the support of the whole Shadow Cabinet. That sounded fine. But it covered up a potentially awkward situation in which the Shadow Cabinet's 'unanimous' endorsement had been extracted by means little short of political blackmail. Fraser was given the job of 'phoning all Shadow Cabinet Ministers to read them the statement. To those who protested he simply replied that the statement was going out anyway. Heath had decided on it and he would not alter it. What he expected now was to be able to say that the whole Shadow Cabinet backed him. It made an almost impossible situation for anyone to refuse without incurring the risk that they would be seen as divisive influences themselves. And right at the end of the campaign too.

'Why issue that statement?' complained one of Heath's colleagues afterwards. 'Enoch's not in the Shadow Cabinet. We never issued a statement when Edward Boyle came out for stopping the South African cricket tour; and that was far worse.' What indeed was far more embarrassing for Heath was that on the same day the text of a speech from Home landed in Conservative Central Office. It was a speech of support for Powell. It was vetoed by the Leader. Later in the week, after Powell had made his impassioned plea on Tuesday night for an all-out Tory vote, an unsuccessful attempt was made to revive the Home speech.

Wilson, that Sunday in Bristol, showed more circumspection in attacking Powell. Yes, he said at an open-air meeting, there were indeed troublemakers about, trying to destroy free speech and the like. And as hecklers tried to drown him, he added: 'And by making that noise you are making my point and, incidentally, Mr. Powell's as well.'

Heath opened his Conference on the Monday morning with a curt reminder that the last three Press Conferences had now spent over an hour on Powell (which was largely his fault, in fact). That, he said, was it, he had *nothing* more to add. He wanted to get back to the real issue of the economy in the remaining three days.

There was an air of stern finality about his comment. It came not a moment too soon. The Leadership had made the absurd mistake of overreacting to Powell and themselves doing precisely what they accused him of—diverting attention from the economic issues. It had all been unnecessary. Going out of their way to attack the people's darling, especially when he was one of their colleagues, was an odd manoeuvre to say the least. It was explicable only by the fierce personal animosity which Heath and several of his closest colleagues felt towards the man himself. Those few days in which the Tory attacks seemed concentrated on Powell rather than the Labour Party were undoubtedly the moment at which the Party came closest to losing the contest. There is good reason to believe that the public was otherwise coming round to the Tory view now that the economy was not in good shape.

The insistence that Powell had to be rebutted was nonsense at the time and even greater nonsense in retrospect. Wilson, after all, had an even greater problem than Heath when it came to colleagues. There was Benn with his Dachau speech. Wilson refused to go far on this beyond saying that he did not write Benn's speeches—but then privately letting it be known that he was 'furious'. This meant that all journalists could get from him publicly was that he was not responsible for Benn's comments. But at the same time the public could be informed in the Press and television that Wilson undoubtedly disapproved. It was an adroit way of handling a difficult situation.

And of course Wilson's ministerial problems were not confined to Benn. After all, Crossman had made a lamentable boob. He had used unfortunate phrases to the British Medical Association. He had talked of cutting agriculture and industrial subsidies. Moreover this was a very senior Minister, not just a prominent back-bencher. But Wilson never allowed himself to be dragged into an open squabble. When one of Crossman's awkward remarks was quoted to him in a television interview, he commented, half humorously: 'We all know Dick anyway when he is answering questions.'

As for his own back-benchers, Wilson had of course far more potential trouble to deal with than Heath. Scores of Labour M.P.s on the Far Left were far wilder figures than Powell could ever be and their election manifestos were full of extremist nonsense. But no one imagined that Wilson would ever let himself be dragged into an open fight with them.

Nor was there much logic in launching a violent attack on Powell for his later speeches in view of his earlier election address, when he had spoken of a threat of 'division and bloodshed on American dimensions'. If that could be ignored, why not the rest? Home was to say pointedly on *Panorama* on the 15th that Powell had not really said anything new in his two most controversial speeches.

Quantifying the damage done to the Tory campaign by the Leadership's tactics will never be possible. Perhaps it was very small. But it is worth noting that letters to Powell remained massively overwhelmingly sympathetic and angry at his treatment. Many were from Party workers. Some were from Party colleagues later to be Ministers, by no means all from the normally Powellite wing.

Having made his very final 'no further comment' on Powell, Heath could now get back to the economic issues for the last three crucial days. If the public had any doubts about the artificiality of the present feeling of prosperity, the Tory Leaders now had extra ammunition accumulating daily for their campaign. In the meantime there was only one distinctly non-economic issue for the campaign organisers and that was Heath's own personality.

Geoffrey Tucker realised the importance of trying to deal with the apparent lack of cosiness which seemed to surround the Leader. So, in a departure from the normal pattern of Party political broadcasts, the Tories' final TV production on Monday night was a brief summary of the life of the man himself, from grammar school to Westminster, with Heath appearing at the end and talking about scarcely any political topics.

It was, partly by luck and partly by design, just what was needed. Heath had seemed less cosy than ever in those past few days. And the electorate was only too glad to get away from the economy for a moment.

Nevertheless the Party managers now knew that they had four economic indicators to make the most of before polling closed on Thursday night. These were: the latest strike figures, the monthly trade figures, the monthly cost of living index and the unemployment figures for June. Only one of these was in any sense a real unknown.

Macleod had made his calculation about the unemployment rate. Ever since he had been Minister of Labour in the late 1950s, he had worked out his own formula for arriving at a national total of unemployed from a sample of the local unemployment rate which was always published earlier in the month. He was now able to predict that the unemployment figure when it came would be the worst for thirty years. He also said emphatically at that Monday Press Conference that the figure would be about 200,000 higher—it certainly sounded impressive—than the average Tory unemployment figure for June. And it was. The Retail Price Index, though it sometimes fell in the summer for seasonal reasons, would almost certainly rise because of the rate in wage inflation. The difficulty with the trade returns was that one month's figures were inclined to be inaccurate.

Because of the latter problem, the Research Department had drawn up a careful table to show the trend over the last six months.

Monday provided the first figures. On strikes. They were

out that morning and showed the number of disputes up by 65% on the same period last year. Heath went on to point out that this meant too that the number of strikes had gone up by 80% in the period since Wilson had abandoned his proposals for Trade Union reforms a year ago.

Trade figures out later that day provided further ammunition. There was a deficit of £31 million. The Tories hammered the lesson home. And Heath himself, in his speech that night at Bradford, once more reiterated that this was 'the housewife's election'. The cost of living was rising. The Index when published on the Wednesday showed that this was still true.

There was also what Labour termed the devaluation scare. Heath moved on this with considerable caution. If he was going to mention the topic, it should obviously not be until very nearly the last day, otherwise the decline in sterling—which other factors were producing anyway—would be blamed on the Tories. The tactics decided on were that a statement would be put out *after* the Leader's Press Conference on Tuesday. That meant that he would not be cross-examined on it until the Press Conference the next day. (It also had the slight disadvantage that since many of the journalists ambling out of 32, Smith Square assumed the hand-outs just to be a repeat of Heath's opening statement, some of the Press did not take or read the document.)

It was in fact a very carefully worded statement. There was a reiteration about all the other warnings which had recently been heard concerning the British economy. It went on to say, in effect, that if the Socialists did the same as before, it could mean another devaluation 'within four years'. It was hardly short-term scaremongering, though Labour Ministers naturally seized on the comment, describing it as cheap and unpatriotic. Wilson was particularly incensed. In fact he rose to the bait too easily. This provided Heath with the opportunity to issue another statement on Tuesday night and to repeat it on Wednesday. Picking his words carefully he said, in effect, that if Labour did the same as before, the outcome would be the same as before. A logician could hardly complain about that.

From Powell himself there came a final speech on the Tuesday night. It was a rallying cry to Tories, though hardly of the orthodox type. He stood before his Wolverhampton audience and bluntly emphasised to them that he had been treated by his life-long political colleagues with a lack of charity and sympathy. And he had received a flood of sympathetic letters from voters saying that they would not vote Tory as a result. 'Don't fool about', he said, addressing his sympathisers. The Election was not about Enoch Powell. It was not even about whether the economy should be 'run by a man with a pipe or a man with a boat'. It was about something deeper and every Tory must get out and vote for his own and his children's future.

Whether this in fact swung many voters or not is impossible to say. But about one-third of the letters Powell received in his still massive postbag after the result came from people who said he had helped the Tories to victory—and some were from Parliamentary colleagues.

For Polling Day itself there were the unemployment figures to come out at midday. And there they were, proving the rightness of Macleod's prediction.

All in all, there was little more the Tories could do in those last three days other than hope that the daily message of warning from Central Office had convinced the country that the apparent surge of prosperity was, as Heath described it, 'sham sunshine'. And with the sun blazing down on the voters as they went to the polling booths, they seemed to agree. The extra few days of plugging away at the one issue which the Tories had decided was the dominant issue from the beginning of the campaign had paid off. And Heath was home and dry.

Had the election been one week earlier, it is hard to avoid

the conclusion that Labour would probably have just won. The last of the economic indicators to be published then would have been the favourable balance of payments results for the first quarter. Indeed, they would have come almost on the eve of the Poll.

Ironically, it was Wilson himself who had coined the now-famous words, ‘a week in politics is a long time’.

GENERAL ELECTION RESULTS

In the alphabetical order of the 630 constituencies in Great Britain and Northern Ireland.

Aberavon
Morris, J. (Lab.) 31,314
Grist, I. (Con.) 10,419
Lab. majority 20,892

Aberdare
Probert, A. R. (Lab.) 22,817
Jones, G. M. (Pl Cymru) 11,431
Lab. majority 11,386

Aberdeen (North)
Hughes, R. (Lab.) 27,707
Williams, D. J. (Con.) 9,807
Lab. majority 17,900

Aberdeen (South)
Sproat, I. M. (Con.) 23,843
Dewar, D. C. (Lab.) 22,754
Con. gain: majority 1,089

Aberdeenshire (East)
Wolridge-Gordon, P. (Con.) 12,866
Farquhar, A. (Scot. Nat.) 9,377
Con. majority 3,489

Aberdeenshire (West)
Mitchell, Lt.-Col. C. C. (Con.) 18,396
Grimond, Mrs. L. (L.) 12,847
Con. gain: majority 5,549

Abertillery
Thomas, J. (Lab.) 22,819
Rendle, J. E. (Con.) 3,478
Lab. majority 19,341

Abingdon
Neave, A. M. S. (Con.) 36,209
Price, N. H. (Lab.) 23,136
Con. majority 13,073

Accrington
Davidson, A. (Lab.) 20,828
Webster, Dr. R. C. (Con.) 20,234
Lab. majority 594

Acton
Spearing, N. J. (Lab.) 13,900
Baker, K. W. (Con.) 13,300
Lab. gain: majority 600

Aldershot
Critchley, J. M. G. (Con.) 33,447
Bogg, R. T. (Lab.) 18,916
Con. majority 14,531

Altrincham and Sale
Barber, A. P. L. (Con.) 27,904
Jones, B. E. (Lab.) 16,671
Con. majority 11,233

Anglesey
Hughes, C. (Lab.) 13,966
'Jones, J. E. (Con.) 9,220
Lab. majority 4,746

Angus (North and Mearns)
Buchanan-Smith, A. L. (Con.) 14,687
Gourlay, J. (Lab.) 5,092
Con. majority 9,595

Angus (South)
Bruce-Gardyne, J. (Con.) 20,439
Slesser, C. G. M. (Scot. Nat.) 8,406
Con. majority 12,033

Antrim (North)
Paisley, I. (Prot. U.) 24,130
Clark, H. (U.U.) 21,451
Prot. U. gain: majority 2,679

Antrim (South)
Molyneaux, J. H. (U.U.) 59,589
Johnston, R. (N.I. Lab.) 19,991
U.U. majority 39,618

Argyll
Noble, M. A. C. (Con.) 13,521
MacCormick, I. (Scot. Nat.) 9,039
Con. majority 4,482

Armagh
Maginnis, J. E. (U.U.) 37,667
Lewis. H. (Nat. Unity) 21,696
U.U. majority 15,971

Arundel and Shoreham
Kerby, Capt. H. B. (Con.) 43,907
Lyne, B. M. (Lab.) 16,531
Con. majority 27,376

Ashfield
Marquand, D. I. (Lab.) 32,372
Kemm, R. N. (Con.) 15,089
Lab. majority 17,283

Ashford
Deedes, W. F. (Con.) 26,649
Bowyer, J. M. (Lab.) 14,037
Con. majority 12,612

Ashton-under-Lyne
Sheldon, R. E. (Lab.) 23,927
Fearn, A. d'A. (Con.) 19,973
Lab. majority 3,954

Aylesbury
Raison, T. H. F. (Con.) 31,084
Mitchell, J. E. (Lab.) 20,441
Con. majority 10,643

Ayr
Younger, G. K. H. (Con.) 22,220
Craigen, J. M. (Lab. & Co-op.) 17,770
Con. majority 4,450

Ayrshire (Central)
Lambie, D. (Lab.) 24,536
Lang, I. (Con.) 19,569
Lab. majority 4,967

Ayrshire (North and Bute)
Maclean, Sir F. (Con.) 18,853
Millar, H. G. (Lab.) 12,459
Con. majority 6,394

Ayrshire (South)
Sillars, J. (Lab.) 23,910
Simpson, N. (Con.) 11,675
Lab. majority 12,235

Banbury
Marten, H. N. (Con.) 36,712
Booth, A. C. (Lab.) 25,166
Con. majority 11,546

Banffshire
Baker, W. H. K. (Con.) 8,457
Watt, H. (Scot. Nat.) 5,006
Con. majority 3,451

Barking
Driberg, T. E. N. (Lab.) 21,097
Pattie, G. E. (Con.) 9,309
Lab. majority 11,788

Barkston Ash
Alison, M. J. H. (Con.) 35,198
Grime, E. K. (Lab.) 23,861
Con. majority 11,337

Barnet
Maudling, R. (Con.) 26,845
Baker, Mrs. J. E. M. (Lab. & Co-op.) 18,166
Con. majority 8,679

Barnsley
Mason, R. (Lab.) 34,956
Godber, R. (Con.) 10,811
Lab. majority 24,145

Barons Court
Richard, I. S. (Lab.) 13,374
Brum, R. E. (Con.) 12,269
Lab. majority 1,105

Barrow-in-Furness
Booth, A. E. (Lab.) 22,400
Miller, H. D. (Con.) 17,536
Lab. majority 4,864

Barry
Gower, H. R. (Con.) 31,957
Allison, J. (Lab.) 23,286
Con. majority 8,671

Basingstoke
Mitchell, D. B. (Con.) 35,138
Carter, D. V. (Lab.) 25,664
Con. majority 9,474

Bassetlaw
Ashton, J. W. (Lab.) 28,959
Lester, J. T. (Con.) 20,698
Lab. majority 8,261

Bath
Brown, Sir E. J. (Con.) 22,344
Young, D. W. (Lab.) 16,493
Con. majority 5,851

Batley and Morley
Broughton, Sir A. D. (Lab.) 23,024
Thompson, D. (Con.) 15,753
Lab. majority 7,271

Battersea (North)
Jay, D. P. T. (Lab.) 11,621
Bradbury, A. V. (Con.) 4,927
Lab. majority 6,694

Battersea (South)
Perry, E. G. (Lab.) 10,925
Samuel, Dr. I. N. (Con.) 9,227
Lab. majority 1,698

Bebington
Cockeram, E. P. (Con.) 31,260
Brooks, E. (Lab.) 30,535
Con. gain: majority 725

Beckenham
Goodhart, P. C. (Con.) 30,763
Bing, I. G. (Lab.) 13,031
Con. majority 17,732

Bedford
Skeet, T. H. H. (Con.) 26,330
Parkyn, B. S. (Lab.) 21,051
Con. gain: majority 5,279

Bedfordshire (Mid)
Hastings, S. L. E. (Con.) 29,670
Harrowell, D. F. (Lab.) 19,035
Con. majority 10,635

Bedfordshire (South)
Madel, W. D. (Con.) 38,085
Roberts, G. E. (Lab.) 33,107
Con. gain: majority 4,978

Bedwellty
Kinnock, N. G. (Lab.) 28,078
Marland, P. (Con.) 5,799
Lab. majority 22,279

Belfast (East)
McMaster, S. R. (U.U.) 26,778
Bleakley, D. (N.I. Lab.) 18,259
U.U. majority 8,519

Belfast (North)
Mills, W. S. (U.U.) 28,668
Sharkey, J. (N.I. Lab.) 18,894
U.U. majority 9,774

Belfast (South)
Pounder, R. (U.U.) 27,523
Coulthard, J. (N.I. Lab.) 11,567
U.U. majority 15,956

Belfast (West)
Fitt, G. (Repub. Lab.) 30,649
McRoberts, B. (U.U.) 27,451
Repub. Lab. majority 3,198

Belper
Stewart-Smith, G. (Con.) 35,757
Brown, G. A. (Lab.) 33,633
Con. gain: majority 2,124

Bermondsey
Mellish, R. J. (Lab.) 13,908
Nicholson, G. H. J. (Con.) 4,172
Lab. majority 9,736

Berwick and East Lothian
Mackintosh, J. P. (Lab.) 21,107
Hardie, J. D. M. (Con.) 20,466
Lab. majority 641

Berwick-upon-Tweed
Lambton, A. (Con.) 15,558
Wareing, R. (Lab. & Co-op.) 8,413
Con. majority 7,145

Bethnal Green
Hilton, W. (Lab. & Co-op.) 15,483
Henriques, O. S. (Con.) 5,578
Lab. majority 9,905

Bexley
Heath, E. R. G. (Con.) 27,075
Cartwright, J. C. (Lab. & Co-op.) 19,017
Con. majority 8,058

Billericay
McCrindle, R. A. (Con.) 47,719
Moonman, E. (Lab.) 43,765
Con. gain: majority 3,954

Bilston
Edwards, R. (Lab. & Co-op.) 27,240
Irving, C. G. (Con.) 26,240
Lab. majority 1,000

Birkenhead
Dell, E. (Lab.) 20,980
Kris, R. (Con.) 15,151
Lab. majority 5,829

Birmingham (All Saints)
Walden, A. B. (Lab.) 12,041
Hollingworth, J. H. (Con.) 7,762
Lab. majority 4,279

Birmingham (Aston)
Silverman, J. (Lab.) 15,456
Hill, A. A. (Con.) 11,894
Lab. majority 3,562

Birmingham (Edgbaston)
Knight, Mrs. J. C. J. (Con.) 23.690
Sever, E. J. (Lab.) 13,047
Con. majority 10,643

Birmingham (Hall Green)
Eyre, R. E. (Con.) 27,319
Keene, T. L. (Lab.) 17,930
Con. majority 9,389

Birmingham (Handsworth)
Chapman, S. B. (Con.) 16,122
Wright, Miss S. R. R. (Lab.) 14,310
Con. majority 1,812

Birmingham (Ladywood)
Fisher, Mrs. D. M. (Lab.) 5,067
Lawler, W. L. (L.) 4,087
Lab gain: majority 980

Birmingham (Northfield)
Carter, R. J. (Lab.) 33,364
Bell, D. W. (Con.) 32,148
Lab. majority 1,216

Birmingham (Perry Bar)
Kinsey, J. R. (Con.) 18,083
Price, C. (Lab.) 16,817
Con. gain: majority 1,266

Birmingham (Selly Oak)
Gurden, H. E. (Con.) 18,281
Hartley-Brewer, M. J. (Lab.) 16,758
Con. majority 1,523

Birmingham (Small Heath)
Howell, D. H. (Lab.) 13,794
Budgen, N. W. (Con.) 6,923
Lab. majority 6,871

Birmingham (Sparkbrook)
Hattersley, R. S. G. (Lab.) 14,773
Mitton, A. E. J. (Con.) 1,427
Lab. majority 3,346

Birmingham (Stechford)
Jenkins, R. H. (Lab.) 22,559
Stevens, J. B. (Con.) 15,848
Lab. majority 6,711

Birmingham (Yardley)
Coombs, D. M. (Con.) 21,827
Evans, I. (Lab. & Co-op.) 21,707
Con. gain: majority 120

Bishop Auckland
Boyden, H. J. (Lab.) 21,257
Wiseman, T. J. (Con.) 13,769
Lab. majority 7,488

Blackburn
Castle, Mrs. B. A. (Lab.) 22,473
Gardner, Mrs. R. T. (Con.) 19,737
Lab. majority 2,736

Blackpool (North)
Miscampbell, N. A. (Con.) 22,298
Callon, W. (Lab.) 13,062
Con. majority 9,236

Blackpool (South)
Blaker, P. A. R. (Con.) 21,273
Hall, P. P. (Lab.) 13,267
Con. majority 8,006

Blaydon
Woof, R. E. (Lab.) 25,724
D'Aguiar, N. H. (Con.) 13,926
Lab. majority 11,798

Blyth
Milne, E. J. (Lab.) 36,118
Blackburn, A. J. (Con.) 12,550
Lab. majority 23,568

Bodmin
Hicks, R. (Con.) 20,187
Tyler, P. A. (L.) 16,267
Con. gain: majority 3,920

Bolsover
Skinner, D. (Lab.) 28,830
Humphrey, I. J. (Con.) 8,371
Lab. majority 20,459

Bolton (East)
Reed, L. D. (Con.) 22,769
Howarth, R. L. (Lab.) 22,298
Con. gain: majority 471

Bolton (West)
Redmond, R. S. (Con.) 19,225
Oakes, G. J. (Lab.) 17,981
Con. gain: majority 1,244

Bootle
Mahon, S. (Lab.) 20,110
Halliwell, G. (Con.) 11,496
Lab. majority 8,614

Bosworth
Butler, A. (Con.) 30,732
Wyatt, W. L. (Lab.) 29,677
Con. gain: majority 1,055

Bothwell
Hamilton, J. (Lab.) 26,431
Highgate, J. B. (Con.) 15,720
Lab. majority 10,711

Bournemouth (East and Christchurch)
Cordle, J. H. (Con.) 31,104
Bisson, T. C. (Lab.) 10,594
Con. majority 20,510

Bournemouth (West)
Eden, Sir J. B. (Con.) 28,714
Bennett, L. F. (Lab.) 14,099
Con. majority 14,615

Bradford (East)
Lyons, E. (Lab.) 17,346
Barr, C. J. (Con.) 8,208
Lab. majority 9,138

Bradford (North)
Ford, B. T. (Lab.) 20,141
Laycock, W. H. P. (Con.) 18,511
Lab. majority 1,630

Bradford (South)
Torney, T. W. (Lab.) 20,985
Bottomley, J. D. W. (Con.) 19,009
Lab. majority 1,976

Bradford (West)
Wilkinson, J. A. D. (Con.) 20,475
Haseldine, C. N. (Lab. & Co-op.) 18,936
Con. gain: majority 1,539

Brecon and Radnor
Roderick, C. E. (Lab.) 18,736
Neale, G. J. J. (Con.) 13,892
Lab. majority 4,844

Brentford and Chiswick
Barnes, M. C. J. (Lab.) 14,051
Wright, Cmdr. O. C. (Con.) 13,538
Lab. majority 513

Bridgwater
King, T. (Con.) 26,685
Billington, R. J. (Lab.) 18,224
Con. majority 8,461

Bridlington
Wood, R. F. (Con.) 25,053
Clarke, H. A. (Lab.) 11,546
Con. majority 13,507

Brierley Hill
Montgomery, F. (Con.) 43,440
Pritchard, T. S. (Lab.) 28,203
Con. majority 15,237

Brigg
Mallalieu, E. L. (Lab.) 31,434
Spokes, Miss A. H. (Con.) 27,449
Lab. majority 3,985

Brighouse and Spenborough
Proudfoot, G. W. (Con.) 22,953
Jackson, G. C. (Lab.) 22,894
Con. gain: majority 59

Brighton (Kemptown)
Bowden, A. (Con.) 24,208
Hobden, D. H. (Lab.) 21,105
Con. gain: majority 3,103

Brighton (Pavilion)
Amery, H. J. (Con.) 24,365
Tonks, F. (Lab.) 13,771
Con. majority 10,594

Bristol (Central)
Palmer, A. M. F. (Lab. & Co-op.) 12,375
Taylor, J. R. E. (Con.) 9,130
Lab. majority 3,245

Bristol (North-East)
Adley, R. J. (Con.) 23,254
Dobson, R. F. H. (Lab.) 22,792
Con. gain: majority 462

Bristol (North-West)
McLaren, M. (Con.) 24,124
Ellis, J. (Lab.) 23,075
Con. gain: majority 1,049

Bristol (South)
Cocks, M. F. L. (Lab.) 24,682
Hunt, D. F. J. (Con.) 15,254
Lab. majority 9,428

Bristol (South-East)
Benn, A. N. Wedgwood (Lab.) 29,176
Reece, N. G. (Con.) 23,488
Lab. majority 5,688

Bristol (West)
Cooke, R. G. (Con.) 20,110
Blackman, D. J. (Lab.) 8,175
Con. majority 11,935

Brixton (Lambeth)
Lipton, M. (Lab.) 13,053
Harkess, J. W. (Con.) 9,727
Lab. majority 3,326

Bromley
Hunt, J. L. (Con.) 22,364
Spellar, J. F. (Lab.) 9,328
Con. majority 13,036

Bromsgrove
Dance, J. C. G. (Con.) 37,544
Davis, T. A. G. (Lab.) 26,670
Con. majority 10,874

Buckingham
Benyon, W. R. (Con.) 28,088
Maxwell, I. R. (Lab.) 25,567
Con. gain: majority 2,521

Buckinghamshire (South)
Bell, R. M. (Con.) 40,039
Davison, K. (Lab.) 16,465
Con. majority 23,574

Burnley
Jones, D. (Lab.) 24,200
Birch, J. (Con.) 14,846
Lab. majority 9,354

Burton
Jennings, J. C. (Con.) 27,428
Truman, R. G. (Lab.) 23,063
Con. majority 4,365

Bury and Radcliffe
Fidler, M. G. C. (Con.) 29,796
Hunt, D. V. (Lab.) 26,592
Con. gain: majority 3,204

Bury St. Edmunds
Griffiths, E. W. (Con.) 36,688
Seager, C. J. V. (Lab.) 23,286
Con. majority 13,402

Caernarvon
Roberts, G. O. (Lab.) 13,627
Lewis, R. (Pl. Cymru) 11,331
Lab. majority 2,296

Caerphilly
Evans, A. T. (Lab.) 24,972
Williams, P. (Pl. Cymru) 11,505
Lab. majority 13,467

Caithness and Sutherland
MacLennan, R. A. R. (Lab.) 8,768
Mackie, G. Y. (L.) 6,063
Lab. majority 2,705

Cambridge
Lane, D. W. S. S. (Con.) 26,252
Scurfield, G. B. (Lab.) 21,191
Con. majority 5,061

Cambridgeshire
Pym, F. L. (Con.) 32,264
Hughes, J. N. (Lab.) 19,993
Con. majority 12,271

Cannock
Cormack, P. T. (Con.) 32,665
Lee, Miss J. (Lab.) 31,136
Con. gain: majority 1,529

Canterbury
Crouch, D. L. (Con.) 33,222
Clother, H. G. N. (Lab.) 15,172
Con. majority 18,050

Cardiff (North)
Roberts, M. H. A. (Con.) 21,983
Rowlands, E. (Lab.) 20,207
Con. gain: majority 1,776

Cardiff (South-East)
Callaghan, L. J. (Lab.) 26,226
Lloyd-Edwards, N. (Con.) 20,771
Lab. majority 5,455

Cardiff (West)
Thomas, T. G. (Lab.) 21,655
Williams, R. C. (Con.) 15,878
Lab. majority 5,777

Cardiganshire
Morgan, D. E. (Lab.) 11,063
Lloyd Williams, H. C. (L.) 9,800
Lab. majority 1,263

Carlisle
Lewis, R. H. (Lab.) 21,866
Marsden, B. A. (Con.) 19,241
Lab. majority 2,625

Carlton
Holland, P. W. (Con.) 39,840
Bennett, C. (Lab.) 27,043
Con. majority 12,797

Carmarthen
Jones, G. G. (Lab.) 18,719
Evans, G. (Pl. Cymru) 14,812
Lab. gain: majority 3,907

Carshalton
Elliot, Capt. W. (Con.) 27,342
Baker, G. S. (Lab.) 16,896
Con. majority 10,446

Cheadle
Normanton, T. (Con.) 39,728
Winstanley, Dr. M. P. (L.) 37,974
Con. gain: majority 1,754

Chelmsford
St. John-Stevas, N. A. F. (Con.) 36,821
Kennedy, G. (Lab.) 23,780
Con. majority 13,041

Chelsea
Worsley, W. M. J. (Con.) 15,852
Madeley, R. J. (Lab.) 5,737
Con. majority 10,115

Cheltenham
Dodds-Parker, A. D. (Con.) 22,823
Godwin, L. G. (Lab.) 14,213
Con. majority 8,610

Chertsey
Grylls, W. M. J. (Con.) 27.239
Slater, C. P. (Lab.) 15,653
Con. majority 11,586

Chester, City of
Temple, J. M. (Con.) 25,877
Crawford, J. (Lab.) 18,872
Con. majority 7,005

Chesterfield
Varley, E. G. (Lab.) 30,386
Ramsden, J. C. (Con.) 16,217
Lab. majority 14,169

Chester-le-Street
Pentland, N. (Lab.) 33,694
Ramshaw, D. (Con.) 13,363
Lab. majority 20,331

Chichester
Chataway, C. J. (Con.) 38,120
Sandelson, N. D. (Lab.) 12,574
Con. majority 25,546

Chigwell
Biggs-Davison, J. A. (Con.) 26,404
Sheaff, W. J. (Lab.) 17,972
Con. majority 8,432

Chippenham
Awdry, D. (Con.) 24,371
Wingfield, Mrs. M. E. (L.) 13,833
Con. majority 10,538

Chislehurst
Hornsby-Smith, Dame P. (Con.) 24,650
Macdonald, A. H. (Lab.) 21,287
Con. gain: majority 3,363

Chorley
Monks, Mrs. C. M. (Con.) 26,577
Forwood, D. A. (Lab.) 24,900
Con. gain: majority 1,677

Cirencester and Tewkesbury
Ridley, N. (Con.) 30,217
Lovell, H. G. (Lab.) 16,131
Con. majority 14,086

Clapham (Wandsworth)
Shelton, W. J. M. (Con.) 16,593
Pitt, Dr. D. (Lab.) 13,473
Con. gain: majority 3,120

Cleveland
Tinn, J. (Lab.) 36,213
Price, P. C. (Con.) 31,130
Lab. majority 5,083

Clitheroe
Walder, A. D. (Con.) 20,430
Bodfish, K. C. (Lab.) 14,158
Con. majority 6,272

Coatbridge and Airdrie
Dempsey, J. (Lab.) 26,117
Rennie, W. J. (Con.) 15,574
Lab. majority 10,543

Colchester
Buck, A. (Con.) 30,562
Bartlett, J. G. (Lab.) 20,325
Con. majority 10,237

Colne Valley
Clark, D. G. (Lab.) 18,896
Wainwright, R. S. (L.) 18,040
Lab. gain: majority 856

Consett
Watkins, D. J. (Lab.) 28,985
Trotter, N. G. (Con.) 11,914
Lab. majority 17,071

Conway
Roberts, I. W. P. (Con.) 16,927
Davies, G. E. H. (Lab.) 16,024
Con. gain: majority 903

Cornwall (North)
Pardoe, J. W. (L.) 19,863
Day, S. J. (Con.) 19,233
L. majority 630

Coventry (East)
Crossman, R. H. S. (Lab.) 36,275
Jones, M. E. (Con.) 24,010
Lab. majority 12,265

Coventry (North)
Edelman, M. (Lab.) 24,004
Tuckman, F. A. (Con.) 18,344
Lab. majority 5,660

Coventry (South)
Wilson, W. (Lab.) 30,010
Gardiner, G. A. (Con.) 27,816
Lab. majority 2,194

Crewe
Allen, S. S. (Lab.) 22,160
Goodlad, A. R. (Con.) 18,678
Lab. majority 3,482

Crosby
Page, R. G. (Con.) 24,042
Caswell, P. J. (Lab.) 18,350
Con. majority 5,692

Croydon (North-East)
Weatherill, B. B. (Con.) 20,351
Elliott, G. F. (Lab.) 16,373
Con. majority 3,978

Croydon (North-West)
Taylor, R. G. (Con.) 19,260
Boden, S. J. (Lab.) 14,687
Con. majority 4,573

Croydon (South)
Thompson, Sir R. H. M. (Con.) 25,986
Winnick, D. J. (Lab.) 22,283
Con. gain: majority 3,703

Dagenham
Parker, J. (Lab.) 31,335
McClancy, H. M. (Con.) 11,976
Lab. majority 19,359

Darlington
Fletcher, E. J. (Lab.) 23,208
Bourne-Arton, A. T. (Con.) 19,447
Lab. majority 3,761

Dartford
Trew, P. J. E. (Con.) 27,822
Irving, S. (Lab. & Co-op.) 27,262
Con. gain: majority 560

Darwen
Fletcher-Cooke, C. (Con.) 26,728
Whittam, B. (Lab.) 17,634
Con. majority 9,094

Dearne Valley
Wainwright, E. (Lab.) 33,966
Cowl, A. B. (Con.) 6,848
Lab. majority 27,118

Denbigh
Morgan, W. G. O. (Con.) 21,246
Roberts, Mrs. A. C. (Lab.) 12,537
Con. majority 8,709

Deptford
Silkin, J. E. (Lab.) 14,672
Brotherton, M. L. (Con.) 7,355
Lab. majority 7,317

Derby (North)
Whitehead, P. (Lab.) 20,114
Roberts, J. W. (Con.) 16,635
Lab. majority 3,849

Derby (South)
Johnson, W. H. (Lab.) 19,407
Greene, R. (Con.) 16,258
Lab. majority 3,149

Derbyshire (North-East)
Swain, T. (Lab.) 38,181
Pashley, J. P. (Con.) 24,550
Lab. majority 13,631

Derbyshire (South-East)
Rost, P. L. (Con.) 32,185
Ryman, J. (Lab.) 29,461
Con. gain: majority 2,724

Derbyshire (West)
Scott-Hopkins, J. S. R. (Con.) 22,692
Inglis, F. C. (Lab.) 13,976
Con. majority 8,716

Devizes
Morrison, C. A. (Con.) 28,475
Faulkner, R. O. (Lab.) 20,442
Con. majority 8,033

Devon, North
Thorpe, J. J. (L.) 18,893
Keigwin, T. C. (Con.) 18,524
L. majority 369

Dewsbury
Ginsburg, D. (Lab.) 22,015
Stansfield, J. M. (Con.) 17,468
Lab. majority 4,547

Doncaster
Walker, H. (Lab.) 22,658
Davies, P. (Con.) 19,431
Lab. majority 3,227

Don Valley
Kelley, R. (Lab.) 42,496
Jackson, T. W. G. (Con.) 18,673
Lab. majority 23,823

Dorking
Sinclair, Sir G. E. (Con.) 25,393
Fahy, W. J. (Lab.) 10,523
Con. majority 14,870

Dorset (North)
James, D. P. (Con.) 28,471
Watkins, P. G. (L.) 12,095
Con. majority 16,376

Dorset (South)
King, E. M. (Con.) 27,580
May, R. G. (Lab.) 20,716
Con. majority 6,864

Dorset (West)
Digby, K. S. D. W. (Con.) 21,081
Sakwa, G. (Lab.) 10,536
Con. majority 10,545

Dover
Rees, P. W. I. (Con.) 30,103
Ennals, D. H. (Lab.) 28,454
Con. gain: majority 1,649

Down (North)
Kilfedder, J. A. (U.U.) 55,679
Young, K. (N.I. Lab.) 14,246
U.U. majority 41,433

Down (South)
Orr, Capt. L. P. S. (U.U.) 34,894
Quinn, J. G. (L.) 7,747
U.U. majority 13,218

Dudley
Gilbert, J. W. (Lab.) 29,499
Williams, W. D. (Con.) 29,163
Lab. gain: majority 336

Dulwich (Camberwell)
Silkin, S. C. (Lab.) 20,145
Mayhew, P. B. B. (Con.) 19,250
Lab. majority 895

Dumfriesshire
Monro, H. S. P. (Con.) 24,661
Donnelly, R. D. (Lab.) 15,555
Con. majority 9,106

Dunbartonshire (East)
McCartney, H. (Lab.) 32,527
Henderson, J. S. B. (Con.) 26,972
Lab. majority 5,555

Dunbartonshire (West)
Campbell, I. (Lab.) 23,009
Adams, W. (Con.) 16,783
Lab. majority 6,226

Dundee (East)
Thomson, G. M. (Lab.) 22,630
Stewart, J. A. (Con.) 19,832
Lab. majority 2,798

Dundee (West)
Doig, P. M. (Lab.) 26,271
Payne, J. A. (Con.) 19,449
Lab. majority 6,822

Dunfermline
Hunter, A. (Lab.) 21,532
Kirkwood, I. C. (Con.) 12,086
Lab. majority 9,446

Durham
Hughes, W. M. (Lab.) 33,766
Greenwood, E. (Con.) 16,707
Lab. majority 17,059

Durham (North-West)
Armstrong, E. (Lab.) 24,245
Page, A. E. (Con.) 10,590
Lab. majority 13,655

Ealing (North)
Molloy, W. J. (Lab.) 23,459
Barter, J. W. (Con.) 23,139
Lab. majority 320

Ealing (South)
Batsford, B. (Con.) 19,326
Rofe, C. (Lab.) 12,042
Con. majority 7,284

Easington
Dormand, J. D. (Lab.) 33,418
Spicer, W. M. H. (Con.) 8,457
Lab. majority 24,961

Eastbourne
Taylor, Sir C. S. (Con.) 30,296
Terrell, S. (L.) 23,308
Con. majority 6,988

East Grinstead
Smith, G. Johnson (Con.) 38,359
Smithers, D. C. B. (L.) 12,343
Con. majority 26,016

East Ham (North)
Prentice, R. E. (Lab.) 11,557
MacFarlane, N. (Con.) 7,735
Lab. majority 3,822

East Ham (South)
Oram, A. E. (Lab. & Co-op.) 13,638
Jackson, C. M. (Con.) 8,402
Lab. majority 5,236

Eastleigh
Price, D. E. C. (Con.) 30,300
Flach, R. T. F. (Lab.) 22,248
Con. majority 8,052

Ebbw Vale
Foot, M. M. (Lab.) 21,817
Donaldson, A. (L.) 4,371
Lab. majority 17,446

Eccles
Carter-Jones, L. (Lab.) 23,913
Boyson, R. (Con.) 18,458
Lab. majority 5,455

Edinburgh (Central)
Oswald, T. (Lab.) 9,561
Rifkind, M. (Con.) 8,000
Lab. majority 1,561

Edinburgh (East)
Strang, G. S. (Lab.) 22,171
Gow, N. (Con.) 16,657
Lab. majority 5,514

Edinburgh (Leith)
Murray, R. K. (Lab.) 12,066
Elliott, W. A. (Con.) 10,682
Lab. majority 1,384

Edinburgh (North)
Dalkeith, Earl of (Con.) 13,005
Cook, R. F. (Lab.) 9,127
Con. majority 3,878

Edinburgh (Pentlands)
Wylie, N. R. (Con.) 21,829
Stewart, E. G. F. (Lab.) 18,646
Con. majority 3,183

Edinburgh (South)
Hutchison, A. M. C. (Con.) 19,851
Henderson, J. (Lab.) 15,071
Con. majority 4,780

Edinburgh (West)
Stodart, J. A. (Con.) 26,864
Foulkes, G. (Lab.) 19,523
Con. majority 7,341

Edmonton
Albu, A. H. (Lab.) 20,626
Hubbard, E. P. (Con.) 18,481
Lab. majority 2,145

Enfield (East)
Mackie, J. (Lab.) 16,433
Weston, Dr. T. E. T. (Con.) 12,403
Lab. majority 4,030

Enfield (West)
Macleod, I. N. (Con.) 21,858
King, H. C. (Lab. & Co-op.) 9,896
Con. majority 11,962

Epping
Tebbitt, N. B. (Con.) 43,615
Newens, A. S. (Lab.) 41,040
Con. gain: majority 2,575

Epsom
Rawlinson, Sir P. A. G. (Con.) 35,541
Wilson, E. G. (Lab.) 12,767
Con. majority 22,774

Erith and Crayford
Wellbeloved, A. J. (Lab.) 23,012
Jackson, H. J. (Con.) 18,158
Lab. majority 4,854

Esher
Mather, D. C. M. (Con.) 37,727
Scorer, R. S. (Lab.) 14,449
Con. majority 23,278

Essex (South-East)
Braine, B. R. (Con.) 41,589
Edwards, D. W. (Lab.) 23,684
Con. majority 17,905

Eton and Slough
Lestor, Miss J. (Lab.) 24,103
Lawson, N. (Con.) 21,436
Lab. majority 2,667

Exeter
Hannam, J. G. (Con.) 21,680
Dunwoody, Mrs. G. P. (Lab.) 20,409
Con. gain: majority 1,271

Eye
Harrison, Sir H. (Con.) 26,099
Manley, R. E. (Lab.) 17,735
Con. majority 8,364

Falmouth and Camborne
Mudd, W. D. (Con.) 21,477
Dunwoody, Dr. J. E. O. (Lab.) 19,954
Con. gain: majority 1,523

Farnham
Macmillan, M. (Con.) 25,113
Stonham, P. M. O. (L.) 10,178
Con. majority *14,935*

Farnworth
Roper, J. F. H. (Lab. & Co-op.) 29,392
Johnston, I. A. (Con.) 20,867
Lab. majority *8,525*

Faversham
Moate, R. D. (Con.) 29,914
Boston, T. G. (Lab.) 26,103
Con. gain: majority *3,811*

Feltham
Kerr, R. W. (Lab.) 21,561
Wallis, Miss B. L. (Con.) 16,006
Lab. majority *5,555*

Fermanagh and South Tyrone
McManus, F. (Unity) 32,832
Hamilton, Marquess of (U.U.) 31,390
Unity gain: majority *1,447*

Fife (East)
Gilmour, Sir J. E. (Con.) 21,619
Ewing, H. (Lab.) 9,756
Con. majority *11,863*

Fife (West)
Hamilton, W. W. (Lab.) 29,929
McLaughlan, G. (Con.) 12,837
Lab. majority *17,092*

Finchley
Thatcher, Mrs. M. H. (Con.) 25,480
Freeman, M. L. (Lab.) 14,295
Con. majority *11,185*

Flint (East)
Jones, S. B. (Lab. & Co-op.) 24,227
Amyes, R. M. (Con.) 20,145
Lab. majority *4,082*

Flint (West)
Meyer, Sir A. J. C. (Con.) 20,999
Evans, J. G. (Lab.) 13,655
Con. majority *7,344*

Folkestone and Hythe
Costain, A. P. (Con.) 27,031
Hyman, N. A. (Lab.) 13,772
Con. majority *13,259*

Fulham
Stewart, M. (Lab.) 16,312
Mactaggart, Sir I. A. (Con.) 12,807
Lab. majority *3,505*

Fylde (North)
Clegg, W. (Con.) 33,667
Hill, R. W. (Lab.) 15,235
Con. majority 18,432

Fylde (South)
Gardner, E. L. (Con.) 39,459
Mahon, D. (Lab.) 13,354
Con. majority *26,105*

Gainsborough
Kimball, M. (Con.) 22,163
Tracy, M. P. (Lab.) 14,454
Con. majority *7,709*

Galloway
Brewis, H. J. (Con.) 14,003
Donaldson, A. (Scot. Nat.) 5,723
Con. majority *8,280*

Gateshead (East)
Conlan, B. (Lab.) 28,524
Wood, P. R. (Con.) 15,489
Lab. majority 13,035

Gateshead (West)
Horam, J. R. (Lab.) 15,622
O'Sullivan, J. (Con.) 7,328
Lab. majority *8,294*

Gillingham
Burden, F. F. A. (Con.) 25,813
Bean, R. E. (Lab.) 18,057
Con. majority *7,756*

Glasgow (Bridgeton)
Bennett, J. (Lab.) 11,056
Gavin, R. (Con.) 3,801
Lab. majority *7,255*

Glasgow (Cathcart)
Taylor, E. M. (Con.) 29,093
Mackay, D. C. H. (Lab.) 24,188
Con. majority *4,905*

Glasgow (Central)
McMillan, T. (Lab.) 7,936
Rennie, G. (Con.) 2,394
Lab. majority *5,542*

Glasgow (Craigton)
Millan, B. (Lab.) 20,872
Wober, W. (Con.) 13,661
Lab. majority *7,211*

Glasgow (Gorbals)
McElhone, F. P. (Lab.) 10,260
Shearer, W. (Con.) 3,071
Lab. majority *7,189*

Glasgow (Govan)
Rankin, J. (Lab. & Co-op.) 13,443
Belton, G. F. (Con.) 6,301
Lab. majority 7,142

Glasgow (Hillhead)
Galbraith, T. G. D. (Con.) 14,674
Cable, V. (Lab.) 7,303
Con. majority *7,371*

Glasgow (Kelvingrove)
Miller, Dr. M. S. (Lab.) 6,106
Dundas, R. E. (Con.) 5,274
Lab. majority *832*

Glasgow (Maryhill)
Hannan, W. (Lab.) 18,925
Murchison, A. K. R. (Con.) 6,638
Lab. majority *12,287*

Glasgow (Pollok)
White, J. (Lab.) 19,311
Wright, E. (Con.) 18,708
Labour gain: majority *603*

Glasgow (Provan)
Brown, H. D. (Lab.) 25,864
Masterton, D. D. M. (Con.) 11,881
Lab. majority *13,983*

Glasgow (Scotstoun)
Small, W. W. (Lab.) 26,492
Mountney, N. J. (Con.) 14,487
Lab. majority *12,005*

Glasgow (Shettleston)
Galpern, Sir M. (Lab.) 17,840
McCue, A. (Con.) 7,969
Lab. majority *9,871*

Glasgow (Springburn)
Buchanan, R. (Lab.) 14,968
Sorbie, J. (Con.) 4,574
Lab. majority *10,394*

Glasgow (Woodside)
Carmichael, N. G. (Lab.) 10,785
MacColl, V. J. (Con.) 9,457
Lab. majority *1,328*

Gloucester
Oppenhemi, Mrs. S. (Con.) 21,838
Diamond, J. (Lab.) 20,777
Con. gain: majority *1,061*

Gloucestershire (South)
Corfield, F. V. (Con.) 35,045
Dalling, M. G. (Lab.) 26,067
Con. majority *8,978*

Gloucestershire (West)
Loughlin, C. W. (Lab.) 22,637
Hopkins, S. H. A. F. (Con.) 21,530
Lab. majority *1,107*

Goole
Jeger, G. (Lab.) 26,424
Bloomer, I. R. (Con.) 17,457
Lab. majority *8,967*

Gosport and Fareham
Bennett, Dr. R. F. B. (Con.) 39,234
Sturges, J. R. (Lab.) 21,262
Con. majority *17,972*

Gower
Davies, I. (Lab.) 26,485
Carter, M. J. (Con.) 9,435
Lab. majority *17,050*

Grantham
Godber, J. B. (Con.) 33,070
Higgins, W. F. (Lab.) 23,296
Con. majority *9,774*

Gravesend
White, R. L. (Con.) 29,924
Murray, A. J. (Lab.) 28,711
Con. gain: majority *1,213*

Greenock
Mabon, Dr. J. D. (Lab. & Co-op.) 19,334
Riddell, W. (L.) 16,100
Lab. majority *3,234*

Greenwich
Marsh, R. W. (Lab.) 20,804
Thom, J. S. (Con.) 13,195
Lab. majority *7,609*

Grimsby
Crosland, C. A. R. (Lab.) 23,571
Spungin, M. F. (Con.) 17,460
Lab. majority *6,111*

Guildford
Howell, D. A. R. (Con.) 27,203
Smith, P. B. (Lab.) 13,108
Con. majority *14,095*

Hackney (Central)
Davis, S. C. (Lab.) 17,380
Lightwood, K. S. (Con.) 9,339
Lab. majority *8,041*

Halifax
Summerskill, Dr. Shirley C. W. (Lab.) 24,026
Turner, G. A. (Con.) 23,828
Lab. majority *198*

Haltemprice
Wall, P. H. B. (Con.) 30,042
Denton, C. M. (Lab.) 15,862
Con. majority *14,180*

Hamilton
Wilson, A. (Lab.) 25,431
Ewing, Mrs. W. (Scot. Nat.) 16,849
Lab. gain: majority *8,582*

Hammersmith (North)
Tomney, F. (Lab.) 16,145
Stewart, B. H. I. H. (Con.) 9,615
Lab. majority *6,530*

Hampstead
Finsberg, G. (Con.) 21,264
Whitaker, B. C. G. (Lab.) 20,790
Con. gain: majority *474*

Harborough
Farr, J. A. (Con.) 44,933
Marshall, J. (Lab.) 25,728
Con. majority *19,205*

Harrogate
Ramsden, J. E. (Con.) 26,167
Greaves, W. (L.) 8,825
Con. majority *17,342*

Harrow (Central)
Grant, J. A. (Con.) 16,525
Judge, A. R. (Lab.) 12,561
Con. majority *3,964*

Harrow (East)
Dykes, H. J. M. (Con.) 19,517
Roebuck, R. D. (Lab.) 15,496
Con. gain: majority *4,021*

Harrow (West)
Page, A. J. (Con.) 24,867
Daniel, T. P. C. (Lab.) 11,462
Con. majority *13,405*

Hartlepools, The
Leadbitter, E. L. (Lab.) 27,704
Marshall, R. M. (Con.) 20,188
Lab. majority *7,516*

Harwich
Ridsdale, J. E. (Con.) 32,754
Phillips, A. W. (Lab.) 19,923
Con. majority *12,831*

Hastings
Warren, K. R. (Con.) 20,364
Kissen, C. B. (Lab.) 13,549
Con. majority *6,815*

Hayes and Harlington
Skeffington, A. M. (Lab.) 19,192
Potier, A. W. (Con.) 13,728
Lab. majority *5,464*

Hemel Hempstead
Allason, J. H. (Con.) 40,417
Fletcher, P. A. (Lab.) 28,067
Con. majority *12,350*

Hemsworth
Beaney, A. (Lab.) 40,013
Tucker, M. C. (Con.) 9,534
Lab. majority *30,479*

Hendon (North)
Gorst, J. (Con.) 18,192
Irvine, A. A. M. (Lab.) 15,013
Con. majority *3,179*

Hendon (South)
Thomas, P. J. M. (Con.) 18,901
Dimson, Mrs. G. F. (Lab.) 12,712
Con. majority *6,189*

Henley
Hay, J. A. (Con.) 33,452
Denby, Miss M. J. (Lab.) 19,310
Con. majority *14,142*

Hereford
Gibson-Watt, D. (Con.) 22,011
Purnell, G. D. (Lab.) 14,410
Con. majority *7,601*

Hertford
Balniel, Lord (Con.) 36,494
Sieve, Mrs. Y. (Lab.) 26,924
Con. majority *9,570*

Hertfordshire (East)
Walker-Smith, Sir D. (Con.) 37,668
Thomas, M. S. (Lab. & Co-op.) 23,601
Con. majority *14,067*

Hertfordshire (South-West)
Longden, G. J. M. (Con.) 32,661
Grocott, B. J. (Lab.) 24,214
Con. majority *8,447*

Heston and Isleworth
Hayhoe, B. J. (Con.) 21,580
Samuel, G. J. (Lab.) 16,981
Con. majority *4,599*

Hexham
Rippon, A. G. F. (Con.) 24,516
Miller, J. E. (Lab.) 16,645
Con. majority *7,871*

Heywood and Royton
Barnett, J. (Lab.) *25,081*
Macgregor, I. (Con.) 24,178
Lab. majority *903*

High Peak
Le Marchant, S. (Con.) 19,558
Jackson, P. M. (Lab.) 18,054
Con. gain: majority *1,504*

Hitchin
Williams, Mrs. S. V. T. B. (Lab.) 40,932
Luce, R. N. (Con.) 37,258
Lab. majority *3,674*

Holborn and St. Pancras South
Jeger, Mrs. L. M. (Lab.) 12,448
Byng, J. M. E. (Con.) 10,125
Lab. majority *2,323*

Holland with Boston
Body, R. (Con.) 33,580
Sackur, R. N. H. (Lab.) 24,241
Con. majority *9,339*

Honiton
Emery, P. F. H. (Con.) 32,885
Trethewey, Mrs. B. V. (L.) 11,330
Con. majority *21,555*

Horncastle
Tapsell, P. H. B. (Con.) 19,299
Skinns, E. A. (Lab.) 8,860
Con. majority *10,439*

Hornchurch
Loveridge, J. W. (Con.) 36,124
Williams, A. L. (Lab.) 30,294
Con. gain: majority *5,830*

Hornsey
Rossi, H. A. L. (Con.) 21,434
Pestell, P. W. (Lab.) 17,645
Con. majority *3,789*

Horsham
Hordern, P. M. (Con.) 41,994
Edwards, A. J. (Lab.) 27,706
Con. majority *14,288*

Houghton-le-Spring
Urwin, T. W. (Lab.) 32,888
Craig-Cooper, F. H. M. (Con.) 11,914
Lab. majority *20,974*

Hove
Maddan, W. F. M. (Con.) 34,287
Nicholas, D. G. (Lab.) 15,639
Con. majority *18,648*

Howden
Bryan, P. E. O. (Con.) 22,102
Graham, J. W. R. (Lab.) 9,567
Con. majority *12,535*

Huddersfield (East)
Mallalieu, J. P. W. (Lab.) 20,629
Holt, J. G. (Con.) 15,632
Lab. majority *4,997*

Huddersfield (West)
Lomas, K. (Lab.) 16,866
Storey, R. (Con.) 16,673
Lab. majority *193*

Huntingdonshire
Renton, Sir D. L. M. (Con.) 27,398
Curran, J. (Lab.) 17,588
Con. majority *9,810*

Huyton
Wilson, J. H. (Lab.) 45,583
Entwistle, J. N. (Con.) 24,509
Lab. majority *21,074*

Ilford (North)
Iremonger, T. L. (Con.) 25,142
Sewell, C. W. (Lab. & Co-op.) 17,352
Con. majority *7,790*

Ilford (South)
Cooper, A. E. (Con.) 18,369
Shaw, A. J. (Lab.) 17,087
Con. gain: majority *1,282*

Ilkeston
Fletcher, L. R. (Lab.) 32,961
Beardsley, R. D. (Con.) 15,870
Lab. majority *17,091*

Ince
McGuire, M. T. (Lab.) 32,295
Coupe, A. R. (Con.) 14,877
Lab. majority *17,418*

Inverness
Johnson, D. R. (L.) 15,052
Wathen, D. A. (Con.) 12,378
L. majority *2,674*

Ipswich
Money, E. D. (Con.) 27,704
Foot, Sir D. (Lab.) 27,691
Con. gain: majority *13*

Isle of Ely
Legg-Bourke, Sir H. (Con.) 28,972
O'Hare, R. E. (Lab.) 19,366
Con. majority *9,606*

Isle of Thanet
Rees-Davies, W. R. (Con.) 33,434
Bishop, L. J. A. (Lab.) 21,709
Con. majority *11,725*

Isle of Wight
Woodnutt, H. F. M. (Con.) 30,437
Boulton, K. W. (Lab.) 13,111
Con. majority *17,326*

Islington (East)
Grant, J. D. (Lab.) 13,980
Devonald-Lewis, R. (Con.) 8,660
Lab. majority *5,320*

Islington (North)
O'Halloran, M. J. (Lab.) 13,010
Pearce, D. A. (Con.) 7,862
Lab. majority *5,148*

Islington (South-West)
Cunningham, G. (Lab.) 12,876
Szemerey, J. (Con.) 6,601
Lab. majority *6,275*

Jarrow
Fernyhough, E. (Lab.) 25,861
Robson, D. J. (Con.) 14,847
Lab. majority *11,014*

Keighley
Hall, Miss J. V. (Con.) 20,957
Binns, J. (Lab.) 20,341
Con. gain: majority *616*

Kensington (North)
Douglas-Mann, B. (Lab.) 13,175
Brittan, L. (Con.) 9,792
Lab. majority *3,383*

Kensington (South)
Rhys Williams, Sir B. M. (Con.) 21,591
Bridges, Mrs. F. M. (Lab.) 6,928
Con. majority *14,663*

Kettering
de Freitas, Sir G. (Lab.) 34,803
Taylor, J. C. (Con.) 30,613
Lab. majority *4,190*

Kidderminster
Brinton, Sir E. T. C. (Con.) 27,667
Smith, G. F. (Lab.) 18,297
Con. majority *9,370*

Kilmarnock
Ross, W. (Lab.) 24,477
Law, G. (Con.) 11,476
Lab. majority *13,001*

King's Lynn
Brocklebank-Fowler, C. (Con.) 23,822
Page, J. D. (Lab.) 23,789
Con. gain: majority *33*

Kingston-upon-Hull (East)
Prescott, J. L. (Lab.) 36,859
Lamont, N. S. H. (Con.) 14,736
Lab. majority *22,123*

Kingston-upon-Hull (North)
McNamara, J. K. (Lab.) 26,302
Townend, J. E. (Con.) 17,912
Lab. majority 8,390

Kingston-upon-Hull (West)
Johnson, J. (Lab.) 24,050
Forrow, T. E. (Con.) 14,537
Lab. majority 9,513

Kingston upon Thames
Boyd-Carpenter, J. A. (Con.) 23,426
Crockett, R. H. (Lab.) 13,090
Con. majority 10,336

Kinross and West Perthshire
Douglas-Home, Sir A. (Con.) 14,434
Whitley, Mrs. E. Y. (Scot. Nat.) 4,670
Con. majority 9,764

Kirkcaldy
Gourlay, H. P. H. (Lab.) 22,986
Hogg, A. M. (Con.) 13,193
Lab. majority 9,793

Knutsford
Davies, J. E. H. (Con.) 33,194
Bennett, A. F. (Lab.) 11,612
Con. majority 21,582

Lanark
Hart, Mrs. J. C. M. (Lab.) 30,194
MacDougall, A. C. S. (Con.) 27,721
Lab. majority 2,473

Lanarkshire, North
Smith, J. (Lab.) 21,982
Black, R. B. J. D. (Con.) 16,963
Lab. majority 5,019

Lancaster
Kellett, Mrs. M. E. (Con.) 18,584
Henig, S. (Lab.) 16,843
Con. gain: majority 1,741

Leeds (East)
Healey, D. W. (Lab.) 28,827
Crotty, P. (Con.) 21,112
Lab. majority 7,715

Leeds (North-East)
Joseph, Sir K. (Con.) 20,720
Patient, A. J. (Lab.) 15,653
Con. majority 5,067

Leeds (North-West)
Kaberry, Sir D. (Con.) 29,227
Woolmer, K. J. (Lab.) 20,795
Con. majority 8,432

Leeds (South)
Rees, M. (Lab.) 19,536
Macpherson, G. K. (Con.) 9,311
Lab. majority 10,225

Leeds (South-East)
Cohen, S. (Lab.) 10,930
Sexton, Mrs. M. (Con.) 5,182
Lab. majority 5,748

Leeds (West)
Pannell, T. C. (Lab.) 21,618
Leitch, A. (Con.) 14,749
Lab. majority 6,869

Leek
Knox, D. (Con.) 27,899
Davies, H. (Lab.) 26,359
Con. gain: majority 1,540

Leicester (North-East)
Bradley, T. G. (Lab.) 15,016
Heneage, P. E. F. (Con.) 14,125
Lab. majority 891

Leicester (North-West)
Janner, G. E. (Lab.) 18,226
Symington, S. J. (Con.) 15,584
Lab. majority 2,642

Leicester (South-East)
Peel, W. J. (Con.) 26,483
Hilbourne, W. (Lab.) 15,788
Con. majority 10,695

Leicester (South-West)
Boardman, T. G. (Con.) 14,611
Grundy, C. (Lab.) 14,505
Con. majority 106

Leigh
Boardman, H. (Lab.) 26,625
McGuire, J. P. (Con.) 15,314
Lab. majority 11,311

Leominster
Bossom, Sir C. (Con.) 17,630
Pincham, R. (L.) 6,462
Con. majority 11,168

Lewes
Beamish, Sir T. V. H. (Con.) 33,592
Barry, Q. (Lab.) 14,904
Con. majority 18,688

Lewisham (North)
Moyle, R. D. (Lab.) 18,235
Samuel, H. R. L. (Con.) 17,208
Lab. majority 1,027

Lewisham (South)
Johnson, C. A. (Lab.) 19,217
Dixon, G. L. (Con.) 13,665
Lab. majority 5,552

Lewisham (West)
Gummer, J. S. (Con.) 19,676
Dickens, J. M. Y. (Lab.) 18,916
Con. gain: majority 760

Leyton
Walker, P. C. G. (Lab.) 23,386
Buxton, R. C. (Con.) 17,906
Lab. majority 5,480

Lichfield and Tamworth
d'Avigdor-Goldsmid, Maj.-Gen. J. A. (Con.) 31,274
Pitt, T. (Lab.) 29,298
Con. gain: majority 1,976

Lincoln
Taverne, D. (Lab.) 20,090
Alexander, R. T. (Con.) 15,340
Lab. majority 4,750

Liverpool (Edgehill)
Irvine, Sir A. J. (Lab.) 14,752
Howard, M. (Con.) 10,804
Lab. majority 3,948

Liverpool (Exchange)
Parry, R. (Lab.) 12,995
Phillips, A. G. (Con.) 4,638
Lab. majority 8,357

Liverpool (Garston)
Fortescue, T. V. N. (Con.) 28,381
Smith, C. J. (Lab.) 21,456
Con. majority 6,925

Liverpool (Kirkdale)
Dunn, J. A. (Lab.) 17,678
Tinné, M. P. (Con.) 13,615
Lab. majority 4,063

Liverpool (Scotland)
Alldritt, W. H. (Lab.) 11,074
Morris, R. H. (Con.) 3,740
Lab. majority 7,334

Liverpool (Toxteth)
Crawshaw, R. (Lab.) 15,276
Keefe, B. M. (Con.) 12,820
Lab. majority 2,456

Liverpool (Walton)
Heffer, E. S. (Lab.) 20,530
Norton, J. (Con.) 16,124
Lab. majority 4,406

Liverpool (Wavertree)
Tilney, J. D. R. T. (Con.) 19,127
Carr, C. E. (L.) 11,650
Con. majority 7,477

Liverpool (West Derby)
Ogden, E. (Lab.) 22,324
Latham, M. A. (Con.) 16,619
Lab. majority 5,705

Llanelli
Davies, D. J. D. (Lab.) 31,398
James, C. R. (Pl. Cymru) 8,387
Lab. majority 23,011

Cities of London and Westminster
Tugendhat, C. S. (Con.) 19,102
Dubs, A. L. M. (Lab.) 10,062
Con. majority 9,040

Londonderry
Chichester-Clark, R. (U.U.) 39,141
McAteer, E. (Nat. Unity) 27,006
U.U. majority 12,135

Loughborough
Cronin, J. D. (Lab.) 22,806
Elton, R. (Con.) 22,272
Lab. majority 534

Louth
Archer, J. H. (Con.) 25,659
Murray, J. (Lab.) 16,403
Con. majority 9,256

Lowestoft
Prior, J. M. L. (Con.) 28,842
Baker, D. A. (Lab.) 23,319
Con. majority 5,523

Ludlow
More, J. E. (Con.) 22,104
Nagington, D. (Lab.) 12,800
Con. majority 9,304

Luton
Simeons, C. F. C. (Con.) 23,308
Howie, W. (Lab.) 21,959
Con. gain: majority 1,349

Macclesfield
Harvey, Sir A. V. (Con.) 29,023
Jeuda, B. S. (Lab.) 18,571
Con. majority 10,452

Maidstone
Wells, J. J. (Con.) 31,316
Graham, K. M. (Lab.) 18,473
Con. majority 12,843

Maldon
Harrison, A. B. C. (Con.) 29,229
Haseler, S. M. A. (Lab.) 22,957
Con. majority 6,272

Manchester (Ardwick)
Kaufman, G. B. (Lab.) 13,728
Paley, I. K. (Con.) 10,726
Lab. majority 3,002

Manchester (Blackley)
Rose, P. B. (Lab.) 21,437
Maguire, A. M. (Con.) 18,838
Lab. majority 2,599

Manchester (Cheetham)
Lever, N. H. (Lab.) 10,912
Arnold, T. R. (Con.) 6,110
Lab. majority 4,802

Manchester (Exchange)
Griffiths, W. D. (Lab.) 8,234
Loftus, W. J. (Con.) 3,341
Lab. majority 4,893

Manchester (Gorton)
Marks, K. (Lab.) 23,679
Kevill, J. A. (Con.) 17,594
Lab. majority 6,085

Manchester (Moss Side)
Taylor, F. H. (Con.) 15,546
Hatton, F. (Lab.) 13,833
Con. majority 1,713

Manchester (Openshaw)
Morris, C. R. (Lab.) 19,397
Allanson, B. M. (Con.) 12,296
Lab. majority 7,101

Manchester (Withington)
Cary, Sir R. A. (Con.) 18,854
Noble, M. A. (Lab.) 15,365
Con. majority 3,489

Manchester (Wythenshawe)
Morris, A. (Lab. & Co-op.) 30,260
Moore, H. D. (Con.) 24,505
Lab. majority 5,755

Mansfield
Concannon, J. D. (Lab.) 30,554
Morton, C. W. H. (Con.) 15,027
Lab. majority 15,527

Melton
Pike, Miss M. (Con.) 38,782
Wood, K. (Lab.) 20,907
Con. majority 17,875

Meriden
Speed, H. K. (Con.) 40,077
Lister, N. P. (Lab.) 35,353
Con. majority 4,724

Merionethshire
Edwards, W. H. (Lab.) 8,861
Wigley, D. (Pl. Cymru) 5,425
Lab. majority 3,436

Merthyr Tydfil
Davies, S. O. (Ind. Lab.) 16,701
Lloyd, T. J. (Lab.) 9,234
Ind. Lab. gain: majority 7,467

Merton and Morden
Fookes, Miss J. E. (Con.) 18,727
May, K. W. (Lab.) 15,244
Con. majority 3,483

Middlesbrough (East)
Bottomley, A. G. (Lab.) 23,581
Laville, N. N. (Con.) 9,623
Lab. majority 13,958

Middlesbrough (West)
Sutcliffe, J. H. V. (Con.) 22,374
Bray, J. W. (Lab.) 21,986
Con. gain: majority 388

Middleton and Prestwich
Haselhurst, A. G. B. (Con.) 25,030
Coe, D. W. (Lab.) 23,988
Con. gain: majority 1,042

Midlothian
Eadie, A. (Lab.) 30,802
Lamotte, J. L. G. (Con.) 18,328
Lab. majority 12,474

Mitcham
Carr, L. R. (Con.) 27,257
Vincent, R. C. (Lab.) 22,047
Con. majority 5,210

Monmouth
Thomas, J. S. (Con.) 28,312
Anderson, D. (Lab.) 26,957
Con. gain: majority 1,355

Montgomery
Hooson, H. E. (L.) 10,202
Williams, D. J. D. (Con.) 7,891
L. majority 2,311

Moray and Nairn
Campbell, G. T. C. (Con.) 13,994
Howe, T. A. (Scot. Nat.) 7,885
Con. majority 6,109

Morecambe and Lonsdale
Hall-Davis, A. G. F. (Con.) 27,442
Garbutt, E. (Lab.) 13,916
Con. majority 13,526

Morpeth
Grant, G. (Lab.) 21,826
Tunnicliffe, K. I. (Con.) 9,515
Lab. majority 12,311

Motherwell
Lawson, G. M. (Lab.) 20,683
Bell, Miss S. (Con.) 12,509
Lab. majority 8,174

Nantwich
Grant-Ferris, Wing-Cmdr. Sir R. (Con.) 20,397
Beetham, D. (Lab.) 15,124
Con. majority *5,273*

Neath
Coleman, D. R. (Lab.) 28,378
Martin-Jones, D. H. J. (Con.) 6,765
Lab. majority *21,613*

Nelson and Colne
Waddington, D. C. (Con.) 19,881
Hoyle, E. D. H. (Lab.) 18,471
Con. majority *1,410*

Newark
Bishop, E. S. (Lab.) 26,455
Allen, D. G. (Con.) 25,235
Lab. majority *1,220*

Newbury
Astor, J. (Con.) 30,380
Sims, T. J. (Lab.) 18,647
Con. majority *11,733*

Newcastle-under-Lyme
Golding, J. (Lab.) 22,329
Winterton, N. R. (Con.) 20,223
Lab. majority *2,106*

Newcastle upon Tyne (Central)
Short, E. W. (Lab.) 13,671
Way, M. (Con.) 4,256
Lab. majority *9,415*

Newcastle upon Tyne (East)
Rhodes, G. W. (Lab. & Co-op.) 20,780
Heselton, P. E. (Con.) 14,832
Lab. majority *5,948*

Newcastle upon Tyne (North)
Elliott, R. W. (Con.) 15,978
Eccles, R. G. (Lab.) 12,518
Con. majority *3,460*

Newcastle upon Tyne (West)
Brown, R. C. (Lab.) 30,805
Lipman, C. (Con.) 21,644
Lab. majority *9,161*

New Forest
McNair-Wilson, P. M. E. (Con.) 36,041
Offenbach, D. M. (Lab.) 13,576
Con. majority *22,465*

Newport
Hughes, R. J. (Lab.) 30,132
Arnold, A. D. (Con.) 22,005
Lab. majority *8,127*

Newton
Lee, F. (Lab.) 34,873
Stanley, J. P. (Con.) 25,863
Lab. majority *9,010*

Norfolk (Central)
Gilmour, I. H. J. L. (Con.) 32,921
Coyne, C. R. (Lab.) 19,030
Con. majority *13,891*

Norfolk (North)
Howell, R. F. (Con.) 24,587
Hazell, B. (Lab.) 19,903
Con. gain: majority *4,684*

Norfolk (South)
Hill, J. E. B. (Con.) 22,614
Shaw, C. (Lab.) 17,172
Con. majority *5,442*

Norfolk (South-West)
Hawkins, P. L. (Con.) 22,220
Potter, L. J. (Lab.) 16,572
Con. majority *5,648*

Normanton
Roberts, A. (Lab.) 28,421
Cargill, D. H. (Con.) 13,132
Lab. majority *15,289*

Northampton
Paget, R. T. (Lab.) 27,424
Parkinson, C. E. (Con.) 26,183
Lab. majority *1,241*

Northants (South)
Jones, A. (Con.) 29,070
Roberts, G. J. (Lab.) 21,131
Con. majority *7,939*

Northwich
Foster, Sir J. G. (Con.) 20,366
Bates, A. (Lab.) 15,746
Con. majority *4,620*

Norwich (North)
Wallace, G. D. (Lab.) 18,564
Turner, A. E. (Con.) 11,868
Lab. majority *6,696*

Norwich (South)
Stuttaford, Dr. I. T. (Con.) 17,067
Ascher, C. F. (Lab.) 16,241
Con. gain: majority *826*

Norwood (Lambeth)
Fraser, J. D. (Lab.) 16,634
Temple-Morris, P. (Con.) 16,003
Lab. majority *631*

Nottingham (Central)
Dunnett, J. J. (Lab.) 17,638
Brook, Partridge, B. (Con.) 14,079
Lab. majority *3,559*

Nottingham (North)
Whitlock, W. C. (Lab.) 25,898
Derbyshire, W. (Con.) 18,616
Lab. majority *7,282*

Nottingham (South)
Fowler, P. N. (Con.) 26,762
Perry, G. H. (Lab.) 23,031
Con. gain: majority *3,731*

Nottingham (West)
English, M. (Lab.) 21,255
Suthers, M. W. (Con.) 19,003
Lab. majority *2,252*

Nuneaton
Huckfield, L. J. (Lab.) 32,877
Lewis-Smith, Miss S. M. (Con.) 18,769
Lab. majority *14,108*

Ogmore
Padley, W. E. (Lab.) 33,436
Gardner, A. F. (Con.) 10,415
Lab. majority *23,021*

Oldbury and Halesowen
Stokes, J. H. R. (Con.) 29,403
Horner, J. (Lab.) 26,499
Con. gain: majority *2,904*

Oldham (East)
Lamond, J. A. (Lab.) 17,020
Holland, H. (Con.) 16,260
Lab. majority *760*

Oldham (West)
Meacher, M. H. (Lab.) 16,062
Campbell, K. B. (Con.) 14,387
Lab. gain: majority *1,675*

Orkney and Zetland
Grimond, J. (L.) 7,896
Firth, J. L. (Con.) 5,364
L. majority *2,532*

Ormskirk
Soref, H. B. (Con.) 40,517
Kilroy-Silk, R. M. (Lab.) 25,486
Con. majority *15,031*

Orpington
Stanbrook, I. R. (Con.) 24,385
Lubbock, E. R. (L.) 23,063
Grant, D. I. (Lab.) 4,098
Con. gain: majority *1,322*

Oswestry
Biffen, W. J. (Con.) 20,361
Turner, N. (Lab.) 10,801
Con. majority *9,560*

Oxford
Woodhouse, C. M. (Con.) 24,873
Luard, D. E. T. (Lab.) 22,988
Con. gain. majority *1,894*

Paddington (North)
Latham, A. C. (Lab.) 11,645
Price, R. S. (Con.) 8,590
Lab. majority 3,055

Paddington (South)
Scott, N. P. (Con.) 10,526
Balfe, R. A. (Lab.) 7,913
Con. majority 2,613

Paisley
Robertson, J. (Lab.) 25,429
Workman, J. (Con.) 15,232
Lab. majority 10,197

Peckham (Camberwell)
Corbet, Mrs. F. K. (Lab.) 17,071
Lawrence, I. J. (Con.) 8,232
Lab. majority 8,839

Pembroke
Edwards, R. N. (Con.) 19,120
Parry, G. S. D. (Lab.) 17,889
Con. gain: majority 1,231

Penistone
Mendelson, J. J. (Lab.) 31,615
Pickup, A. (Con.) 14,897
Lab. majority 16,718

Penrith and The Border
Whitelaw, W. S. I. (Con.) 23,800
Longworth, R. (Lab.) 10,256
Con. majority 13,544

Perth and East Perthshire
MacArthur, I. (Con.) 21,860
Friel, Miss V. A. (Lab.) 9,972
Con. majority 11,888

Peterborough
Nicholls, Sir H. (Con.) 30,227
Ward, M. J. (Lab.) 25,662
Con. majority 4,565

Petersfield
Quennell, Miss J. (Con.) 30,414
Horrocks, K. (Lab.) 10,307
Con. majority 20,107

Plymouth (Devonport)
Vickers, Dame J. H. (Con.) 21,843
Taylor, F. K. (Lab.) 20,471
Con. majority 1,372

Plymouth (Sutton)
Owen, Dr. D. A. L. (Lab.) 29,383
Goss, J. M. (Con.) 28,636
Lab. majority 747

Pontefract
Harper, J. (Lab.) 31,774
Deslandes, I. A. (Con.) 10,687
Lab. majority 21,087

Pontypool
Abse, L. (Lab.) 27,402
Bell, W. M. (Con.) 8,869
Lab. majority 18,533

Pontypridd
John, B. T. (Lab.) 28,414
Withers, M. C. (Con.) 8,205
Lab. majority 20,209

Poole
Murton, H. O. (Con.) 31,100
Campbell, I. S. (Lab.) 17,610
Con. majority 13,490

Poplar
Mikardo, I. (Lab.) 16,520
Denney, R. C. (Con.) 4,036
Lab. majority 12,484

Portsmouth (Langstone)
Lloyd, I. S. (Con.) 43,733
Kenward, R. R. (Lab. & Co-op.) 26,492
Con. majority 17,241

Portsmouth (South)
Pink, R. B. (Con.) 23,962
White, J. (Lab.) 13,847
Con. majority 10,115

Portsmouth (West)
Judd, F. A. (Lab.) 17,169
Clarke, Brig. T. H. (Con.) 16,214
Lab. majority 955

Preston (North)
Holt, Miss M. (Con.) 20,102
Atkins, R. H. (Lab.) 17,140
Con. gain: majority 2,962

Preston (South)
Green, A. (Con.) 20,480
Mahon, P. (Lab.) 19,149
Con. gain: majority 1,331

Pudsey
Hiley, J. (Con.) 24,308
Mann, J. (Lab.) 18,313
Con. majority 5,995

Putney (Wandsworth)
Jenkins, H. G. (Lab.) 25,162
Wakeham, J. (Con.) 23,768
Lab. majority 1,394

Reading
Vaughan, Dr. G. F. (Con.) 23,598
Lee, J. M. H. (Lab.) 22,444
Con. gain: majority 1,154

Reigate
Howe, R. E. G. (Con.) 28,462
Farley, M. P. (Lab.) 15,433
Con. majority 13,029

Renfrewshire (East)
Anderson, Miss M. B. H. (Con.) 29,163
Carnegie, Mrs. J. (Lab.) 16,062
Con. majority 13,101

Renfrewshire (West)
Buchan, N. F. (Lab.) 22,999
Fletcher, A. M. (Con.) 20,699
Lab. majority 2,300

Rhondda (East)
Davies, G. E. (Lab.) 19,602
James, G. (Pl. Cymru) 6,931
Lab. majority 12,671

Rhondda (West)
Jones, T. A. (Lab.) 18,779
Davies, H. V. (Pl. Cymru) 3,528
Lab. majority 15,251

Richmond, Surrey
Royle, A. (Con.) 20,979
Palmer, A. R. (Lab.) 12,981
Con. majority 7,998

Richmond, Yorks
Kitson, T. P. G. (Con.) 30,471
Aldrich, M. J. (Lab.) 12,702
Con. majority 17,769

Ripon
Stoddart-Scott, Sir M. (Con.) 21,211
Daniel, D. (Lab.) 9,147
Con. majority 12,064

Rochdale
McCann, J. (Lab.) 19,247
Smith, C. (L.) 14,076
Lab. majority 5,171

Rochester and Chatham
Fenner, Mrs. P. E. (Con.) 30,263
Kerr, Mrs. A. P. (Lab.) 24,922
Con. gain: majority 5,341

Romford
Leonard, R. L. (Lab.) 27,899
Neubert, M. J. (Con.) 25,139
Lab. majority 2,760

Ross and Cromarty
Gray, J. H. N. (Con.) 6,418
Mackenzie, A. R. (L.) 5,617
Con. gain: majority 801

Rossendale
Bray, R. W. T. (Con.) 20,448
Boothroyd, Miss B. (Lab.) 18,568
Con. gain: majority 1,880

Rotherham
O'Malley, B. K. (Lab.) 25,246
Cooke, E. R. (Con.) 12,770
Lab. majority 12,476

Rother Valley
Hardy, P. (Lab.) 44,322
Durrant, R. A. B. (Con.) 17,418
Lab. majority 26,904

Rowley Regis and Tipton
Archer, P. K. (Lab.) 25,001
Smith, P. M. (Con.) 15,537
Lab. majority 9,464

Roxburgh, Selkirk and Peebles
Steel, D. M. S. (L.) 19,524
Fairgrieve, R. (Con.) 18,974
L. majority 550

Rugby
Price, W. G. (Lab.) 25,041
Griffith, J. H. P. (Con.) 22,086
Lab. majority 2,955

Ruislip-Northwood
Crowder, F. P. (Con.) 24,247
Silverman, B. H. (Lab.) 11,541
Con. majority 12,706

Runcorn
Carlisle, M. (Con.) 25,272
Taylor, M. J. E. (Lab.) 16,204
Con. majority 9,068

Rushcliffe
Clarke, K. H. (Con.) 30,966
Gardner, A. J. (Lab.) 24,798
Con. gain: majority 6,168

Rutherglen
Mackenzie, J. G. (Lab.) 17,751
Hutchison, P. C. (Con.) 14,710
Lab. majority 3,041

Rutland and Stamford
Lewis, K. (Con.) 22,803
Toch, H. (Lab.) 15,136
Con. majority 7,667

Rye
Irvine, B. G. (Con.) 32,300
Fountain, H. A. (Lab.) 9,031
Con. majority 23,269

Saffron Walden
Kirk, P. M. (Con.) 24,549
Weetch, K. T. (Lab.) 14,885
Con. majority 9,664

St. Albans
Goodhew, V. H. (Con.) 24,503
Beaumont, C. H. (Lab.) 16,629
Con. majority 7,874

St. Helens
Spriggs, L. (Lab.) 31,587
McGaw, I. D. (Con.) 16,509
Lab. majority 15,078

St. Ives
Nott, J. W. F. (Con.) 18,581
Castle, Dr. M. E. (Lab.) 9,913
Con. majority 8,668

St. Marylebone
Hogg, Q. McG. (Con.) 17,639
Morrell, K. W. (Lab.) 8,325
Con. majority 9,314

St. Pancras (North)
Stallard, A. W. (Lab.) 16,497
Moorhouse, C. J. O. (Con.) 10,648
Lab. majority 5,849

Salford (East)
Allaun, F. (Lab.) 15,853
Lack, J. B. (Con.) 9,583
Lab. majority 6,270

Salford (West)
Orme, S. (Lab.) 16,986
Clark, A. E. (Con.) 14,310
Lab. majority 2,676

Salisbury
Hamilton, M. A. (Con.) 26,549
Waugh, A. (Lab.) 17,493
Con. majority 9,056

Scarborough and Whitby
Shaw, M. N. (Con.) 26,154
Pitts, M. F. (L.) 16,517
Con. majority 9,637

Sedgefield
Reed, D. (Lab.) 36,867
Beck, A. A. (Con.) 24,036
Lab. majority 12,831

Sevenoaks
Rodgers, Sir J. C. (Con.) 32,654
Ovenden, J. (Lab.) 15,376
Con. majority 17,278

Sheffield (Attercliffe)
Duffy, A. E. P. (Lab.) 26,482
Santhouse, Miss P. M. (Con.) 10,986
Lab. majority 15,496

Sheffield (Brightside)
Griffiths, E. (Lab.) 23,941
Newton, A. H. (Con.) 8,572
Lab. majority 15,369

Sheffield (Hallam)
Osborn, J. H. (Con.) 25,134
Broadley, A. H. (Lab.) 12,884
Con. majority 12,250

Sheffield (Heeley)
Spence, J. D. (Con.) 27,950
Hooley, F. O. (Lab.) 27,237
Con. gain: majority 713

Sheffield (Hillsborough)
Darling, G. (Lab. & Co-op.) 18,775
Patnick, C. I. (Con.) *11,445*
Lab. majority 7,330

Sheffield (Park)
Mulley, F. W. (Lab.) 23,302
Renton, R. T. (Con.) 7,024
Lab. majority 16,278

Shipley
Fox, J. M. (Con.) 20,938
Free, N. (Lab.) 16,161
Con. majority 4,777

Shoreditch and Finsbury
Brown, R. W. (Lab.) 14,474
Sims, R. E. (Con.) 7,166
Lab. majority 7,308

Shrewsbury
Langford-Holt, Sir J. (Con.) 22,619
Kent, P. A. (Lab.) 13,413
Con. majority 9,206

Skipton
Drayson, G. B. (Con.) 20,817
Targett, K. (Lab.) 12,011
Con. majority 8,806

Smethwick
Faulds, A. M. W. (Lab.) 16,077
Rathbone, B. B. (Con.) 13,968
Lab. majority 2,109

Solihull
Grieve, W. P. (Con.) 37,756
Gray, D. (Lab.) 13,181
Con. majority 24,575

Somerset (North)
Dean, A. P. (Con.) 38,975
Mitchard, J. T. (Lab.) 28,121
Con. majority 10,854

Southall
Bidwell, S. J. (Lab.) 19,389
Reeves, K. G. (Con.) 15,166
Lab. majority 4,223

Southampton (Itchen)
King, Dr. H. M. (The Speaker) 29,417
Bray, E. (Nat. Dem.) 9,581
Majority 19,836

Southampton (Test)
Hill, S. J. A. (Con.) 24,660
Mitchell, R. C. (Lab.) 22,858
Con. gain: majority 1,802

Southend (East)
McAdden, Sir S. J. (Con.) 24,025
Clyne, P. R. (Lab.) 17,065
Con. majority 6,960

Southend (West)
Channon, H. P. G. (Con.) 29,304
Burstin, M. (Lab.) 12,419
Con. majority 16,885

Southgate
Berry, A. G. (Con.) 22,963
Bastin, R. B. (Lab. & Co-op.) 9,389
Con. majority 13,574

Southport
Percival, W. I. (Con.) 22,950
Fearn, R. (L.) 13,809
Con. majority 9,141

South Shields
Blenkinsop, A. (Lab.) 30,191
McKee, Dr. J. (Con.) 19,960
Lab. majority 10,231

Southwark
Gunter, R. J. (Lab.) 16,834
Gordon, J. (Con.) 7,040
Lab. majority 9,794

Sowerby
Houghton, A. L. N. D. (Lab.) 16,583
Burman, W. G. (Con.) 16,114
Lab. majority 469

Spelthorne
Atkins, H. E. (Con.) 27,266
Cheney, P. L. (Lab.) 18,239
Con. majority 9,027

Stafford and Stone
Fraser, H. C. P. J. (Con.) 30,056
Stanworth, M. J. K. (Lab.) 20,380
Con. majority 9,676

Stalybridge and Hyde
Pendry, T. (Lab.) 22,226
Rogerson, Col. J. E. (Con.) 19,377
Lab. majority 2,849

Stepney
Shore, P. D. (Lab.) 18,993
Greenway, H. (Con.) 4,922
Lab. majority 14,071

Stirling and Falkirk
MacPherson, M. (Lab.) 22,984
Anderson, D. R. (Con.) 15,754
Lab. majority 7,230

Stirlingshire (East and Clackmannan)
Douglas, R. C. (Lab. & Co-op.) 23,729
Fairlie, J. (Con.) 13,178
Lab. majority 10,551

Stirlingshire (West)
Baxter, W. (Lab.) 18,884
Glen, J. (Con.) 11,465
Lab. majority 7,419

Stockport (North)
Owen, I. W. (Con.) 18,132
Gregory, A. (Lab.) 17,261
Con. gain: majority 871

Stockport (South)
Orbach, M. (Lab.) 16,747
Howson, C. (Con.) 14,679
Lab. majority 2,068

Stockton-on-Tees
Rodgers, W. T. (Lab.) 22,283
Radford, P. V. (Con.) 17,960
Lab. majority 4,323

Stoke Newington and Hackney, North
Weitzman, D. (Lab.) 20,446
Boast, J. R. (Con.) 11,298
Lab. majority 9,148

Stoke-on-Trent (Central)
Cant, R. B. (Lab.) 18,758
Ashley, Mrs. E. (Con.) 11,227
Lab. majority 7,531

Stoke-on-Trent (North)
Forrester, J. S. (Lab.) 20,642
Heath, J. S. (Con.) 10,542
Lab. majority 10,100

Stoke-on-Trent (South)
Ashley, J. (Lab.) 20,770
Apps, R. J. (Con.) 13,344
Lab. majority 7,426

Stratford
Maude, A. E. U. (Con.) 28,106
Tombs, P. E. (Lab.) 11,393
Con. majority 16,713

Streatham (Wandsworth)
Sandys, D. (Con.) 19,215
Ward, Mrs. A. S. (Lab.) 13,593
Con. majority 5,622

Stretford
Churchill, W. S. (Con.) 28,629
Davies, E. A. (Lab.) 24,614
Con. gain: majority 4,015

Stroud
Kershaw, J. A. (Con.) 27,089
Wheatley, R. D. (Lab.) 19,158
Con. majority 7,931

Sudbury and Woodbridge
Stainton, K. M. (Con.) 32,393
Orriss, B. (Lab.) 19,829
Con. majority 12,564

Sunderland (North)
Willey, F. T. (Lab.) 25,779
Reay-Smith, J. M. (Con.) 16,738
Lab. majority 9,041

Sunderland (South)
Bagier, G. A. T. (Lab.) 26,840
Orde, D. A. (Con.) 20,722
Lab. majority 6,118

Surbiton
Fisher, N. T. L. (Con.) 17,359
Kerr-Waller, R. D. (Lab.) 10,469
Con. majority 6,890

Surrey, East
Clark, W. G. (Con.) 35,773
Meyer, P. W. (L.) 11,749
Con. majority 24,024

Sutton and Cheam
Sharples, R. C. (Con.) 23,957
Dowsett, J. (Lab.) 11,261
Con. majority 12,696

Sutton Coldfield
Lloyd, G. W. (Con.) 36,774
Tebbutt, P. M. (Lab.) 18,134
Con. majority 18,640

Swansea (East)
McBride, N. (Lab.) 28,183
Murphy, M. J. (Con.) 8,191
Lab. majority 19,992

Swansea (West)
Williams, A. J. (Lab.) 24,622
Rees, J. E. H. (Con.) 21,384
Lab. majority 3,238

Swindon
Stoddart, D. L. (Lab.) 25,731
Ward, C. J. F. (Con.) 20,155
Lab. gain: majority 5,576

Taunton
du Cann, E. (Con.) 26,158
Mama, S. (Lab.) 17,823
Con. majority 8,335

Tavistock
Heseltine, M. R. D. (Con.) 25,846
Banks, M. E. B. (L.) 10,397
Con. majority 15,449

Thirsk and Malton
Turton, R. H. (Con.) 30,892
Bradshaw, J. R. (Lab.) 15,309
Con. majority 15,583

Thurrock
Delargy, H. J. (Lab.) 30,874
Bright, G. F. J. (Con.) 19,486
Lab. majority 11,388

Tiverton
Maxwell-Hyslop, R. (Con.) 24,689
Hewetson, R. (Lab.) 10,823
Con. majority *13,866*

Tonbridge
Hornby, R. P. (Con.) 31,890
Colquhoun, Mrs. M. M. (Lab.) 17,897
Con. majority *13,993*

Torquay
Bennett, Sir F. M. (Con.) 33,996
Bryers, P. S. T. (Lab.) 15,948
Con. majority *18,048*

Torrington
Mills, P. M. (Con.) 21,328
Lacey, L. A. (L.) 11,455
Con. majority *9,873*

Totnes
Mawby, R. L. (Con.) 31,519
Blank, R. (Lab.) 16,429
Con. majority *15,090*

Tottenham
Atkinson, N. (Lab.) 17,367
Simmonds, L. T. (Con.) 10,975
Lab. majority *6,392*

Truro
Dixon, P. (Con.) 24,894
Cuss, R. C. (Lab.) 16,684
Con. majority *8,210*

Twickenham
Jessell, T. (Con.) 28,571
Grant, J. H. W. (Lab.) 16,950
Con. majority *11,621*

Tynemouth
Ward, Dame I. (Con.) 30,773
Beecham, J. H. (Lab.) 23,927
Con. majority *6,846*

Ulster, Mid
Devlin, Miss B. (Ind. Unity) 37,739
Thornton, N. (U.U.) 31,810
Ind. Unity majority *5,929*

Uxbridge
Curran, C. (Con.) 23,414
Ryan, J. (Lab.) 19,768
Con. gain: majority *3,646*

Vauxhall (Lambeth)
Strauss, G. R. (Lab.) 13,046
Jones, C. W. (Con.) 7,477
Lab. majority *5,569*

Wakefield
Harrison, W. (Lab.) 27,352
Smith, D. (Con.) 15,668
Lab. majority *11,684*

Wallasey
Marples, A. E. (Con.) 24,283
Wells, C. J. (Lab.) 21,172
Con. majority *3,111*

Wallsend
Garrett, W. E. (Lab.) 39,065
White, E. M. (Con.) 24,650
Lab. majority *14,415*

Walsall (North)
Wells, W. T. (Lab.) 27,543
Barnes, J. (Con.) 20,128
Lab. majority *7,415*

Walsall (South)
d'Avigdor-Goldsmid, Sir H. J. (Con.) 35,545
Rea, G. S. (Lab.) 24,196
Con. majority *11,349*

Walthamstow (East)
McNair-Wilson, R. M. C. (Con.) 14,260
Tomlinson, J. E. (Lab.) 13,732
Con. majority *528*

Walthamstow (West)
Deakins, E. P. (Lab.) 12,472
Silvester, F. J. (Con.) 7,870
Lab. gain: majority *4,602*

Wandsworth (Central)
Cox, T. M. (Lab.) 19,776
McLaughlin, Mrs. F. P. A. (Con.) 16,830
Lab. majority *2,946*

Wanstead and Woodford
Jenkin, C. P. F. (Con.) 20,065
Barker, A. P. (Lab.) 8,522
Con. majority *11,543*

Warrington
Williams, W. T. (Lab. & Co-op.) 20,970
Gooch, A. B. (Con.) 11,647
Lab. majority *9,323*

Warwick and Leamington
Smith, D. G. (Con.) 36,994
Watkinson, J. T. (Lab.) 21,355
Con. majority *15,639*

Watford
Tuck, R. H. (Lab.) 19,698
Clarke, D. W. (Con.) 19,622
Lab. majority *76*

Wednesbury,
Stonehouse J. T. (Lab. & Co-op.) 23,998
Harman, D. M. (Con.) 20,627
Lab. majority *3,371*

Wellingborough
Fry, P. D. (Con.) 27,459
Mann, J. H. (Lab.) 25,107
Con. majority *2,352*

Wells
Boscawen, R. T. (Con.) 25,106
Thompson, F. R. (Lab.) 16,335
Con. majority *8,771*

Wembley (North)
Bullus, Sir E. E. (Con.) 18,345
Childerhouse, K. (Lab.) 11,916
Con. majority *6,429*

Wembley (South)
Russell, Sir R. S. (Con.) 16,578
Elliott, M. N. (Lab.) 14,336
Con. majority *2,242*

West Bromwich
Foley, M. A. (Lab.) 23,412
Hawkins, G. (Con.) 18,976
Lab. majority *4,436*

Westbury
Walters, D. M. (Con.) 26,524
McLaren, J. (Lab.) 17,413
Con. majority *9,111*

Western Isles
Stewart, D. J. (Scot. Nat.) 6,568
Macmillan, M. K. (Lab.) 5,842
Scot. Nat. gain: majority *726*

West Ham (North)
Lewis, A. W. J. (Lab.) 17,664
Shearman, W. J. (Con.) 7,130
Lab. majority *10,534*

West Ham (South)
Jones, Sir F. E. (Lab.) 18,899
Balcomb, B. C. (Con.) 5,422
Lab. majority *13,477*

Westhoughton
Price, J. T. (Lab.) 29,674
Unsworth, Dr. C. A. (Con.) 23,847
Lab. majority *5,827*

West Lothian
Dalyell, T. (Lab.) 29,360
Wolfe, W. C. (Scot. Nat.) 15,620
Lab. majority *13,740*

Westmorland
Jopling, T. M. (Con.) 21,253
Pease, J. G. (L.) 9,426
Con. majority *11,827*

Weston-super-Mare
Wiggins, A. W. (Con.) 33,816
Palmer, Miss S. (Lab. & Co-op.) 14,473
Con. majority *19,343*

Whitehaven
Cunningham, J. A. (Lab.) 22,974
McKay, Dr. W. G. (Con.) 16,418
Lab. majority *6,556*

Widnes
MacColl, J. E. (Lab.) 28,384
Pierce, G. H. (Con.) 20,841
Lab. majority *7,543*

Wigan
Fitch, E. A. (Lab.) 28,102
Daniels, A. (Con.) 12,882
Lab. majority *15,220*

Willesden (East)
Freeson, R. (Lab.) 20,073
Cutler, H. W. (Con.) 15,564
Lab. majority *4,509*

Willesden (West)
Pavitt, L. A. (Lab. & Co-op.) 21,918
Dyason, R. F. (Con.) 10,163
Lab. majority *11,755*

Wimbledon
Havers, R. M. O. (Con.) 15,285
Holmes, R. C. (Lab.) 8,554
Con. majority *6,731*

Winchester
Giles, Rear Adm. M. C. M. (Con.) 25,249
Perry, C. (Lab.) 11,773
Con. majority *13,476*

Windsor
Glyn, Dr. A. (Con.) 32,264
Sullivan, T. D. (Lab.) 16,214
Con. majority *16,050*

Wirral
Lloyd, J. S. B. (Con.) 38,655
Paterson, R. G. (Lab.) 22,197
Con. majority *16,458*

Woking
Onslow, C. G. D. (Con.) 37,220
Taylor, R. M. (Lab.) 18,652
Con. majority *18,568*

Wokingham
van Straubenzee, W. R. (Con.) 43,183
Helm, C. A. R. (Lab.) 22,630
Con. majority *20,553*

Wolverhampton (North-East)
Short, Mrs. R. (Lab.) 17,251
Wright, G. I. (Con.) 15,358
Lab. majority *1,893*

Wolverhampton (South-West)
Powell, J. E. (Con.) 26,220
Bamfield, J. A. N. (Lab.) 11,753
Con. majority *14,467*

Wood Green
Butler, Mrs. J. S. (Lab. & Co-op.) 18,666
Malynn, M. P. R. (Con.) 14,022
Lab. majority *4,644*

Woolwich (East)
Mayhew, C. P. (Lab.) 19,423
Cope, J. A. (Con.) 10,259
Lab. majority *9,164*

Woolwich (West)
Hamling, W. (Lab.) 21,036
Gaffney, M. P. (Con.) 20,418
Lab. majority *618*

Worcester
Walker, P. E. (Con.) 29,717
Jones, P. (Lab.) 21,275
Con. majority *8,442*

Worcestershire, South
Nabarro, Sir G. D. N. (Con.) 30,648
Bailey, A. E. (Lab.) 12,839
Con. majority *17,809*

Workington
Peart, T. F. (Lab.) 24,975
Turner-Bridger, M. F. (Con.) 15,532
Lab. majority *9,443*

Worthing
Higgins, T. L. (Con.) 33,051
Bartlett, Mrs. S. M. (Lab.) 8,989
Con. majority *24,062*

Wrekin, The
Trafford, Dr. J. A. P. (Con.) 26,282
Fowler, G. T. (Lab.) 25,764
Con. gain: majority *518*

Wrexham
Ellis, R. T. (Lab.) 31,089
Patterson, B. (Con.) 15,649
Lab. majority *15,440*

Wycombe
Hall, J. (Con.) 40,151
Jones, B. S. (Lab.) 23,341
Con. majority *16,810*

Yarmouth
Fell, A. (Con.) 23,088
Gray, H. (Lab.) 19,931
Con. gain: majority *3,157*

Yeovil
Peyton, J. W. W. (Con.) 27,689
Elswood, J. A. (Lab.) 20,621
Con. majority *7,068*

York
Lyon, A. W. (Lab.) 29,619
Askew, B. (Con.) 27,422
Lab. majority *2,197*

For reasons of space, we have included only the winning candidate, and the candidate who polled the second highest number of votes.